Praise for *The Financial Times Guide to Management*

'Practical, concise and full of tips every manager needs to know, *The Financial Times Guide To Management* provides a powerful guide for leaders at every level.'

Arianna Huffington, *Chairman, President and Editor-in-Chief of the Huffington Post Media Group*

'Amidst the myriad of books on leadership, this guide presents an unusually concrete, comprehensive and practical set of principles and learnings for managers at every level.'

John Pepper, *Former CEO & Chairman, P&G; Former Chairman, Walt Disney*

'This is clear, encouraging and packed with good sense – just like its author. A winner.'

Eleanor Mills, *Editorial Director,* The Sunday Times

'Management means bringing out the best in people, but who brings out the best in a manager? Ann Francke's book deserves to become an important part of the answer.'

Gavin Patterson, *CEO, BT*

'Great compilation of management theory and best practice, with good input from influential practitioners.'

Cilla Snowball, *Group CEO and Group Chairman, AMV BBDO*

'*The FT Guide to Management* is an excellent resource for anyone interested in becoming a better manager, wherever they are in their career.'

Paul Geddes, *CEO, Direct Line Group*

'A resource and guide for every manager with the hum insights and experiences of those who took the troubl

Dame Carol Black, *Chairman, Nuffield Trust; Pr*

D0228106

'If you are looking for sound, practical, enlightening advice on management, this is the book for you.'

Peter Ayliffe, Chairman, Monitise; Former CEO, VISA

'A primer on running a business, a sort of everyman's MBA.'

Chris Warmoth, *Executive Vice President, Heinz*

'Ann's agile journey through today's management landscape is inspiring and accessible; an invaluable asset for aspiring, newly appointed and more experienced managers alike.'

Rebecca Taylor, Dean, Open University Business School

'Ann Francke's *FT Guide to Management* is a readable, well grounded guide to management and the role of the manager. The book combines insights based on research with anecdotes from experience to provide both food for thought and practical guidance for present and aspiring managers.'

Kai Peters, CEO, Ashridge Business School

'A practical and comprehensive guide on what it takes to lead and inspire others and manage for success in today's increasingly volatile and complex world.'

Paul Polman, CEO, Unilever

The Financial Times
Guide to Management

The Financial Times Guide to Management

How to make a difference and get results

Ann Francke

Harlow, England • London • New York • Boston • San Francisco • Toronto • Sydney • Auckland • Singapore • Hong Kong
Tokyo • Seoul • Taipei • New Delhi • Cape Town • São Paulo • Mexico City • Madrid • Amsterdam • Munich • Paris • Milan

PEARSON EDUCATION LIMITED

Edinburgh Gate
Harlow CM20 2JE
United Kingdom
Tel: +44 (0)1279 623623
Web: www.pearson.com/uk

First edition published 2014 (print and electronic)
© Pearson Education (print and electronic)

Pearson Education is not responsible for the content of third-party internet sites.

ISBN: 978-0-273-79286-4 (print)
 978-0-273-79473-8 (PDF)
 978-0-273-79474-5 (ePub)
 978-1-292-00572-0 (eText)

British Library Cataloguing-in-Publication Data
A catalogue record for the print edition is available from the British Library

Library of Congress Cataloging-in-Publication Data
Francke, Ann.
 The Financial Times guide to management : how to make a difference and get results / Ann Francke. -- 1 Edition.
 pages cm. -- (Financial Times guides)
 Includes index.
 ISBN 978-0-273-79286-4 (pbk.) -- ISBN 978-0-273-79473-8 (PDF) -- ISBN 978-0-273-79474-5 (ePub) -- ISBN 978-1-292-00572-0 (eText)
 1. Management. 2. Communication in management. 3. Leadership. 4. Organizational change. I. Title.
 HD31.F6863 2013
 658--dc23
                            2013040020 <tel:2013040020>

10 9 8 7 6 5 4 3 2 1
17 16 15 14 13

Cover image © Richard Packwood/Getty Images
Typeset in 9pt Stone Serif by 3
Printed by Ashford Colour Press Ltd., Gosport

NOTE THAT ANY PAGE CROSS REFERENCES REFER TO THE PRINT EDITION

For Barry and Izzy

Contents

Acknowledgements

This book owes its existence to a very modern-day management tool: specifically it came to pass because Nicole Eggleton, the FT's Commissioning Editor, contacted me on LinkedIn shortly after I had joined CMI as CEO. I thank her here – as she had the foresight to think that someone who had been a manager and was now responsible for leading a Chartered Management Institute might have both experience of and interest in the subject. She was right! And she proved a lovely editor to work with. Insightful, positive, and with the ability to know just how much commentary to provide in order to shape the manuscript and make it better. And thanks to all of the colleagues at Pearson for making the manuscript a book. And to Peter Ayliffe, the CMI's President, for his support in encouraging me to do this alongside my day job.

Once I got over the surprise and panic that accompanies agreeing to an undertaking of this size, I realised that in my 25-plus years as a management practitioner with some of the world's best companies I'd absorbed rather a lot on the topic. So the biggest acknowledgement and thanks has to go to those who have managed me and those whom I have managed, as well as to the colleagues near and far I've interacted with or observed. I've been inspired by and learned from all of them over the years, and their collective wisdom shapes this book. The best of these folks have been generous enough to share their thoughts on management which I've pulled together in the last chapter – so a special thank you to each one of them! You, readers, will benefit from their invaluable views and insights directly.

There are many others who deserve special thanks: Petra Wilton, for helping to shape, edit and comment on the manuscript at every stage, Nick Parker, Michele Jenkins, Sarah Childs and Robert Orton for their very thorough and useful research for each of the chapters, and Shae Kuehlmann, for her positivity, proofreading and oversight (she was my 'book nag'). Thanks, too, to Simon Newlyn, Richard Coles and Phil Wood for helping with the graphics and to Phil Whitely for helping to reduce and reshape the final version. Thanks to Chris Warmoth, Mike Harrison, Stephen Hess and Louise Bevan for reading early drafts and giving me comments. Finally, I thank Barry, my husband, for putting up with the many nights and weekends I spent messing up the dining room table and for his kindness, patience and support.

Publisher's acknowledgements

We are grateful to the following for permission to use copyright material:

Figure 2.1 courtesy of the Chartered Management Institute; Figure 8.1 from COBIT © 2007, IT Governance Institute. All rights reserved. Used with permission; Figure 10.2 adapted and reprinted with permission of *Harvard Business Review*, from 'Strategies of Diversification' by Ansoff, I., 1957. Copyright © 1957 by the Harvard Business School Publishing Corporation; all rights reserved; Figure 11.2 adapted and reprinted with permission of *Harvard Business Review*, from 'What is Strategy?' by Porter, M. E., 1996. Copyright © 1996 by the Harvard Business School Publishing Corporation; all rights reserved; Figure 14.1 courtesy of Kotter International (www.kotterinternational.com); Figure 14.2 from Fisher, J. M. 'A Time for Change', *Human Resource International*, vol 8:2 (Taylor & Francis Ltd, http://www.tandf.co.uk/journals, 2005); Figure 15.1 courtesy of Jim Riley (www.tutor2u.net); Figure 15.2 © The British Standards Institution 2010; Figure 16.1 courtesy of Richard Ellis, CSR Director, Alliance Boots. Used with permission; Figure 16.3 adapted from the Southbeach Notation Model (www.southbeachinc.com); Figure 22.2 adapted and reprinted with permission of *Harvard Business Review*, from 'How Competitive Forces Shape Strategy' by Porter, M. E., 1979. Copyright © 1979 by the Harvard Business School Publishing Corporation; all rights reserved.

Articles in Chapter 21: 'Ryanair volte-face shows feedback is best given face-to-face', by Kellaway, L., *Financial Times*, 29 September 2013; 'Profits are the route to sustainable business', by Hill, A., *Financial Times*, 23 September 2013; 'Mandela's lessons in how to negotiate', by Skapinker, M., 31 July 2013; 'Management – overview', by Hill, A., 12 June 2013; 'The multilingual dividend', by Hill, A., 14 March 2013; 'I've finally found a piece of good corporate guff', by Kellaway, L., 18 February 2013; 'If you have to reject me, tell it to me straight', by Kellaway, L.,

23 January 2013; all articles © 2013 The Financial Times Ltd. All rights reserved; 'The value of mentors who have been there', by Skapinker, M., 4 January 2012 © 2012 The Financial Times Ltd. All rights reserved.

Text on pages 124–5 from 'Don't Let Strategy Replace Planning', by Roger Martin, HBR Blog Network, 5 February 2013 (http://blogs.hbr.org/cs/2013/02/dont_let_strategy_become_plann.html); reprinted courtesy of Roger Martin and *Harvard Business Review*.

In some cases we have been unable to trace the owners of copyright material, and we would appreciate any information that would enable us to do so.

About the author

As Chief Executive Officer of CMI, Ann brings her extensive global management experience and her proven track record of developing people and delivering innovative strategies that result in sustainable growth. At CMI, she uses her experience in leading organisations to promote best practices in management and leadership and improve the performance and quality of working life in organisations. Ann speaks frequently at conferences and in the media on all aspects of management, and blogs for Huffington Post UK and other publications.

Prior to CMI, Ann was Global Managing Director at the British Standards Institution, where she led the training and certification businesses to create a more customer-facing organisation.

Before BSI Ann held executive management board positions at FTSE 100 companies Boots Group and Yell and was European Vice President at Mars with responsibility for the pet care portfolio. Ann began her career at Procter & Gamble and managed a variety of international brands including Pampers, Always and Olay before rising to global general manager. She has a BA with distinction from Stanford University and MBA and MS degrees from Columbia University in New York.

Ann is a member of the Lancaster University Management School Advisory Board, WACL, and is a founding member of the *Guardian*'s Women in Leadership. She is also a Woman of Influence for Cancer Research UK and advises WhiteCap LLC, a brand fund.

Ann lives in West London with her husband; her daughter attends university in the USA. A UK/US citizen, Ann also speaks German and Russian.

About CMI

The CMI is the only UK chartered body with the mission to promote better managed and led organisations by increasing the number and quality of professionally qualified managers. Founded in 1952, the CMI has over 100,000 in its membership community, and partners with 600 learning organisations and over 450 employers to provide best-practice content, toolkits and nationally recognised qualifications. We produce many thought-leading research reports on management and leadership topics and are the only professional body authorised to award the 'practical MBA' and coveted hallmark of Chartered Manager.

Introduction

What is management?

When I was studying business and journalism at Columbia University in New York, I won an internship with a major movie studio. However, this apparently perfect placement turned into a perfect storm. On the Friday evening before the Monday of my final presentation to the Board, my then boss, who had hardly spoken with me all summer, red-lined my entire presentation. Although it was backed by evidence, he felt it contradicted his point of view. At about 4.00 a.m. that Sunday morning, after hours of staring at my computer screen locked up in the plush Fifth Avenue offices, it dawned on me that I didn't have to put up with this. I could have redone the whole thing to appease my boss, but I quit instead.

Two years later, as a newly minted graduate, I was in Germany and had just been offered a job with Procter & Gamble. I was in the fortunate position of having another job offer, which I was on the point of accepting. Before making the final decision, the doorbell rang and a telegram arrived with a bouquet of flowers. It was from Procter & Gamble's Werner Geissler, the executive who had interviewed me, repeating the company's offer and emphasising how much they would like me to join. It was an easy choice. I embarked upon almost fourteen years of a very successful career with Procter & Gamble – a place that taught me the value of great leadership and management. It didn't matter that I was starting as a mere brand assistant; I was consistently made to feel that I could always make a difference, always learn, and always improve. Incidentally, today Werner Geissler is Procter & Gamble's Vice Chairman. And I can still count on his advice.

More than twenty-five years have since passed, in which time I have witnessed similar events time after time, involving both myself and others. The context varies, but the fundamental dynamic hasn't. It comes down to the same issue: are you managing well or are you managing badly? We have all worked for bad bosses and know that they can make life miserable. Equally, I hope you have worked for good managers who have inspired you. This book, then, is about how to recognise the difference between good and bad management and develop your skills as a good manager. As you do, you can make a positive difference for those whom you manage as well as for the organisation to which you belong.

Defining management

What is management and what do managers do? I have been managing for over twenty years and yet I still cannot answer this question easily. My favourite definition came ten years ago, when, as a senior manager for Mars, I was sent on a course at the Center for Creative Leadership in Colorado Springs. There, I learned that management was about creating the conditions for others to succeed. This is as good a short definition as you can find.

For those of you who still hunger for more theory, I have summarised the top twenty-five management thinkers in Chapter 22, 'A guide to the gurus'. I do not intend to explain all the gurus' definitions here. Instead, I will focus on capturing the core elements of what, why and how:

- **WHAT managers do** Managers plan, direct, coordinate and monitor the overall activities of organisations, or units within organisations.[1]

- **WHY they do it** The *purpose* of management: to provide direction, gain commitment, facilitate change and achieve results through the efficient, creative and responsible deployment of people and other resources.[2]

---

[1] International Labour Organization (2008). International Standard Classification of Occupations.
[2] Management Standards Centre (commissioned by UKCES), 2008, National Occupational Standards for Management and Leadership.

■ **HOW they do it** Managers make others more effective through better planning and organising. They bring out the best in other people. This involves setting goals, planning how to achieve them, motivating others, coordinating and evaluating activities and directing these activities to accomplish a task or objective.

In recent times the focus on management has moved away from planning and organising resources as part of a disciplined chain of command towards the skills of motivating, directing and coaching others to succeed. In reality both ways of working have their place. Patients in a hospital, for example, will want a good level of command and control over the storage and administration of medicines. In many contexts, however, 'command and control' is less effective. I will explore this in Chapter 3.

Who is a manager?

Managers plan: they direct, they organise, they decide, they act, they allocate, they motivate, they evaluate, they adapt, and they achieve results through others. Yet many with these responsibilities still don't see themselves as managers. I am always surprised when I am speaking on a topic such as the quality of managers today and my audience assumes that I am talking about some distant 'other' – a boss in an ivory tower. I'm not. I'm talking about them.

In the UK, the number of managers in 2010 is estimated at 3 million (UKCES[3]), and it will grow. By 2020, according to a government report, there will be an increase of almost 20 per cent to 3.6 million, requiring an extra 544,000 managers by the end of the decade. This trend is even truer globally, where growth in developing and emerging markets will create many managerial posts.

The 'accidental manager'

One reason people often don't see themselves as managers is that they 'fell' into management 'by accident'. They may have been promoted

[3] UKCES, *Working Futures 2010–2020*, 2012.

into management positions due to technical expertise or specialist skills. Suddenly, they are responsible for leading teams and budgets, but have not been trained in either area. Another reason that management is more difficult to identify with is that it is not always recognised as a profession in its own right. For example, whilst Chartered Accountants have existed since 1854, Chartered Managers have only existed since 2001. You do not need a licence to practise, such as in law or medicine. It is estimated that only around one in five managers is professionally qualified. However, the expectation is far different: as many as four out of five managers believe that managers *should* be professionally qualified.[4] I will talk about management qualifications in Chapter 1.

So you think you can manage

The fact that so many people are 'accidental managers' may explain why people often think they are better than they truly are at management. The best way to evaluate how effective you are is to ask those you manage. Unfortunately, when you look at UK surveys on this topic, the results are pretty dismal.

According to a 2012 survey conducted by CMI and Penna:[5]

- 43 per cent rated their managers as ineffective or highly ineffective.

- 21 per cent rated their managers as highly effective.

- 36 per cent rated their mangers as effective.

It is not just individuals who find their managers' skills don't measure up. Nearly three-quarters (72 per cent) of organisations in the UK reported their managers lacked skills, with nearly two-thirds (65 per cent) saying this was true of senior managers and a huge 85 per cent reporting deficiencies in the management skills of junior managers.[6]

---

[4] Bradley, M., Woodman, P. and Hutchings, P., *The Value of Management and Leadership Qualifications*, Chartered Management Institute, 2012.
[5] McBain, R. et al., *The Business Benefits of Management and Leadership Development*, Chartered Management Institute, 2012.
[6] CIPD, *Learning and Talent Development*, 2012.

Nature versus nurture

Contrary to some views, management skills can be learned and developed. Nine out of ten managers said that a management qualification improved their performance, and eight out of ten said this also improved the performance of their team.[7] Fortunately, the attitude that successful leaders and managers were born with a set of innate traits is dying out. Today, most would agree that management can be learned. As Henry Mintzberg,[8] author of the first CMI Management Book of the Year, said: 'It is time to recognise that management ... is a practice, learned primarily through experience and rooted in context.'

Types of managers

There are many different types of managers. Some specialise in certain functional areas such as marketing, operations, human resources, information or finance; others are general managers across all business areas. In this book we are focused on the skills and tools needed in general management although we do touch on certain specialist areas such as finance and marketing. That is because in today's increasingly complex and interdependent world it is virtually impossible to manage in isolation. Therefore understanding more about other functional areas will help you perform your role better, whether you are a general manager or more specialised. Different management styles are also more associated with different roles. (I will talk about styles in Chapter 1.)

The other aspect to consider is at what level of management you are. Managers and leaders exist at all levels – something that is often overlooked, as people tend to focus on those at the top. But officially, according to the National Standards, there are at least four levels:

1 **Team leaders** Entry-level roles with tightly defined duties, carried out according to existing practices. Team leaders organise others' work and disseminate information, as well as monitor and support performance of team members.

---

[7] Bradley, Woodman and Hutchings, *The Value of Management and Leadership Qualifications*.
[8] Mintzberg, H., *Managing*, Berrett-Koehler Publishers, 2011, p. 9.

Examples: Shift supervisor at restaurant or store; Call Centre team leader; Hospital Floor supervisor.

2 **First-line managers** Implement the plans of more senior managers in line with the vision and targets of an organisation. Often have resource responsibility and implement performance management. Primarily internally focused on delivering customer requirements.

Examples: Beauty Department Manager, Brand Manager, Call Centre Manager, Department Head at Hospital.

3 **Middle managers** Coordinate activities and solve problems. Have wider strategy-setting and decision-making powers, and have a budget. Do an operating plan. Manage the team leaders and first-line managers. Develop relationships across the organisation with other specialists. Outcomes meet internal and external stakeholder needs.

Examples: Digital Marketing Manager, Store Manager, Branch Manager, Area Manager, Category Manager, Assistant Principal.

4 **Senior managers/directors/business owners** Lead the organisation, primarily inspiring and guiding others and coaching to improve their performance. Develop and communicate strategy. Key people responsible for setting the direction the organisation or specialist area will take.

Examples: Head Teacher, Vice Chancellor, Marketing Director, Operations Director, European Director, UK Managing Director, Owner, Chief of Staff at Hospital.

Levels of management: rule of seven

Of course, many companies and organisations add in their own levels. There can be as many as twelve, which most would agree is too many. At Procter & Gamble, for example, when I was there, they generally tried to keep the number of levels between the entry level and the CEO down to seven; at Mars, managers' levels were known as 'zones'. Zone 1 referred to the owners, John and Forrest Mars, and Zone 7 or 8 was entry level. Whenever the number of levels between the top and the bottom went into double digits, you knew a restructuring wasn't far off.

exercise

Can you map the levels in your organisation from entry to the CEO?
Do you know where you fit?

The 'management versus leadership' debate

Many people love discussing the difference between managers and leaders, often implying that leaders are somehow superior. Yet both activities are necessary, and the best people are good at both. Most of the leading practitioners I know share this view. I will refer again to Henry Mintzberg[9] on this topic:

> It has become fashionable to distinguish leaders from managers ... One does the right things, copes with change; the other does things right, copes with complexity ... Frankly, I don't understand what this distinction means in the every-day life of organisations. Sure, we can separate managing and leading conceptually. But can we separate them in practice? Or, more to the point, should we even try? How would you like to be managed by someone who doesn't lead? [W]hy would you want to be led by someone who doesn't manage?

But for those of you who really cannot live without a conceptual distinction, I offer you one of the leading international thinkers on the topic, John Kotter:

> **Management** Makes systems of people and technology work well day after day, week after week, and year after year:
> - organising and staffing;
> - planning and budgeting;
> - controlling and problem-solving;
> - taking complex systems of people and technology and making them run efficiently, effectively and continuously.

---

[9] Mintzberg, *Managing*, p. 8.

Leadership Creates the systems that managers manage and changes them in fundamental ways to take advantage of opportunities and to avoid hazards:

- creating vision and strategy;

- communicating and setting direction;

- motivating action;

- aligning people;

- creating systems that managers can manage and transforming them when needed to allow for growth, evolution, opportunities, and hazard avoidance.

Kotter[10] sees management and leadership as complementary, and this is the approach taken for this book.

Traits that count

While managers are largely made not born, and competencies and skills can be learned, there are certain traits and behaviours which will help you be a better manager, and make it *easier* to succeed.

Six good traits for effective managers and leaders:[11]

1 **Drive** the desire to move forward and accomplish goals.

2 **Integrity** honesty and a sense of moral purpose.

3 **Self-confidence** a strong sense of self worth, but not arrogance.

4 **Curiosity** a questioning, inquiring mind that asks how things can be made better and is interested in others and the environment.

5 **Passion** a 'fire in the belly' – the desire to make a difference.

6 **Grit** the ability to stick out tough situations. To persevere and not give up.

---

[10] Kotter International. http://www.kotterinternational.com/kotterprinciples/management-vs-leadership

[11] Bennis, W., *On Becoming a Leader*, ReadHowYouWant Publishers, 2009, pp. 33–5; Kirkpatrick, S. and Edwin, A., *Leadership: Do Traits Matter?*, Academy of Management Executive, 1991; also, my own experience.

If you can combine these traits with a reasonable level of intelligence, plus knowledge of the business or organisation, you will be well placed to succeed.

Context counts

Just as there are different types and levels of managers, there are also different contexts. Managing in a start-up business is different to managing in a multinational organisation. I have worked in both, and the difference is huge. In a start-up, you wear many hats, are always doing everything yourself, and there is less structure. You can get lonely, and be afraid to ask for help. Things move very quickly, or as soon as you can get to them. In a multinational, you will be moved along in a structure, and will master one task or project before moving on to the next. There will be set ways of doing things that you will learn, and often you will be developed, though not always. Getting things done will take longer, as so many more people are involved.

It also matters what sort of sector you work in. There are traditional sectors, like heavy industry and manufacturing; service sectors like finance and healthcare; and the 'new' economy of technology start-ups. In heavy industry and manufacturing the core skills are likely to be engineering and operational skills; in service sectors they are likely to concern managing information and data; but people skills are critical in all sectors.

Who owns the business makes a difference as well. Private companies manage for profit, as do publicly held companies. In private companies the owner may well be the boss. In public companies, you have shareholders and generally more external stakeholders. In these companies performance is usually measured by the financial success of the company, and bonuses may be awarded to incentivise managers to achieve these targets. The bonus may be in stock, if it is a public company, or in cash.

Social enterprises are a new form of private company that manages for profit but reinvests the profit in community enterprises. These are gaining rapidly in popularity and appeal. Leading managers and thinkers, including Unilever CEO Paul Polman and Harvard's Michael Porter, believe that shared value – combining private enterprise profits with social enterprise benefits – is the next business model for capitalism and will help us to sustain and improve the quality of life in our world. I agree with them. Chapter 13, which looks at measuring results, talks about how to look beyond financial terms when evaluating your organisation's performance.

Public sector managers are a huge part of the population in any country, including the UK, as the government is often the largest single employer. In the public sector, you are not managing for profit, but for achieving a better result in terms of the quality or efficiency of a service or outcome, such as better education or healthcare, more effective town planning, or a lower crime rate. Your budget is allocated to you as part of government spending, so you don't have to worry so much about revenue generation. Nonetheless, questions of funding are of paramount concern to public sector managers, given the huge cuts in public sector spending recently.

The third sector refers to charitable and other non-profit organisations. These can be in the arts, those that help the less fortunate; and institutions that educate such as museums. If you are managing here, you are trying to provide a community service for free; you are also trying to raise money as well. You also work with many stakeholders and rely heavily on unpaid workers or volunteers.

All these factors will affect the objectives, styles and measurements of where you manage. But in all of these environments you are still a manager. Generally speaking, in more uncertain, fluid environments, the organisation will be more decentralised, and in more stable environments will be more formal and centralised. One of the biggest challenges confronting managers today is how to combine both kinds of cultures and organisations within the same enterprise: the stable and predictable with the fluid and more agile.

Why management matters

So, does management actually matter? And how much difference does improving management make? The answers are, respectively, 'Yes' and 'Probably far more than you imagine'. Benefits can be transformational.

They assist the organisation, the customer, the economy and society, not just process efficiencies.

Good management:

- improves business performance;
- improves employee performance;
- makes people healthier and happier;
- improves the survival rates of business;
- improves society in terms of ethical and sustainable benefits.

In February of 2012, CMI and Penna[12] undertook the biggest study ever on the benefits of management and leadership in the UK. The study showed that organisations that invest effectively in management and leadership performed on average 23 per cent higher than those that didn't. This can mean the difference between success and failure.

Global studies also show the difference good management makes. A 2011 study by McKinsey and the London School of Economics showed that a single point improvement in management practice (on a five-point scale) is associated with the same increase in output as a 25 per cent increase in the labour force or a 65 per cent increase in invested capital. In other words, good management is like having more people or having more money![13] The opposite is also true, as incompetent management by company directors causes over half of company failures.[14]

Perhaps as importantly, good management improves people's performance, both in terms of their engagement and their wellbeing. And people in growing companies are more likely to be managed well, whereas people in declining companies and organisations are less likely to benefit from good management.

People who are well managed are happier and healthier than those who are not. By contrast, people who are poorly managed are often poorly themselves, suffering stress, and other illness. It is estimated that poor

[12] McBain et al., *The Business Benefits of Management and Leadership Development.*
[13] Department for Business, Innovation and Skills, *Leadership and Management in the UK – The Key to Sustainable Growth*, 2012.
[14] Ibid.

management costs UK business over £19 billion per year in reduced productivity.[15]

Finally, good management makes a similar difference everywhere. The global study we cited above showed that across the world in twenty countries firms that applied best practices were more profitable, grew faster and survived longer than those who didn't in every country looked at.[16]

What the world needs now is better managers

The global financial crisis of 2008 and the ensuing economic recession has brought into question the trustworthiness of business managers. One survey showed that trust in business and government declined sharply in 2012 in all eighteen countries surveyed, with double-digit declines registering in most mature markets. The main cause of irresponsible behaviour was poor management.[17] Unlike other professions, such as medicine or law, which explicitly recognise a commitment to serving the greater good and formally espouse a strict code of conduct, management has yet to define either.

Widespread views of management often focus on the maximisation of short-term financial returns, and emphasise a narrow view of managerial responsibilities as serving the interest of shareholders over clients, employees, or society at large. These views misrepresent the full complexity of the management profession and its role in driving global prosperity and, as we have painfully learned, can have disastrous economic consequences. Recent events in the UK highlight this – the scandal at Barclays concerning fixing LIBOR (the London Inter-Bank Offered Rate), and the Leveson inquiry into misconduct by elements of the media.

In order to rebuild trust in business and government institutions,

---

[15] Cooper, C. and Worrall, L., *The Quality of Working Life*, Chartered Management Institute, 2012.

[16] Bloom, N., Genakos, C., Sadun, R. and Ven Reenen, J., *Management Practices Across Firms and Countries*, Harvard Business School, 2011.

[17] Edelman Global Trust Index 2012.

create economic growth and build sustainable businesses, and develop a happier and healthier society, we need to develop more good managers. This guide is designed to help achieve this. More immediately, this guide is designed to help *you* to be a better manager for yourself, others and your organisation, wherever you may work.

part

1

Managing yourself

1

What kind of manager are you?

What you will learn in this chapter

- What kind of personality and management style you have and why it matters
- Understanding and using your strengths to have a positive impact on others
- How to develop an ethical framework for taking management decisions
- How to handle stress and maintain a work–life balance

Who are you?

The answer to the question, 'What kind of manager are you?' begins with who you are as a person. Yet one of the most difficult tasks for a manager is developing self-awareness. That is why so much of modern management development focuses on psychological profiling to help managers better understand themselves.

The most widely used of these personality assessments is called Myers Briggs.[1] Indeed, every organisation I have worked for has used this tool as part of its management development programme. It has been taken by over 50 million people and used by over 10,000 companies, 2,500 universities and 200 government agencies in the US alone.[2] Originally

---

[1] http://www.myersbriggs.org/
[2] http://www.washingtonpost.com/leadership

developed to help women enter the workforce during World War II, it is based on the theories of Carl Jung and has sixteen distinct personality types.[3] Which one you are is defined by four different areas:

1 To recharge, do you spend time with people (Extrovert) or your thoughts (Introvert)?

2 Do you perceive information more through your senses – tangible things you see and touch such as data and details – in the present (Sensing), or more through your gut-feeling, hunches and concepts with a view towards the future (Intuitive)?

3 Do you make decisions primarily based on analysing situations (Thinking) or more on how your emotions are responding (Feeling)?

4 Do you prefer to have a plan and act? (Judging) or stay open and adapt (Perceiving)?

The resulting four-letter combination defines your personality: for example, I am an ENTP (where N stands for intuitive).

Whether you use this or another personality assessment, understanding more the kind of person you are is a vital element to becoming a better manager.

The concept of being you at work is a powerful one. Suppose that you are a natural right-hander but you are forced to write with your left hand. You would find that awkward. Now imagine that you had to produce a book for work, and so had to write with your 'wrong' hand, day in day out, for hours at a time. The same is true for management. If we cannot be ourselves, and have to subvert or redirect who we really are, we quickly become more stressed and less effective. That is because too much of our energy is invested in suppressing who we naturally are and pretending to act in a way that we would not normally do.

Now imagine the opposite: you are totally in synch with yourself, doing what comes naturally, able to focus completely on the people and tasks around you without being self-conscious, achieving a great deal in what seems like very little time. That is called Flow. It leads to greater hap-

---

[3] Jung, C.G., *Psychological Types, Collected Works*, Vol. 6, Princeton University Press (1971 [1921]).

piness and fulfilment, as well as increased productivity. Be yourself at work and 'go with the Flow'.[4]

Management styles

As a manager, one of your key responsibilities will be to ensure your department, team or area of the business delivers its objectives. The way in which you deal with people will have a big impact on how successful you are as a manager. Therefore, becoming aware of your management style and its impact on others is really important.

There are many theories of management style. For me, the best of these deploy the simple idea of people and tasks. If you are focused on both the people and the task, you are going to get the best results. If you are focused on neither, you are going to get no results. If you are only focused on the task, you may get things done but risk harming relationships. If you are only focused on the people, they may like you but you probably won't get much done.

One summary of this is called the Management Grid, developed in the 1950s and 1960s by Robert Blake and Jane Moulton. It describes different management styles as follows:[5]

1 **Impoverished management** Little concern for either the task or the people. This style involves little more than going through the motions, doing only enough to get by. These are called the 'slackers' or those who are 'disengaged'.

2 **Authority-obedience** High levels of concern for task and low for people. This represents a controlling style, close to the traditional 'command and control' approach, but runs the risk of damaging human relationships. If you are a nice guy, then this style can also be benevolent, autocratic or paternalistic.

3 **Country club leadership** High levels of concern for people and low for task. This is seen as accommodating – it may create a warm and friendly working environment but at the cost of getting the job done efficiently. This is the guy or gal who takes all his or her reports

---

[4] Csikszentmihaly, M., *Flow: The Psychology of Optimal Experience*, Harper Perennial, 1990.
[5] Blake, R. and Mouton, J., *The Managerial Grid: The Key to Leadership Excellence*, Houston: Gulf Publishing Co., 1964.

out for endless team lunches, team-building days and drinks, but doesn't really manage their output.

4 **Team management** High levels of concern for both task and people. This is seen as the most effective style with the potential for high achievement. Of course, you also need to manage various individuals, as well as teams.

5 **Middle of the road management** Moderate level of concern for task and people. This achieves a balance between task and performance but is likely to perpetuate the status quo rather than achieve notable success. It can also be quite bureaucratic and resistant to change.

I have seen all of these styles at work over the years. Do you recognise yourself and your colleagues?

Plot yourself on the graph in Figure 1.1. Then ask one peer, one direct report and your boss to do the same. Do the descriptions of your style match up? What are the key differences? Ask for specific examples and feedback to explain them.

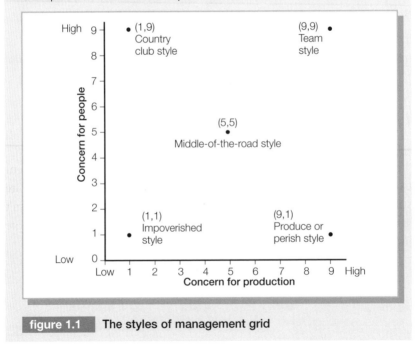

figure 1.1   **The styles of management grid**

Situational leadership

How you manage also depends on the situation, and you need to flex your style accordingly. Doing so is called situational leadership. If you are in a crisis, you may need to be more directive – you don't want to ask people which fire exit they prefer or hold a vote on who should leave the burning building first. The style you apply can change over time, and, indeed, managers should change their style over time to reflect the shifting capabilities of their people and the organisation. The skill levels of people also matter, as does their motivation. If you are overseeing lots of unengaged, low-skilled people, then you will need to behave differently than if you are in charge of highly motivated and qualified people who have been working together a long time. Our One Minute Manager guru, Ken Blanchard, also thinks that how you manage others depends on who you are leading and their skill level and commitment, as he explains below:[6]

- A **telling/directing** style when they are both unwilling and unable.

- A **selling/coaching** style when there is some competence but a lack of commitment.

- A **participating/supporting** style where they are competent but unwilling or insecure.

- A **delegating** style where competence and commitment are both high.

Which style is most effective? The answer is it depends on both the situation and the context, but, generally speaking, high concern for both people and task will get the best results. This is a shift away from the 'command and control' or paternalistic styles that were very prevalent earlier. Sadly, however, the most common styles in the UK and US are still autocratic-bureaucratic. And we wonder why the economy isn't growing.[7] We will explore how to develop each of these styles more fully in Chapters 7 and 8.

---

[6] http://www.kenblanchard.com
[7] http://www.managers.org.uk/workinglife2012

Leading from strengths

We all have innate strengths, so one would think that we would rely very heavily on these in our role as managers. And yet we don't. According to a Google lecture by Carolyn Foster, when Gallup, the famous opinion poll organisation, asked 1.7 million people all over the world whether they could use the things they were best at in their workplace every day, only 20 per cent said yes.[8] When we do performance reviews, far too many of us focus on areas where we need to improve, and spend too much time trying to 'fix' weaknesses rather than grow strengths. We should focus on using the things we are good at, more effectively. We can use our strengths to mitigate our weaknesses.

Think about your talents – things that come naturally to you. Think, too, about talents that you do not use much but would like to develop. There's a useful survey at http://www.viame.org/survey/Account/ Register 'Values In Action', created by Dr Seligman.[9] Any strength, however, taken to the extreme, becomes a weakness. For example, if your natural strength is to be able to seek harmony, this can lead you to shy away from taking difficult decisions. Try to use offsetting characteristics to keep your strengths from becoming too much of a good thing, and ask people for feedback to help you. It also helps to have diversity of strengths in teams as discussed in Chapter 9.

In addition to strengths that are uniquely yours, there are some 'freebies' – strengths we can all access if we choose, and which increase our levels of satisfaction in working and personal lives.[10] These are:

1 **Zest** This is about unbridled enthusiasm and vitality, fuelled by the ability to make a difference in our world.

2 **Curiosity** Our intrinsic interest in our internal and external environments.

---

[8] Carolyn Foster, 'Leading from strength: making a difference as only you can', Google Tech Talk, 29 Jan. 2008, citing Buckingham, Marcus and Clifton, Donald O., *Now, Discover Your Strengths*, Free Press, 2001.

[9] Ibid.

[10] Authentic happiness, in Foster, 'Leading from strength: making a difference as only you can'.

3 **Optimism** Thinking that troubles are transient, limited and controllable.

4 **Gratitude** Go thank someone. Write down three things to be grateful for twice a week – apparently this is the most effective discipline of all.

5 **Giving and receiving appreciation** Remember, the absence of recognition is why people leave jobs. So this is vitally important.

Once you start to know your strengths, don't try to do everything at once. Take it a step at a time. Otherwise you'll be overwhelmed, as will those around you, and you may end up being less effective.

Be aware of impact

How you behave will have a great impact, and it is the simple things that matter. Saying 'good morning' and 'thank you' – sincerely – is crucial to getting people behind you. I learned this lesson early in my career as a brand manager. I was overseeing a major launch, and after two years we were ready. The $200 million factory had been built; over 50 million samples were ready to go, and the competitors were at our door with their versions of the product. It was tense and the stakes were high. I had become obsessed with getting this task executed perfectly. I had three young brand assistants working for me – all very different people. One day, they all came knocking at my door.

'We need to speak to you', they said, coming into my office and shutting the door behind them. 'You never say "Hi" to us, or address us as people. Each day, you just storm into the office, head down, straight into your own office, and shut the door. It's terrible. You make us feel like you don't care. Like you don't value us.'

That was a wake-up call. I changed my behaviour after that, and we went on to build a really strong team, and together launched one of Procter & Gamble's most successful regional brands ever.

In today's digital world, the human touch is arguably even more important. Recently I led a session at a company where the employees were not feeling engaged because the managers did not make them feel valued. At a workshop asking which behaviours could improve, the common element across all the groups was recognition – often in the form of simple everyday actions.

The importance of ethics and values

In 2013, we are still feeling the effects of a global financial crisis and a recession predicted to last another several years. What is its root cause? Bankers, insurers and government regulators all behaving badly, according to many people. Why and how did this happen? What can we do differently as managers to make sure we don't slip into selfish, harmful ways? The answer is to develop a moral compass – and that means to develop ethics and values, and ensure we take them with us to work.

Ethics and values are about doing what's right and having some form of principles alongside just profits or progress. But which principles are right and how should we decide? One approach to this very timely subject uses the concepts of 'Ethicability and Moral DNA'. In his book, *Ethicability*, Roger Steare talks about three different forms of ethics: the Ethic of Obedience, the Ethic of Reason and the Ethic of Care.[11]

The Ethic of Obedience is about obeying rules of law or codes of conduct; the Ethic of Reason is about analysing what is wise and exercising self-discipline; and the Ethic of Care is about what is helping humanity, respecting human dignity and showing empathy for others. All of these ethical dimensions have been recognised by philosophers since Aristotle and Confucius, although what is new is what Steare does with them. He started testing people along all three dimensions, using an online tool he calls Moral DNA. Based on the results of over 50,000 people from all over the world, he makes some pretty interesting observations:

■ We are different people at home than at work. At work we have more obedience, more reason and less care than at home.

■ Women generally have higher levels of all three ethical dimensions than men; this is especially true of the ethic of care.

[11] http://www.ethicability.org/

▦ As we get older, our ethic of care stays more or less constant, whilst our ethic of obedience declines and our ethic of reason increases.

Given that most of the bankers and executives involved in the financial crises were older males, it seems that it was very easy for them to be more selfish, less caring and to write their own rules. The UK Labour politician Harriet Harman MP famously said, 'Financial crises might have been avoided if we'd have had Lehman Sisters.'

So how should we ensure we bring ethical decision-making back into our workplace?

Steare offers up something he calls the RIGHT[12] acronym. It means we ask ourselves the following:

▦ What are the **R**ules?

▦ Are we acting with **I**ntegrity?

▦ Who is this **G**ood for?

▦ Who could we **H**arm?

▦ What's the **T**ruth?

Steare's work also suggests that if we behaved more authentically, more in tune with our 'at rest' selves with regards to ethics, we would make better, more ethical decisions. Companies sometimes try to bridge the gap between work and home by encouraging employees to use their personal values in making workplace decisions. Examples of this include encouraging employees to spend the companies' money as if it were their own, and not cutting corners on quality, and introducing 'buddy' programmes to help new people on board. By bridging the gap between individual and corporate values, many companies feel they will be creating more ethical workplaces.

High standards of professional conduct and competence are at the heart of good ethics in management, wherever practised in the world. Being professional means that you behave appropriately for the culture and the situation. If you are new to a culture, ask someone who has worked there before to explain a few basic norms and expectations.

---

[12] Steare, R., *Ethicability*, Roger Steare Consulting Limited, 2011.

How you present business cards and organise business dinners is different in Shanghai from in Chicago.

Of course, some good practices are universal. You should not bully or insult others or behave in a way that could be construed as harassment of any sort. Nor should you use email in the wrong way – whether it's to boast of your colleagues' sexual prowess or to ask everyone on the site if they have seen the sausages you put in the staff fridge. If you're unsure whether your behaviour is professional, ask someone for feedback, or imagine what your grandmother would say! The Confucian interpretation of the golden rule is also helpful: do not do anything to anyone else that you wouldn't want them to do to you.[13]

Trust is a fundamental element of any relationship between a manager and others. It can take a long time to establish, yet only moments to destroy. Establishing a working relationship that is based on trust goes a long way to improving morale, motivation and employee engagement, which in turn leads to increased productivity and performance.

There are two sides to trust within a relationship. There can be:

■ trustworthy behaviour (i.e. responding to trust others place in you);

■ trusting behaviour (i.e. putting your trust in others).

Trustworthy behaviour involves:

■ communicating – keeping people informed;

■ keeping promises;

■ being honest;

■ not misleading people;

■ admitting when you are wrong;

■ showing concern for others;

■ keeping confidences;

■ not talking behind others' backs.

---

[13] Confucius, *Analects*, 43, Aspen Institute Germany Seminar Readings, 2012 edn, p. 275.

What to do when you are under pressure

Limited resources, time, training, money and equipment can add to stress levels. A certain level of pressure can be effective in keeping people motivated. However, when it gets beyond this level problems often arise and stress ensues. Recognising that you are pressurised before stress takes hold will enable you to assess your activities and processes with a clear head. Try to work smarter by streamlining processes and decide how better to manage time and resources. Eliminate 'waste'. Accept the elements that are outside your control, and work on the problems you *can* change.

Consider the following steps for identifying and reducing the causes of stress and pressure:

- **Recognise your symptoms** Health, behaviour and attitude to work.

- **Identify the sources** What is making you feel pressured? This could be home life as well as work life.

- **Know your response** Knowing how to adapt and adjust.

- **Identify the strategies that help you cope** Such as breaking down a work task, removing or reducing outside pressure; taking a walk; taking a holiday.

- **Begin to make the necessary changes** To yourself, your relationships and your activities.[14]

The work environment

Once upon a time, industrial estates and office parks were bleak and faceless environments, showcased in series like *The Office*. But thank goodness, that's starting to change. Increasingly, office parks are trying to create environments and programmes that help managers enjoy work. One such park, near where I live, has even made 'Enjoy Work' its credo, equipping office park staff with sunny yellow jackets, golf carts and umbrellas emblazoned with the slogan Enjoy Work. Built around a lovely setting with a bridge, waterfall, lake and birds and fish, there are

---

[14] *Stress Management: Self First*, CMI Checklist Series, no. 34, 2011.

constant activities that encourage people to mingle – everything from massages and Chinese tarot to soccer games, concerts, barbecues and fireworks. Outside seating areas and temporary 'chillax' zones provide plenty of places for enjoying nice weather. A health club and restaurants onsite complete the vibrant atmosphere. (Note: this complex just won an award for creating a first-class work environment!)

Keeping balance

Maintaining a work–life balance, and a workload balance, will significantly help to prevent stress and burn-out. Research shows that those who experience wellbeing at work are more productive, and work–life balance is an essential part of wellbeing. Find time to relax and unwind. Improve your own efficiency in such key areas as time and energy management, avoiding information overload, and delegation.

In today's 24 × 7 world, managers' stress increases as they are always accessible by Smartphone or iPad. In fact, experts say that this accessibility is increasing stress levels and diminishing productivity. So don't expect your team to answer emails at all hours. And make sure your boss has reasonable expectations. A friend of mine quit her job as company President because her boss expected her to have her phone on by her bed every morning from 6.00 a.m. and every evening till midnight. Go on. Switch It Off!

Top tips: best ideas for work–life balance

1 Focus on outcomes not office time.

2 Encourage your employer to adopt flexi-time and flexible working.

3 Take a walk break once an hour ('Management by Walking Around').

4 Plan your week to balance family, work and fun activities.

5 Put your health and family first.

If all else fails – try a career break. I recently took three years out from corporate life to help my family, moving continents to do so. Of course it was tough to re-enter the working world, but the time spent putting my family first gave me a valuable perspective and helped to re-frame my focus when I did return.

Top tips, pitfalls and takeaways

Top tips

▥ Know Yourself. Know Others. Know your Style.

Top pitfalls

▥ Forgetting the impact of your behaviour on others and its impact on the climate, morale and performance.

▥ Losing balance and effectiveness through burn-out.

Top takeaway

▥ Style matters. How we manage others at work has the biggest impact on their job satisfaction. People leave people, not jobs.

Getting things done

What you will learn in this chapter

- How to set objectives and prioritise
- How to monitor progress towards objectives
- How to accept ownership of tasks and responsibilities, and own up to mistakes
- How to make decisions and communicate them

As a manager, regardless of your style, you need to accomplish things through yourself and others. In this chapter, we discuss getting things done: how to set goals, plan your time, make decisions, and cope when it all goes wrong – as it will from time to time. Your ability to do all of these things lies in the degree to which you are willing and able to take responsibility for your actions.

Getting things done

We all struggle with this one. It's a universal part of being human, let alone being a manager. A useful three-word reminder is: 'Do, Don't Stew!' – spend less time mulling over your burden, and more time reducing it. The classic scenario is when you wake up in the middle of the night worried about a big presentation, meeting or project. The task looms large, but there is nothing you can do about it at 3.00 a.m. However, if you do have important insights as to how you might tackle the issue, it can help to jot them down. So keep a pad and pen by the bed.

Even if you have achieved a calm mental state and have planned everything, something unexpected may happen. But by better planning, and anticipating that things may misfire, you can achieve better management of tasks and of time. This reduces work pressures so that you will feel more relaxed; moreover, others will be more likely to perceive you as calm and well-organised.

Consider how you currently use your time. An analysis of your activities could reveal that a significant proportion of your working day is being 'wasted' on unimportant tasks. An analysis could include some of the following:

▓ **Be clear about how you spend your time** Keep a log of your activities and compare how it maps versus the Priority Grid (p. 21).

▓ **Be clear about your objectives and priorities** Understand what is required of you and when you are expected to deliver.

▓ **Ascertain what your potential problem areas may be** What is making you use time inefficiently? What is getting in the way of getting things done?

▓ **Tackle the enemy without** Those external factors that are outside your control such as the work of other departments, constant phone ringing, emails arriving, etc.

▓ **Tackle the enemy within** Personal inefficiency such as lack of planning and prioritising the less urgent work; tendency to waste time surfing favourite websites, checking emails, etc.

▓ **Make time to play** Decrease pressure and stress by aiming to allocate some time to relax.

▓ **Make time to think** Allocate time to yourself where you won't be interrupted so that you can think and plan with a clear head.[1]

---

[1] *Managing Your Time Effectively*, CMI Checklist Series, no. 16, 2011.

Manage energy as well as time

You might also think about managing your energy levels as well as your time. If you are feeling low, no amount of time management will inspire you to produce a winning presentation. Similarly, should you find yourself in full flow on that important presentation when lunchtime beckons, try to finish the task while your energy is high and eat lunch a little later; maybe treat yourself to something special as a reward. Most of us have body clocks and know our peak and low times. Try to fit in tasks accordingly.

Deadlines

Deadlines help get things done by setting an agreed timescale and sharing this with those involved in the task. They should be realistic, however, to reduce unnecessary pressure. Instinctively, most of us will focus on the task with the closest deadline and tackle this first. However, don't be guided by dates alone. Rather, consider how long each task is estimated to take. Establish if there is any leeway with the deadline set. Avoid the temptation to prioritise easy or enjoyable tasks at the expense of complex or less favourable ones.

As well as considering a deadline date, take into account the start date too,[2] estimating how long a task will take to complete so it can be started in plenty of time. When many deadlines loom at once, workloads can become insurmountable. Prioritising tasks in advance and creating a clear plan for time management will lower stress and make tasks more manageable, and enjoyable. Remember to build in some contingency time to allow for unexpected events.

Setting objectives

Objectives help you to steer individuals and teams in the right direction for the collective good of the organisation. They ensure that everyone in the organisation understands what they are working towards and the

---

[2] Bittel, Lester R., *Right on Time! The Complete Guide for Time-Pressured Managers*, McGraw-Hill, 1991, p. 63.

responsibility each has in meeting expectations. They also clearly high-light how results will be measured, providing a framework for feedback and performance.

Objectives should provide challenge and clarity, motivating employees to realise their potential and promote positive impact. Setting unre-alistic objectives can have the negative effect of disengaging people; setting vague ones can lead to confusion. It is important that indi-vidual, team or departmental objectives are set in the wider context of the organisation's goals.

A common framework for goal-setting follows the SMART acronym. Objectives should be: Specific; Measurable; Achievable; Results-focused; and Time-bound:[3]

> **S**pecific – objectives should clearly describe and define the required result.
> **M**easurable – an agreed process, system or method for identifying when an objective has been met.
> **A**chievable – challenging but achievable in terms of resources, funding, skills, time, and so on.
> **R**esults-focused and **R**elevant – goals should have outcomes that will make a positive and lasting impact to the organisation and contribute to its strategy.
> **T**ime-bound – a timeframe for accomplishing the objectives should be set.

Keep your objectives simple, using 250 words or fewer. Avoid jargon, or going into the micro-detail of your individual or departmental tasks, and the macro detail of the overall organisational mission. Under- or over-shooting objectives is a common mistake.

Unless you measure progress towards objectives you will never know whether you are on the way to achieving them. I am amazed by how few managers actually routinely measure progress towards objectives and projects they set themselves and their teams – except for the week right before the annual performance appraisal. It may be that the objec-tives set aren't the right ones, or the measurements are too complicated,

---

[3] *SMART Objectives*, CMI Management Models Series.

or inappropriate, or too vague. Make sure when you set objectives for yourself with your boss and then with your team, that you agree on the measurements and how often you will review progress towards these. Do it at least once a month.

Later I will share more formal ways of evaluating and measuring performance objectives, programmes and initiatives (in Parts 3 and 4).

exercise

Set your objectives using the SMART approach with your boss. Then ask your team members to do the same. See if they link with your own objectives and those of the organisation to which you belong. Now, do all of you understand how your individual objectives are contributing to the overall organisational goals? If not, where are the gaps? The overlaps? Where are things unrealistic or unclear?

Clear priorities

Once your objectives are set, you will need to prioritise which things to do when. There will be many interruptions and other features of your working day which don't directly contribute or relate to your objectives. A simple 'urgent versus important' grid can help prioritising.

Important tasks are those which contribute to your long-term goals and objectives. If you are not clear about what your aims are, establishing these should be your starting point. Tasks which are urgent and important might include: emergencies, customer complaints, meetings and appointments or reports that need to be delivered within a specific time frame. These must to be carried out straight away or delegated to someone else if appropriate. It is vital to plan time slots in advance for tasks which are important but not urgent. This will ensure you will have time to give them the attention they deserve and to complete them successfully.

If you judge that tasks are urgent but not important – requests from others, interruptions and distractions, for example – you should assess

Important and urgent	Not important and urgent	Do now	Delegate or reject
Important and not urgent	Not important and not urgent	Plan to do	Discard

figure 2.1   A simple urgent versus important grid

Source: Chartered Management Institute.

them carefully and try to avoid them if you can. You may be able to delegate them or to explain sensitively why you are unable to complete them.

Tasks which are neither important nor urgent are ones which you should try to exclude whenever possible. Cross them off your task list, and keep that list so you know what's been crossed off. If, in six months' time, you or someone else feels an impact from you not having done those things, then you may want to revisit.

The importance of ownership and responsibility

Taking ownership for your areas of responsibility will help others to see that you operate with integrity and can be trusted to follow through on your commitments. The opposite is also true. Lack of ownership, or 'passing the buck', is a management scourge. Just think about how many managers passed the buck when it came to the major scandals. The flip side of taking the glory when things go right is taking the flak when things go wrong.

Taking ownership of tasks and responsibilities gives your role clarity. It enhances your credibility and lends a degree of authority, as you are perceived as the 'go-to' person for a given task or problem. For collaborative working, the RACI Matrix is an effective way of clarifying roles. RACI represents: **R**esponsible, **A**ccountable, **C**onsulted, **I**nformed.[4] Such tools can prevent blurring the lines of responsibility, ensuring that everyone knows what areas they are personally accountable for and what is expected of them. I explore this tool further in Chapter 8.

It is also important to understand what you can and cannot reasonably influence. The power to influence others may be key to being a successful manager, but it is important that you understand your own sphere of influence. The time-honoured Serenity Prayer is helpful: 'God, grant me the serenity to accept the things I cannot change, the courage to change the things I can, and the wisdom to know the difference.'[5]

However careful and conscientious we are, we all make mistakes. What matters is our response. If you want to gain the respect of your employees, your peers and your superiors then you have to take ownership of any mistakes made. This could sometimes even mean having the responsibility of dealing with mistakes made by others if they work for you, or if you are part of a team or division that has missed an important milestone. Blaming others for a bad outcome is a sure-fire way to create a toxic atmosphere. So *always* own up to your mistakes. If you have made a mistake, apologise to all affected. Devise a plan to rectify the mistake and endeavour to resolve it swiftly and to the satisfaction of everyone involved. Saying sorry can be a very liberating experience, and it is amazing how it can take the heat out of situations with others.

Making mistakes is often a spur to innovating better products or services.[6] MIX, the Management Innovation Exchange, rates submissions which recount mistakes and what was learned as far more valuable than those that share glowing accounts of individual and corporate heroism.[7]

---

4 *RACI Matrix*, CMI Management Models Series.

5 http://www.thefix.com/content/serenity-prayers-desperate-origins-Niehbur-Bonhoeffer-Tillich9965

6 Pearn, Michael, Mulrooney, Chris and Payne, Tim, *Ending the Blame Culture*, Gower, 1998, p. 106.

7 http://www.managementexchange.com

Similarly, responding to a setback in a positive way may force you to consider how you might tackle a particular issue differently, which could lead to a more favourable outcome in the longer term. Sometimes, it's best to take a break. You can recover, regain perspective and bounce back. I guarantee you that every good manager has experienced many failures. Try asking your mentor or someone you admire what their greatest setback was and what they learned from it. You'll be surprised how open people will be in sharing their 'failure' stories. Also, by asking others what they learned from their setbacks, you will gain more insight into how to learn from your own.

Making good decisions

Management is all about taking decisions, and yet many people struggle with this. Sometimes the issue seems too complex, or the decision is spread across many different areas. Sometimes we are afraid to take decisions for fear of reprisal, either from our bosses, our reports, or external stakeholders such as customers. But chronic indecisiveness is a key reason for poor results. Decisions can be rational, or 'gut', simple or complex, or a combination. They can be made individually, or as a group, consensually, consultatively or autocratically. They require you to identify issues, weigh up the problems and consequences, and to use the best information available, knowing that it will never be perfect. You will also need to identify who will be affected by your decision and the risks involved, in order to assess whom to consult or include in the process.

So how can you become more decisive? Here are six simple steps:

1 Identify the issue: Understand what it is you are trying to decide.

2 Decide how to decide.

3 Decide: Use an evidence-based approach, plus your own judgement and experience.

4 Communicate what you've decided.

5 Implement your decision.

6 Monitor the impact and results and adjust as required.

1. Identify the issue

What is it that you are trying to decide? Are you sure you are tackling the right issue? Being clear on the problems that require solving is valuable. Try asking, 'Why?' until you get to the nub of the issue. This is analogous to tackling the disease rather than the symptom; it's also called root cause analysis.

2. Decide how to decide

In order to decide how simple or complex your decision process should be, try asking yourself the following questions:

> How much information do you need?
> What are the risks of getting it wrong?
> Who will be affected by the decision?

If the decision is not that important, you can probably decide it yourself. On the other hand if it is going to have an impact on others, needs others to help in its implementation or has high consequences, you will need to involve others in the decision-making process, if only to get their input and information.

> How urgent is it? How much time do you have?

If you don't have a lot of time, you may need to involve fewer people or settle for less information, or consider fewer alternatives.

3. Use an appropriate process

The fundamental process for decision-making involves:

◼ **Involve the right people and information** Try to include *all* those who have good information and/or are affected by the decision.
◼ **Generate alternatives** Weigh up different ways of solving the problem. Be sure to consider things from a variety of functional and stakeholder perspectives.
◼ **Evaluate the alternatives** Which best meets the objective? What is the impact? Is the outcome ethical? Agree a framework for evaluating alternatives that is objective and transparent, and uses

evidence wherever possible. Be sure to include the risks as well as the rewards. Frequently, costs versus benefits or high/low impact and effort frameworks can help here. You can also assign rating scores based on the degree to which alternatives meet key needs. When evaluating alternatives, try to avoid 'groupthink', and bias.

▩ **Choose the best alternative** Ultimately, you have to select your preferred option. Too often managers will present papers that weigh up all the options but never set out any clear decisions, or they attempt to combine too many options into a combined decision. I call this last bit a 'kitchen sink' decision. Avoid it! It's muddled and won't work.

▩ **Check it against your original objective and the impact.**

▩ **Check it against your judgement and experience.**

4. Communicate your decision

This step is sometimes overlooked. It is essential that you communicate your decision to all who are affected. If you forget this, you may create confusion or disengagement, and encourage behaviours that will undermine the effectiveness of your decision.

5. Implement

Now that you've invested all the time and effort in taking the decision, don't forget to do it! This will almost always be the hardest part to get right.

6. Monitor the results and impact

Rational decision-making has its limits. It can be very time-consuming and resource intensive, and it can lead to paralysis. No decision will ever have perfect information. Counter-intuitively, it can lead to the wrong decision, particularly if it contravenes the 'gut' feel of any number of participants. Therefore, increasingly, 'gut' methods such as that advocated by Malcolm Gladwell in *Blink*, as well as more collaborative, agile, iterative trial and error methods are gaining in popularity. These will be explored further in Chapter 15.

Top tips for making decisions

1 Know what you are deciding.

2 Separate gut from evidence in decision-making.

3 Be clear in your decision. Can you explain why you took it?

4 It's OK to decide not to decide – for a time. But not forever.

Top pitfalls in decision-making

1 Don't let your preconceived preferences influence the process.

2 Don't cut corners, especially if the decision has far-reaching implications.

3 Don't cherry pick from too many options, or try to solve too many things at once, or you may end up in a muddle.

4 Don't ignore your gut.

Additional resources: http://productivemuslim.com/productivity-ninja/

Top tips, pitfalls and takeaways

Top tips

■ Use SMART objectives. Make sure you revisit your progress against these at least once a month.

■ Manage your energy as well as your time. Do the big stuff when you have the most energy.

■ Learn from failures.

Top pitfalls

■ Vague objectives and decisions, kitchen sink decisions and non-decisions all lead to underperformance of individuals and organisations.

■ Forgetting to apologise when you have made a mistake. If you do things you will make mistakes. Get over it.

Top takeaways

■ Prioritise. Focus on what's important and urgent, and make time to do what is important but not urgent. Do or delegate the urgent but not important and avoid the not urgent and not important.

■ To get things done, you and your employees need clarity. Clarity of objectives, responsibilities and decisions.

3

Managing your career

What you will learn in this chapter

- How to manage your career and move onward and upward
- How qualifications help develop skills
- How to use social media, branding and other techniques to make yourself attractive to new employers
- How to handle redundancies and second careers

Careers today are very different than they were 100 years ago, or even ten years ago. The internet almost takes geography out of the equation. You can apply for an internship in London if you are sitting in a small town somewhere in North Carolina. If you are based in Europe and looking to hire a bookkeeper, you could find the person in India. There have also been shifts in attitudes. The parents of baby boomers (Westerners born between around 1945 and 1962) expected a job for life, but later generations have experienced waves of downsizings.

Switching careers is more common – not only out of necessity as one job disappears, but also because people are living longer and retirement savings may be insufficient, so people extend their working lives. I'm a good case in point: I've switched careers, sectors and countries several times over the years, having gone from being a European general manager at Procter & Gamble based in Germany to writing this book, and have been a FTSE 100 executive board member, an entrepreneur in America, a global business services director and social enterprise CEO in between.

I've always learned things from previous positions I can apply in new roles. Equally, I can say with conviction that the principles and practices of good management – and bad – are very consistent across sectors, cultures and careers.

How to move onwards and upwards: getting promoted

When you join an organisation you should always ask about career opportunities within it. Many organisations, including professional services firms and multinationals, will have set, transparent career paths and promotion levels – so make sure you ask this question before joining and before any job transition, so you know what it looks like. Smaller, growing firms also have career paths, although these are much less predictable. But whether you are in a large or small organisation, one common characteristic applies: *you own your promotion opportunities.*

The people who spend their time working hard, head down, hoping to get noticed will almost always lose out to those who keep their head up, market themselves and their results and actively seek out new opportunities and challenges.

Here are five simple things you can do to maximise your chances of promotion:

1 **Keep track of your accomplishments** When you are in conversation, you can refer to your contributions. Don't brag, just be factual. Know the value you have added and be able to express it in terms of outcomes: I saved £X or grew the business by Y per cent.

2 **Be visible** Attend your organisation's events and social outings, and volunteer to help on important projects. Don't take on more than you can handle, but being a 'can-do' proactive person will help far more than being the one who never contributes outside their immediate remit. This will bring you into contact with others in different areas. When it comes time to discuss promotions, people will always favour those whom they perceive have been active and whom they recognise. By contrast, 'invisible' employees are harder to endorse.

3 **Complement your boss with your work skills** If your boss is a whiz at presentations but hates detail, try to complement him or her by being in charge of the detailed reporting. He or she will appreciate your value even more

4 **Apply!** When new opportunities come up, most companies today post them internally. Even if you are not sure you are 'ready' for the promotion, give it a go. You will get yourself noticed and you will also build your profile and flag you are interested in advancement (NB: This is especially true for women – put yourself out there!). Use the 'matching checklist' – see the box below – to help you prepare for internal job interviews.

Matching job requirements to your experience: the matching checklist

When you apply for a job, one of the best techniques you can use is a matching checklist. This takes the key requirements in the job description and lists them on the left-hand side of the page. For each of these, list on the right-hand side of the page your relevant examples and experience. This is a very effective technique as it impresses recruiters with how well you have thought through your suitability for the job and provides them with concrete examples of why you're the best choice.

Source: As adapted from Stork & May

---

5 **Consider advancing your skills** By taking on better qualifications through your employer's programme or other relevant offers, you signal that you are willing and able to learn new skills.

Negotiating a salary increase

1 *Know why you deserve a raise*. Outline the arguments, assemble the evidence: Have you excelled at cost savings? Delivered sales over budget? Won an important client? Use concrete examples.

2 *Benchmark*. Know the salary ranges of others doing similar work in your industry.

3 *Book a meeting to discuss with your boss*. Be calm, and don't do it at a bad time for them.

4 *Know your company policy*. Many companies can only give raises at certain times of the year or within certain percentage bands. Be realistic in respect of your company's performance and the general economic situation.

5 *Consider alternative benefits*. Work on a new project, more holidays, a sabbatical, or a special development programme.

6 *Don't expect an answer right away*. Give your boss time to consider and consult – but make sure you agree a time when you will follow up the discussion.

Switching jobs

Today's managers are far more mobile than their predecessors. Indeed, the average manager will change jobs every three to five years, and even CEOs only last an average of two and a half years. In part this reflects a more global, plugged-in workforce; and in part the climate of economic austerity that makes redundancies and downsizings more prevalent. These same factors make job switching easier than ever before. So if you are stuck in your current job, have discussed advancement opportunities and done the above all to no avail, it may be time to look elsewhere.

Management qualifications

As mentioned above, gaining additional qualifications can signal that you are interested in developing yourself and hence ready for promotion. They are also a great way to help make you better at managing.

Less than one in five managers in the UK is qualified, and that percentage is about the same globally. So what are your options if you aim to be one of those in the qualified elite? The most common is the MBA; however, there are also other qualifications, including undergraduate degrees in business studies, professional qualifications, and other sector specific awards and certificates. In a recent survey, managers rated MBAs and professional qualifications such as Chartered Manager the most effective.[8] Here I offer a brief summary of the most popular.

The MBA

Back when I was in business school in 1985, most considered the MBA an automatic entry ticket to a high-paying management job. No more. According to the *Wall Street Journal*, the number of MBAs in the US has risen by 75 per cent in the last decade, and the costs have risen by almost 25 per cent in the last three years.[9] Increasingly, competition comes from a rising number of global business schools and online offerings. Some of the most common reasons given for doing MBAs include:

▥ The breadth of management education available on MBA programmes.

▥ It is valued by employers.

---

[8] *Value of Qualifications*, CMI, 2012.
[9] *Wall Street Journal*, 12 Dec. 2012.

■ Networking and business opportunities with fellow students.

■ A chance to reflect and potentially refocus your career.

■ Better career and pay prospects.

■ The best MBAs give an international outlook.

MBAs are still regarded by most as the most worthwhile business degree, but it is important to examine what the main reason is for choosing your MBA, and that you do some thorough research. The *FT* ranks all business schools, and maintains separate rankings for global business schools, European business schools and executive education MBAs. Studies have shown increases in salary post-MBA,[10] but these are not as great as they once were. If you are not fortunate enough to be able to gain admission to and afford a top-tier business school, you may want to consider other qualifications. There have also been several criticisms of the MBA, most notably by the management guru Henry Mintzberg. He argues that there needs to be more focus on learning from and using one's practical experience.[11]

Professional management qualifications: Chartered Manager

Many of the advantages of MBAs, such as making contacts, can also be gained by undertaking alternative qualifications. One interesting alternative to consider is a professional qualification in management such as Chartered Manager. Research by professional bodies shows that the public trust the chartered designation more than any other. The UK offers a broad palette of professional bodies, as do many other countries. Many of these are recognised internationally. There are also numerous short course, executive courses, and, increasingly, specialised courses to consider.

---

[10] Walker, L., *The MBA Equation*, Professional Manager, 2012.
[11] Mintzberg, H., *Managers Not MBAs*, Pearson Education, 2004.

The 'practical' MBA: four things Chartered Managers do

1 Make a proven, positive, and practical impact in their world of work.

2 Have a recognised management qualification (usually a Level 5 or above in the UK National Framework).

3 Sign a code of conduct on ethics.

4 Are committed to continued professional education.

Research by CMI on Chartered Managers shows an impressive satisfaction rate of over 90 per cent, and 68 per cent say it has improved their performance.

Source: The Impact of Chartered Managers, CMI, 2012

Using social media: personal branding and network building in the digital age

Today you can search for information on any company, almost anywhere, from work or your own home. You can locate decision-makers, potential customers, suppliers and subject-matter experts and contact them. You can highlight your interests on LinkedIn, job sites, and alumni associations. You can build your own brand by posting blogs, or tweeting regularly. A 2011 report from Experian found that 91 per cent of online adults used social media at least once a month[12] – but how many of us really reflect on the networks we are using and what we use them for? Social media can be a powerful tool for career advancement and continuing professional development. So how do you make sensible use of technology in managing your career?

Use online resources to help cultivate good relationships externally. Take industry associations, professional bodies and the trade press, for example: offer to be helpful in connecting them with others, joining, providing background information, and contributing to message boards. If you are in a position of responsibility, identify the key associations and trade journalists in your space and share information that you think will make their lives easier. If you are given the opportunity, offer to speak at events, or help to organise them, or summarise their outcome and share with the organisers. You are creating content for others that will also build your brand.

[12] http://www.experian.com/assets/simmons-research/brochures/2011-social-media-consumer-report.pdf

Whether you are looking to recruit, find a job, build customers or network, a LinkedIn profile is vital. It will bring you to the attention of others. When you create your profile, look at others' – find one you like and emulate it. You might want to consider keyword searches; people are looking for concrete key words. Recruiters are typically looking for information on: job title, job sector or industry, function, and size of budget, staff, or other concrete dimensions of responsibility. Terms like: CMO, CEO, IT Software programmer, leading innovation, global, are more likely to get searched.

Building a network

Think about people you know. They are easy to find on LinkedIn. You can then send out invitations. And most profile settings will give you access to their connections. Scroll through those to see if there are people whom you know that you can connect with. It's always best to connect with people you know. This is because otherwise your connections may not be meaningful. Of course, if you have a specific request for information, LinkedIn allows you to send a message asking for advice. Look for quality not quantity. And don't be afraid to reach out to your contacts when it is useful. If you use the endorsement feature, be wary of having too many.

A learning tool

Continuing professional development shouldn't just mean attending training courses.[13] Via social media you have the chance to learn from some of the best people in business and public life. You can read blog posts from thought leaders in your industry; you are also able to gain a real insight into the views and opinions of colleagues, employees and stakeholders. Consider taking part in online conversations via Twitter or the groups on LinkedIn. You can also sign up for and get regular free content from thought-leadership institutions such as McKinsey and the *Harvard Business Review*. Try Googling what you are interested in – B2B marketing, for example – and you will find free white papers to download, emails to sign up for and discussion forums to join. Of course they are using this to generate leads but that is not necessarily a downside;

---

[13] See Hyland, L., 'Move aside CPD – UPS is on its way!', *Training Journal,* June 2009.

there may be material that is worth paying for. This kind of use of the web can lead to genuine 'win–win' connections.

Online reputation

It is vital that you consider carefully what information you put online, and who can access it. For example, do you want to add your colleagues as friends on Facebook and have them see personal photos and communication with your non-work friends? It is well known that most employers will Google anyone they are thinking of hiring. There is no right or wrong answer to what information you share, but you need to think about how your manager or a recruiter might perceive your online profile, and whether your organisation has a social media policy. The safest rule is: if you wouldn't want your boss or grandmother to see it, then don't put it there. More companies are springing up that allow you to manage your own online reputation. They do this by allowing you to place your preferred content higher up on Google.

How to cope with redundancy, getting fired and job search

Every good manager I know has been fired at least once! I've been fired for reasons such as a boardroom coup or cost-cutting. It does not carry the stigma it may have once done. Try not to take it personally – bounce back and do something better! Take time to do so. The following tips can help:

1 **Let go** Say goodbye and accept that your employment has ended and see it in perspective, with both the good and the bad.

2 **Don't burn bridges** Unless you are truly the victim of discrimination and have strong evidence, then try to maintain a good relationship with your former employer. Discrimination suits may result in more money in the short term, but it can hamper the ability to get a good reference. Nor should you underestimate the trauma that fighting your employer will put you under. If your relationship with your boss was not the best, try seeking a reference from a supportive peer, or even a boss of your boss.

3 **Make a positive transition** Sort out the practicalities for your new life – your legal entitlements, your finances, and focus on establishing a new routine and getting yourself organised; build your confidence – focus on your skills and achievements. Do the things that were difficult while you were employed – go to the gym, take up yoga, learn a new language.

4 **Move forward** Take stock of who you are: likes and dislikes, skills, experience, training needs, values, priorities and family constraints. Start redesigning your future and considering different options, such as starting your own business, studying, travelling, or a career break.[14]

5 **Seek out new networks and old colleagues/friends for mutual benefit** This is a great opportunity to get in touch with former colleagues and friends and explore possibilities with them. Avoid asking them for a job – instead, ask them how they are, and then share your current situation. Ask them if they can make an introduction. Also, think about ways in which you might be able to help them.

6 **Consider joining or forming a support group** When I found myself wanting to re-enter the job market after a family sabbatical, I teamed up with senior women in a similar position. We called ourselves CREW – Career Renaissance for Executive Women. It was great to share experiences. We are still good friends today, and we have all been through several career transitions since.

7 **Wait until you are in a positive frame of mind before beginning your job search** Potential employers and head-hunters will pick up on a defensive or victimised attitude. Also, you will need to think about what you will say about why you left your last position. Write it down, and practise it. Similarly, you should think about what your previous employer will say. Counter any negative references with positive ones from previous employers, colleagues and direct reports.

8 **Consider Career Outplacement** This refers to support that your employer provides, usually via an external company, which helps you find new employment. Support services vary but can include

---

[14] Adapted from *Dealing with Redundancy, CMI Checklist Series*, no. 218, 2011.

counselling, assistance with writing a CV and interview preparation. They will help you to be proactive and prevent you from falling into the trap of feeling sorry for yourself. The best will also have contacts, content and networks. If you are interested in outplacement don't forget to ask your employer to make it part of your settlement package. Most employers will want to see you land on your feet and will be willing to consider this.

Job sources

Most of us are aware that job hunting, like much else, has been transformed by the internet. But plan your approaches as if you weren't online. Think about what you want to do and why. Write down your activities and things you have done; be sure to focus on results, outcomes and stories you are proud of and can share. Focus on your strengths; the things you are good at. Make sure you have facts to prove this.

Think about the kind of job and company you would like: Are you looking for freelance virtual work? Or are you looking to join a company? Large or small?

Think about companies that might fit your bill. And then search for information on the people that might run the areas you are interested in.

Once you've got their names, see if you can find a way in using your networks. If not, consider approaching them directly, by doing your research about them and highlighting an area of shared interest or expertise. Email them a personal cover note and your CV, and follow up with a phone call. Ask for their advice rather than a job. If you can get in to see them great, otherwise, a phone call can work. This is more likely to work than posting your résumé on countless job sites.

There are a number of other tools and methods that could be of use:

▨ **Networking** Make use of contacts you have in previous jobs. Two-thirds of jobs are said to be found this way. See 'The power of networking', in Chapter 5.

■ **Head-hunters and recruitment agencies** Find out about the key head-hunters and recruiters for your industry. There are two types of search consultants: those who operate on a retained basis and those who do things on a speculative, success-fee-only basis. The first are the reputable search consultants and include all the big global names. Most of these recruiters belong to AIESC and you can join this organisation as well and gain access to them. You need to be wary of the second, as they will be attempting to aggressively market you, often to the wrong sorts of people.

■ **Interim or temporary assignments** This will get you into an organisation in addition to building your esteem; it will make it easier for you to transition into full-time work. Interim management is offered by many leading head-hunting firms.

■ **Social media** Many companies now advertise their vacancies on social media. You can also use social media to let people know you are looking; however, you might want to do that in a targeted fashion rather than broadcast your availability too publicly. You can also attend networking events and create a profile for yourself online. Offer to speak at conferences in your industry, or contribute content to online forums.

■ **Maintain good relationships with head-hunters even if you are not looking for a job** It is always a good idea to stay in touch with head-hunters. Often, they will call you asking for your recommendations of potential candidates for a position. It's in your interests to oblige. The more you help them, the more likely they are to reach out to you. Then when you need them, or are thinking of switching, they are more likely to take your call, meet with you, or suggest others with whom you might speak.

Career changes

Very few people have the same job or work for the same organisation throughout their career, and some seek a career change. Members of the armed forces, and of the police and fire services, for example, have always retired early enough to have time for a second career. This could include starting your own business or becoming freelance: one former executive I know successfully reinvented herself as a children's book author. Another former retail professional pursued her dreams of becoming a scuba diving instructor in the Maldives. More commonly, many professionals choose to enter into careers as executive coaches, consultants, charity workers or teachers. As you plan your second career, ask yourself these questions:

- Do you really want a second career?

- What is it that you like doing and what skills would you like to develop?

- Will future career changes require you to undertake further education or training?

- Are you willing to move down the ladder in order to enter a new field?

- Are you able to support yourself financially in the short-, medium- and long-term?

- What do people around you think?

So-called 'parallel careers' can end up creating second careers. The term 'parallel careers' relates to a secondary job or activity that is undertaken by an individual alongside their existing career. There are many examples of people whose second career remains a rewarding hobby – such as the CEO who coaches little league baseball – or those whose second career eventually overtakes the first, such as the TV producer who became a bestselling author having begun writing fiction as a hobby, and self-published *Fifty Shades of Grey*.

Top tips, pitfalls and takeaways

Top tips

- Use social media to build your personal brand and expand your network.

- Do a 'matching checklist' when applying for jobs to ensure you highlight relevant experiences.

- Reach out to others in the same boat for support during career transitions.

Top pitfalls

- Burning bridges when you experience a difficult change, such as being made redundant.

- Forgetting the reality of a career transition will often result in a loss of status, success and 'starting over'. Make sure you factor this in; don't be too romantic about your switch!

Top takeaways

- Changing careers is increasingly common and can be very rewarding.

- Careers today are more fluid than ever before. You need to be adaptable, be prepared to move to different organisations and continually learn new skills.

Developing skills that make a difference

4

Communicating well

What you will learn in this chapter

- The importance of communication for leadership and management
- The many different aspects of communication, including listening, body language and lingual clarity
- Some practical tips on how to communicate effectively

What is communication? Most of us take communication for granted, thinking that it's about what we say and how we say it. True communication, however, really concerns what the person or people receiving your message understood. It happens only when the message you intended to send is the same as the message your audience received. This is surprisingly rare.

I once had a top boss who enjoyed talking in a whisper, often using odd phrases that were barely audible. He did this deliberately, so people would have to lean in to understand him. Like Marlon Brando in *The Godfather* he was asserting power over everyone, saying 'I'm important, so you better try really hard to listen to me and I am not going to make it easy.' People spent many hours trying to decipher his phrases and second-guess what he actually meant. What a waste of time and energy!

I am sure you can think of a boss or colleague who didn't communicate clearly. Writing is even worse. How many of us don't understand what a boss says in a meeting, or what a colleague's memo means, but are too afraid to ask?

Communication goes wrong when:

■ The message isn't clear in the mind of the person sending it.

■ The words don't express what the sender means.

■ The body language doesn't match the words.

■ The person receiving the message doesn't understand the message.

■ The preconceived notions of the receiver get in the way of the message.

Communicating well and clearly is one of the most powerful things you can do as a manager. It improves your efficiency, promotes clearer, more structured thinking, and reduces the frustration that arises from misunderstandings.

It can actually make the difference between success and failure.

So why is it so hard? In order to communicate well and clearly, you need to do the following seven things:

1   Think about your audience.

2   Keep it simple, stupid (KISS).

3   Avoid jargon and catchphrases.

4   Listen actively.

5   Pay attention to body language.

6   Say what you mean.

7   Watch the positive to negative ratio.

You can do this with practice. Most people would say I am a good communicator, but it wasn't always so. In my first performance review, my boss told me I needed to improve my presentations as I wasn't clear. So I spent the next few years doing lots of presentations.

Think about your audience

Clear communication involves putting yourself in the other person's shoes – something we often don't think about before we speak or write. For example, someone who uses flowery, grandiloquent language in a roomful of non-native English speakers is bound to be misunderstood. Equally, someone who is speaking really softly on a conference call won't be heard.

Think about your audience and try to imagine how they would receive your message. It also helps, I find, if you pretend you are talking to non-native English speakers, or a group of ten-year-olds. It will help you to express yourself more clearly and enunciate better.

If you are addressing a group of analysts or shareholders it's different to when you are addressing your colleagues from different departments. Keep your audience in mind, and try to imagine how what you say will be understood – or not understood – by them.

exercise

Write a five-minute presentation on your most important project which will gain support from each of the following three audiences:

■ the CEO;

■ a peer whose team members you need to get the project done;

■ a new recruit joining your department.

How has your audience's perspective changed your presentation in each case?

KISS

Keep it simple, stupid.

This is one of the phases I have most often used in my professional life. We tend to overcomplicate things: maybe we think we are somehow being more professional or more strategic or more important. But we're not; we are simply making it harder for people to understand.

I once got someone in to lead a workshop on 'Clear Communication' in a company I worked for. What that person did was simple but very effective. He asked everyone to write down what they felt was the mission statement of the organisation. Then he had people read them aloud. They were full of long, windy sentences and big words. He then had everyone write the statement using one-syllable words with six letters or less. What a difference it made! Remember – you are not writing a novel. You are trying to get your message understood.

Try to express your message in as few words of one syllable as possible. Use active, not passive voice. And keep it short.

'The most valuable of all talents is that of never using two words when one will do.'

Thomas Jefferson

Effective presentations

Presenting well is something all good managers have to learn. It will materially impact your success – as those who shine at communicating well are often those who advance in an organisation.

Good presentations are to the point. They avoid death by PowerPoint. They don't overload with facts, figures and more facts. They tell a story. They use humour and sincerity. Consider involving your audience at key points. Ask them a question rather than give them the answer.

Well-structured presentations help your audience to remember your key points. An old adage is: tell them what you are about to tell them. Tell them. And then tell them again what you have just told them. It works! Also, I find that sharing things in groups of threes keeps things digestible.

If you are using slides, make sure you have no more than three bullet points per slide. Try to make one or two main points per slide. Do not overload your slides! Keep them simple – avoid lots of words and charts and numbers. If you want people to remember a number, highlight it. Try simple pictures that capture what you want to say. But make sure your slides reinforce your words – otherwise, people will wonder why your visuals don't match your words. And avoid just using pictures to 'sex up' content that have no relationship to what you want to say.

Make sure you use a clear voice with lots of expression. Always practise beforehand. If you run into trouble at a transition point, change your presentation so it flows better. If it's too long, cut it! Try never to speak for more than 25 minutes. Most people will click out after 30 minutes even if you are an accomplished speaker.

Video yourself presenting. With today's Smartphone technology this is really easy. And very helpful. If you shuffle too much, move around, speak too quickly or too slowly, your video will enable you to see that objectively and practise to fix it.

Avoid jargon and catchphrases

All businesses use jargon far too much. One company I worked for used numbers to refer to everything. Anyone who didn't work there hadn't the foggiest notion what they were on about. It really got in the way of what they were trying to sell – which was business improvement tools. Worse still, this jargon was all over their website. So no one really understood what they did. Now thank goodness, there's been a major programme to eliminate the jargon, so that customers are much clearer on what the company sells.

exercise

Find a document you really think is full of jargon and ask your team to rewrite it together so that a stranger can understand it. You'll be surprised at how much clearer it is. I guarantee you will uncover different meanings and understanding for different phrases that you all assumed you understood, clearing up your communication in the process. Indeed, jargon can have disastrous consequences. In his bestselling book, *The Big Short*, Michael Lewis implies that overuse of complex jargon, and people's inability to admit they didn't know what it meant, was responsible for the biggest financial meltdowns of recent history.[1]

Tip

Read aloud what you've written. If it doesn't make sense, fix it.

[1] Lewis, Michael, *The Big Short: Inside the Doomsday Machine*, Allen Lane, 2010.

Equally annoying are catchphrases and filler words. If every second word is 'like' or 'you know', people tune out and stop listening.

Listen actively

Think of a boss you liked working for; someone you really admire. Now list the qualities of that person. I bet being a good listener is on your list. It is a real trait of almost every inspiring leader, manager and teacher. Now, think of a bad boss and do the same. I bet that he/she doesn't listen.

Listening is not the same as hearing. Hearing is passive, while listening involves making sense of what we hear. It is an active process that demands complete attention. When you listen to someone you are saying, 'I value you – it's important that I understand what you have to say.'

It is quite clear when someone is not listening to what you have to say. They demonstrate:

▪ a lack of sufficient eye contact;

▪ a glazed expression;

▪ interrupting;

▪ not being able to reply to questions;

▪ turning their body away;

▪ showing impatience.

So how do you listen actively? A simple mnemonic, LISTEN, can help:

▪ Look interested – maintaining eye contact with the speaker helps you to concentrate; an alert, interested expression will actually make you feel more interested (in the same way that it is difficult to feel angry about something if you are smiling and laughing).

▪ Inquire with questions, to check your understanding. Don't make assumptions.

▪ Stay on target, using any slack thinking time to consider the implications of what the speaker is saying.

▪ Take notes, to help you concentrate and refresh your memory later.

▪ Evaluate the whole message, watching body language as well as hearing the words.

▪ Neutralise your feelings, acknowledging to yourself any prejudices you may have.

In the end, try summarising your understanding of what someone has said. By reflecting back to check your understanding, you are giving someone conclusive proof that you've listened to them. You can also use this in reverse. Try asking someone to summarise their understanding of what you've said.

Pay attention to body language

In face-to-face communication, research suggests that only about 10 per cent of the words make up the message that is understood. The other 90 per cent consists of your body language, gestures, facial expressions, posture, your tone of voice and non-verbal utterances like sighs. If your words are spoken in a way that isn't matched by your body language and tone they will be misunderstood. If you say 'I agree' in a meeting with clenched jaw looking down at the floor with your arms crossed, do you think people will be convinced?

Consider how you pick up on messages from other people, even when they are not talking. We look for eye contact, we consider their posture and gestures, and we look at their facial expressions, and react to their use of space and touch.

Body language is very difficult to control and some people claim they can tell whether someone is telling the truth or not by their body language. But you will undoubtedly be a better listener and communicator if you take it into account. And remember: people with highly developed skills of interacting are more likely to become most successful.

The tone you use to say things dramatically influences your message. The way you are feeling is conveyed in your voice through the way it affects pitch, the rate of speech and volume. Variations in the emphasis which we place on words can also result in completely different messages being conveyed, even though we might use the same words in both situations. Remember, most people will rely on the message conveyed by how you have said it rather than by the words you have used.

When your message is not what people expect to hear, take particular care to match non-verbal communication with your words. Bear in mind that people often hear what they expect, or want, to hear. Ask them to summarise what you have said back to you in these cases to ensure they have understood your message.

> **Tip**
>
> Mirror image others – and yourself.

Mirror imaging others

You can be a more effective communicator by becoming a subtle 'mirror image' of the person with whom you are communicating. This is called 'Pacing'. 'Pacing' means that you playback the tone, body language, facial expressions and tempo of the person with whom you are communicating in your own actions. Try practising this at home first. It can be very effective, especially to improve communication with someone where there is conflict or misunderstanding.

Mirror imaging yourself

Before you give an important talk, practise it in front of the mirror. Watch how you say things. Watch how you stand and practise your tone of voice. You can also give presentations to your family or partner and ask them to critique.

Say what you mean

I often read documents, or listen to presentations, where the author or presenter isn't being clear. They are relying on fancy language, using too much jargon, or 'organisation-speak', rather than saying what they really mean to say. Make sure you check what you are going to say before you say it by saying it out loud. If it doesn't sound right, correct it.

The same is true for interviews. If someone asks you a question and you blurt out a lot of stream of consciousness, it will not impress people. So if you are anticipating an important meeting, like an interview, try jotting down potential questions and answers in bullet points form to capture what you are going to say before you say it.

Email etiquette

Emails have become a scourge of modern working life. Remember how they were supposed to make life easier and more effective? The opposite has happened. Far too many of us spend too much time on too many emails that add little or no value to our work. Here are four simple dos followed by four simple don'ts:

Do think about whether an email is the best means of communicating. Will a phone call do? Or a face-to-face conversation? Especially if the person works in the same building.

Do keep your emails short and to the point. A simple one, three to five sentences, should suffice. Avoid more than seven sentences. People don't want to wade through long emails. And do ensure your attachments are a reasonable length – or use other means to share such as Dropbox.

Do DISCIPLINE YOUR USE OF EMAILS. Try to put aside set times to answer/write emails once or twice daily rather than interrupt what you are doing each time your inbox goes ping. Consider an email-free Friday.

Do keep on top of your inbox. Try to delete your emails regularly and archive the ones you wish to keep.

Don't feel obligated to answer every email you receive. Many will be unimportant, unnecessary, or just junk. Ignore them. If they are important, whoever sent the email will be back in touch.

Don't cc: all on your replies. It's a big warning sign to colleagues that you are point-scoring, politicking, insecure, or all three. Keep your recipients list to a minimum and reply to the sender only, unless asked to do differently.

Don't engage in endless long email trails. If there are more than three replies back and forth it's time to pick up the phone.

Don't rant and rave on email. It you must vent via a poison pen email, do so. It can be therapeutic. But then hit DELETE! If you send it you will regret it.

Further resources

http://www.presentationmagazine.com/effective-presentation-techniques-the-top-10-149.htm

http://www.shutupandsaysomething.com/

Praising

The final point to remember is to watch your positive to negative ratio in communicating with others. Researchers have measured the number of positive statements in communication (things like 'that is a good idea' or 'yes, let's try that'), versus the number of negative statements ('we have tried that before and it failed' or 'that's not what I was looking for'). It turns out that teams who achieve a ratio of over five positives to each negative are much more likely to be high performing; medium performing teams had a ratio of two positives for every negative, and low-performing teams had more negatives than positives.[2] Another Nobel-winning psychologist, John Gottman, monitored the conversations between newly-weds. Those with a positive to negative ratio of over five stayed married, whereas those with a positive to negative ratio of less than one (i.e. more negative than positive) got divorced.[3]

What does it mean for you? When you are communicating with people, try to say five positive things for every negative one. It will pay dividends in building stronger, more effective relationships with both those at work, and at home.

Top tips, pitfalls and takeaways

Top tips

- ■ Before giving a talk or presentation, practise out loud in front of a mirror.

- ■ Learn how to listen well; it is at least as important as speaking clearly and honestly.

Top pitfall

- ■ Using organisational or professional jargon.

---

[2] Losada, M. and Heaphy, E., 'The role of positivity and connectivity in the performance of business teams: a nonlinear dynamics model', *American Behavioral Scientist*, 2004.

[3] http://www.gottman.com/

Top takeaways

■ Communication is not a side issue: it is of fundamental importance for all managers and can make a difference between success and failure in commercial projects.

■ Communication is multi-dimensional, involving indirect forms of communication such as body language.

5

Understanding others

What you will learn in this chapter

- The importance of emotional intelligence, or EQ, in effectiveness as a manager
- How to use emotional intelligence to build your negotiating skills
- How to build a personal network, and your personal brand
- The importance of a network within the organisation you work for

The cornerstone of success in management is based on two simple thoughts: know and control yourself, know and deal with others. The most successful people are not necessarily the smartest, or nicest, or even the most driven. They are the ones with the highest EQ. This stands for emotional intelligence – the ability to perceive and understand your own feelings and those of others. It involves self-awareness, empathy and self-restraint. It can be developed by managers throughout their career.

EQ became prominent in business thinking largely thanks to Daniel Goleman. He developed a framework that includes five different aspects:

1 **Self-awareness** Examining how your emotions affect your performance; awareness of strengths and weaknesses; being self-confident and certain about your capabilities, values and goals.

2 **Self-regulation** Controlling your temper; controlling your stress by being more positive and action-centred; retaining composure and

the ability to think clearly under pressure; nurturing trustworthiness and self-restraint.

3 **Motivation** Enjoying challenge; seeking out achievement; commitment; ability to take the initiative; optimism; and being guided by personal references in choosing goals.

4 **Empathy** The ability to see other people's points of view; behaving openly and honestly; avoiding the tendency to stereotype; and being culturally aware.

5 **Social skills** The use of influencing skills such as good communication; listening skills; negotiation; cooperation; dispute resolution; ability to inspire and lead; capacity to initiate and manage change; and ability to deal with others' emotions – particularly group emotions.[1]

Empathy: knowing others and understanding what motivates others

One of the most common mistakes to make is to assume that everyone is similar to you in personality and drivers. That's why a personality profiling exercise like Myers Briggs, for yourself and your team, can be very useful (see Chapter 1). An extroverted thinker will be very action-focused and adopt a 'let's get it done now' approach, whereas an introverted feeler will want to go for well-thought-through consensual solutions. Both approaches have their value. Having different types of personalities in teams and departments will often help you to get better results. We will talk more about this later in Chapters 9 and 15.

It is also helpful to think about personal circumstances that may drive motivation. For example, not everyone is motivated by career ambition or money. Some people are more motivated by fear of failure, or by the need for recognition from others. Understanding key drivers is vital to developing empathy. Once you understand what motivates someone, try expressing things in a way that focuses on their motivation.

---

[1] Goleman, Daniel, *Emotional Intelligence*, Bantam Doubleday, 1996, p. 2.

For example, you want to implement a new method for forecasting sales.

- For the fear of failure person, you could say: If we do this, our chances of missing the forecast will be much less.

- For the person who is motivated by recognition, you could say: If we do this, we can enter into the sales team of the year award.

- For someone motivated by money, you might say: If we do this, we'll hit our target more easily and get our bonus.

Make the mapping of personality types and motivations of your team the subject of a team meeting. How do the insights help you to become more effective together? What will you do differently as a result?

Online resources to help you: http://www.personalitypathways.com/ type_inventory.html

Source: www.authentichappiness.edu

Letting people know where they stand

It is very important that you as a manager are clear with people about where they stand. This is vital for building trust and improving performance, and yet it is one of those things that managers struggle with most. Recently, the global head of talent for a major bank told me he was running a session for the top 150 managers – people with enormous educations, positions, and pay cheques – on exactly this topic, 'how to have the difficult conversation', because they avoided it. Don't you! Try being really clear with your reports when you sit with people to review progress. If you have negative feedback, give it clearly and constructively, with examples and a commitment to help them improve. People genuinely appreciate clarity and honesty – they want to know where they stand.

Negotiating

Negotiating happens whenever you are discussing something with a department, a colleague, a customer or supplier, and you need something to be considered or implemented by someone else. Negotiating can of course also be about discussing complex deals, transactions, and agreements or settling disputes.

Think win–win

The fundamental premise of negotiating is about coming up with solutions that benefit both parties. This is known as 'win–win' behaviour. The worst sort of negotiation is one in which neither party wins – the 'lose–lose'. In the middle, but generally not a good outcome, are the win–lose or lose–win scenarios. That's because a one-sided victory can potentially lead to negative consequences. If winning comes at the expense of a damaged relationship or reputation, then it will be very short-lived indeed. [2]

Try to think about ways in which you can get what you want and give the other party something that will benefit them. This requires that you understand what is important to you and the other party before you enter into the negotiation. It may be that what is very valuable to you is an easy thing for them to give up. Or vice versa. Know your priorities, in terms of your 'must-haves' versus your 'nice to haves', in advance.

Build the emotional bank account

Negotiating is a routine part of management, so how you negotiate will directly affect your reputation and influence. A helpful technique is to think in terms of a bank balance. When you do things that result in benefits for others, or deliver against your promises, your bank balance gains a deposit – an emotional 'credit'. Conversely, when you do things that disadvantage others, or don't deliver, your bank balance loses and you have an emotional 'debit'. The key is to build up a positive

---

[2] Kennedy, Gavin, *Negotiation: An A–Z Guide*, *The Economist* in association with Profile Books, 2009, p. 250.

'emotional bank balance' with your colleagues over time. That will help you enormously in building your influence and negotiating ability, such as the ability to call in favours when you need them.

An aspect of good negotiating skills is knowing when to compromise. Concessions on certain things, especially when they are not that important to you but are important to someone else, will distinguish you as a reasonable person and build your emotional bank account. Of course, it's also important not to be a 'doormat', or someone who gives in too easily. The key is to know when it is worth letting someone 'win', because it will help you gain an advantage when negotiating for something bigger. An example might be that you extend the deadline on a project with your supplier, but lock in a lower price. Or give your colleague the bigger office, but take the most talented junior manager into your department.

Five tips for negotiating[3]

1 Don't give a range on numerical metrics. Clearly if you say, 'I'll pay between £50,000 and £60,000', anyone in their right mind is going to go for the higher number. Or if you say, 'I need this in a week or two', the person is going to give it to you in two.

2 Don't say: 'It's up to me and I'll decide right now.' This can put people off. Moreover, it can be useful to say that you need to discuss things with another party before you make a final decision. Everyone benefits from thinking things through, and it will prevent you from being cornered. You will often genuinely need to check what you want to agree with a boss or colleague.

3 Never take it personally. Professionals never get flustered. By acting as if what's at stake isn't really all that important to you and by staying calm, even if the other person gets angry, you can gain an advantage.

4 Don't say: 'We've just got to get this done.' If you are under time pressure and feel the need to close something quickly, you will end up making concessions that you may wish you hadn't.

---

[3] Adapted after Mike Hoffman, 11 Jan. 2012, Inc.com, Mansueto Ventures LLC.

5 If you are a seller, make the first offer. Research shows that the price is higher when the seller, not the buyer, makes the first bid.

Role play. Try to role play negotiating between two sides, say supplier and customer, or one department and another. Switch roles and genuinely try to uncover the other side's motivations and needs.

Influencing

Power gives people automatic influence in any negotiation. At Procter & Gamble they used the phrase 'higher paid judgement'. That meant that if you were arguing on matters of opinion, then the boss would win. But there are other ways of building influence if you don't have power.

If you don't hold a position of authority within the organisation, your ability to influence and persuade can be developed. Your negotiating position will be strengthened if you:

■ communicate your case clearly and concisely, and with confidence;

■ support your position with evidence and facts;

■ show respect for others and listen to their points of view;

■ encourage an engaging and meaningful two-way conversation;

■ gain the full support of senior managers. With this backing secured beforehand you can effectively use others' positions of authority to garner influence.

Generally speaking, if you communicate well, are trying to be helpful to others, and assist people in achieving their goals you will quickly build influence.

Networking – why you need to ...

I once got a call out of the blue from a former boss of mine whom I'd worked for in Germany. He was a lovely man, very personable, with a

John Cleese type of humour (which stood out all the more as he was a Brit in Germany), and we'd had a good working relationship. I'd lost touch with him over the years, although we'd both since relocated to the UK. After we had exchanged pleasantries he continued: 'No doubt you're wondering why I've suddenly gotten back in touch, after all these years. The truth is, Rob suggested I give you a ring because I'm new to the UK and need to start networking. Rob said you're really good at it. Could you give me some pointers?'

I was both flattered and confused. Flattered because it's always nice to be asked for advice, especially from a former boss. Confused, because I'd never thought about whether or why I was good at networking. But I knew it wouldn't have been easy for him to make that call. Of course I was happy to help.

That little vignette contains many of the key points about networking. First, everyone needs to do it. Secondly, you never know when or how former contacts will be useful. Thirdly, most people are eager to help others if they ask for it. Fourthly, networking, like other aspects of management, is a skill that can be learned.

The power of networking

You need a good network to develop new knowledge and skills, uncover new opportunities, further your career, garner business intelligence and leads, and identify potential role models. Networking is also interesting. Done well, it can be a real source of learning and motivation. If you regard it as a chore, or a mercenary exercise, you will neither enjoy it nor gain much benefit.

Networking can be face-to-face, in work settings or socially, or online. Be prepared by practising the answer to the key networking question, 'What do you do?' And developing a tiny USP for yourself. Always be ready to take an opportunity that comes your way. You might answer the questions depending on who is asking and how they ask: you may refer to your family and hobbies; it depends on the context. Always have your business card handy. These days, you can also ask to connect on LinkedIn while the meeting is still fresh in your mind.

But also remember the cardinal rule of networking: sell yourself, not your stuff.

Business networking is about building up mutually beneficial relationships. It's not about selling. I once made the mistake of approaching a leading director on the dance floor at the club Christmas gala to mention that our organisations were discussing a potential business deal. 'I know,' she said brusquely. 'But we are not going to discuss it here!' and discoed away. We didn't get the deal and that person still avoids me to this day.

Heather Townsend, author of the *FT Guide to Networking*, describes networking in a formula:

Opportunity = Credibility x (Personal Brand + Visibility + Social Capital)

While I wouldn't necessarily be that formulaic, she has a point. So let's look at each one briefly:

■ **Credibility is simple** Do you do what you say you will? Are you trustworthy? Are you a gossip? The more you can answer yes to the first two and no to the third, the higher your credibility will be.

■ **Personal brand is about how you come across** What are your personal values and what do you stand for? A positive personal brand is a great thing. I know many people who, although not particularly powerful within their own organisations, are at the top of every external list of influential people because they have mastered the art of networking and have built an immensely powerful personal brand in the process.

■ **Visibility** For many people, the issue will be about being visible as opposed to invisible. So how do you build visibility? The first thing to ask is: Who are the right people? Define your target audience. Is it a functional industry sector such as the marketing community? The City? Is it a sector network? Such as healthcare, the defence department, or fashion? Or is it movers and shakers in the educational world? Or is it a geographic community, such as the Midlands or Humberside, or the Middle East? Once you've done that, it is time to uncover who influences that target audience, so you can adopt a strategy of influencing the influencers. This involves researching the individuals and organisations that are most influential to your chosen target so that you can raise your visibility with them.

■ **Social capital** This concept is very similar to the emotional bank account discussed earlier. It's about building your positive bank balance with people more broadly. Volunteer for projects that will help your organisation or industry association. You can also be a connector, or a super connector as Malcolm Gladwell calls them. Super connectors are constantly using their networks to introduce people who may benefit from the introduction, often at no benefit to themselves. Most people are happy to help others, and if you are perceived as someone who likes to connect and help other people, then they will naturally think of you when opportunities occur. In addition, you will improve your own happiness.

---

case study   Madonna to Max Factor

One fine spring day in the mid 1990s my account team at Leo Burnett, the agency that handled Max Factor, and I were in a room kicking around ideas on how to make the brand more relevant and hip, as we were definitely in the older age demographic. They turned to me and said we have a great idea: let's sign Madonna. Some quick research convinced us that their idea was great. The only problem was how to get Madonna to agree. Max Factor was big in the UK, but not exactly hip in LA where Madonna lived at the time. And also, although we had a contract with one of her make-up artists, that didn't give us the clout to ring up the woman herself and make a proposal. We decided to take our time, and started targeting people whom Madonna would listen to. Fashionistas like Philip Treacy and the late, great Isabella Blow. Our approach to them was very genuine, as they too could help Max Factor become hip. So we sponsored Isabella's then protégé at Fashion Week. We listened to Isabella as she said Swarovski crystals were going to be the next big thing (and indeed she was right). We let her design our new colours. Equally we asked Philip to direct our Max Factor commercials for London Fashion Week. All of this proved great fun, and really helped the brand (it helped that it was also before the time when associating with artists and fashion was as widespread as it is today). The result of all of this was that by the time we approached 'Madge', or M as she likes to be known, we knew that when she did her research on Max Factor we'd come out well. Because the people whom she asked trusted us. I also spent a lot of time cultivating a good relationship with her then manager.

Finally, in summer 1997, we flew to LA to make our pitch. Sure enough, when we did finally get round to asking her, Philip, Isabella, Mario Testino and others put in a good word. I'm sure that helped her say yes. Max Factor got great coverage throughout the world and it was a key element in building the brand. No doubt, it also built my brand, as I was often quoted on the signing.

The point is that this is a great 'influence the influencer' example. As for what Madonna was really like? Well, suffice it to say she was very professional. She shook my hand and thanked me for believing in her. She started and finished on time. Also, Gwyneth Paltrow came to the film set. And she liked my pashmina.

Build your network within your organisation

Don't overlook networking opportunities within your own organisation. Every organisation is characterised by 'key players' – those who have the ability to influence or possess the knowledge most valued by others. Be mindful that it isn't only those occupying senior positions; those in less senior positions often possess valuable knowledge, or are the gatekeepers to it. Although it isn't easy to recognise such people, by discreetly asking colleagues who they recommend for x or y, you begin to build up a picture. It is likely that the same name or group of names is mentioned time and time again. By connecting with influential people you can then begin to tap into their network of contacts to further extend your own sphere of influence too.

Event networking: a simple how-to guide

Many of us – most of us – dread going to events full of folks we mostly don't know. We are all in the same boat here. If you follow this advice you will soon feel comfortable and always much happier after than before the event.

When you go to an event, make a list beforehand of three to five people whom you would like to meet. Research them, so you know about them. Then actively look for them. Start off talking about them, not you. For example, asking open-ended questions like, 'What did you think of the speaker?', 'What is your interest in x?' or, 'I know you are very involved with *x*. How is that going?' are all good openers. Sincere flattery also works. But remember, it's about linking their interest to yours – not leading with your own agenda.

Maintain eye contact and listen actively to your networking companion. There is nothing worse than someone who is actively looking around the room away from you. If your companion is doing this it's a sure sign you aren't connecting. Try a different tack or move on.

Avoid monopolising people. Five to ten minutes is usually plenty at receptions. Once you've had your conversation, ask to exchange business cards or contact details. Make your exit gracefully by saying, 'I've so enjoyed this conversation but I want to let you get on – I'm sure there are many other people here you need to see. I will be in touch to follow up on *x* that we discussed.'

Be open to the chance encounter as well as your 'pre-list'. Some of the best results come from people whom you meet by chance and have a naturally engaging conversation with.

Don't forget to actually follow up quickly afterwards – via LinkedIn or an email. Refer briefly to your shared interest in either of these. Always pick up guest lists at events. If you didn't get a chance to meet your 'target' on the night, reach out afterwards with a friendly short email or via LinkedIn. Share your specific mutual interest in common and request a follow-up conversation. Most people will say yes. And don't be afraid to email or call at least three or four times. People forget and are often swamped – don't jump to the conclusion that they are ignoring you. Be polite but persistent.

When you meet them afterwards, again make sure you look for common interests. Try a light touch initially – something easy for them to do. Ask more questions. If there are synergies it will be obvious, and they will feel it has been their idea. It will make getting things done easier.

exercise

Develop a networking plan for the next three months. How will you build your visibility and social capital among your key target audience? What will you do to engage them? How will you identify the key players in your organisation? After three months, see where you are in your plan. Has networking become easier? I bet the answer is yes.

Top tips, pitfalls and takeaways

Top tips

- Listen to others when you network; let them speak.

- Use the concept of the emotional bank account: when you help someone, you gain an emotional 'credit' – a store of goodwill for the future.

- If you cannot deal directly with someone, influence the influencers.

Top pitfalls

- Going into 'sales' mode in a social setting, or too early in a relationship.

- Thinking you are too important for someone – for example, a journalist in the trade press.

Top takeaways

- Understanding others is a vital part of core business skills such as negotiating, as well as cultivating a network.

- Negotiating can involve a win for both sides.

part

3

Managing others

6

Coaching, motivating and developing others

What you will learn in this chapter

- Why coaching has become both popular and valuable
- Key disciplines of a coaching style of management, and how it can boost team performance over time
- Some tips on motivating others

Coaching has become big business. According to a 2012 report,[1] it defied the recession and continued to grow globally. According to Anne Scoular, author of *The FT Guide to Business Coaching*,[2] demand for coaching is caused by 'cognitive (over)load': we simply have too much information coming at us, creating too many choices, across much larger spaces, with less time to process, fewer trusted sources to refer to, and the same size of brain to deal with it all. She defines coaching as pulling things out of people rather than pushing them in: 'Traditional mentoring, or advising, or consulting, puts in advice, content, and information. Coaching ... pulls out the capacity people have within.... It uploads rather than downloads.'[3]

---

[1] http://www.coachfederation.org.uk/
[2] Scoular, Anne, *Business Coaching*, FT Guides, Pearson Education Ltd, 2011.
[3] Scoular, *Business Coaching*, pp. 2–7.

In this chapter, I talk about how you as a manager can coach your colleagues, and how you can be effectively coached. I also cover how to recognise and use what motivates others and steps you can take to develop those you work with.

The manager as coach

Most companies do not teach their line managers to be coaches, and in fact actively discourage it. When we set our objectives with our boss, there are usually quantitative performance targets like cost reduction, productivity, market share or customer satisfaction. Rarely is it about coaching and developing people. An exception is Procter & Gamble (P&G). Everyone is measured on two things: how they develop the business, and how they develop their people. I am surprised that more businesses do not follow the example.

According to many studies, the leadership style we use least is the coaching style.[4] This is often because of the cognitive (over)load referred to. Coaching takes time, effort and patience, and when you're under pressure to deliver these are often the first things to go. It's much easier to tell someone what to do, or do it for them. But that will lead you both to work harder, not smarter.

So how do you develop coaching skills? Scoular cites four key basic disciplines.[5] These are echoed by Steven Covey in his book, *The Seven Habits of Highly Effective People*:

1 Listening.

2 Questioning.

3 Being non-directive.

4 GROW model.

Let's take a closer look at how each of these can help you to become a better coach.

---

[4] http://www.managers.org.uk/workinglife2012 and Goleman, Daniel, *Leadership that Gets Results*, cited in Scoular, *Business Coaching*, p. 13.

[5] Scoular, *Business Coaching*, p. 61.

Listening

How do you listen? By not talking, it's true; but this is difficult. One individual I know was trying to get his clients, top lawyers, to listen. For five minutes. It proved nigh on impossible. After 30 seconds, the lawyers started interrupting, asking questions, and getting to a situation where they could tell the client what to do. But by listening to people you can get a lot more done. Try the techniques for active listening, such as summarising what's been said, using good body language and eye contact (see Chapter 4). Try not to interrupt. Listening is also a great influencing technique.

Questioning – and being non-directive

Asking good questions is critical: the trick is to ask short, open-ended questions that cannot be answered yes or no. Here are some examples:

■ What would you like to talk about?

■ Why do you think that's important?

■ How do you think your colleagues would respond?

■ What do you think the best thing to do is?

There are times when you would simply like to tell someone what to do. But remember, if you are always telling people what to do, they won't learn to think for themselves. Before long they are back at your door, asking you to tell them what to do. I like to run one-to-one sessions with my direct reports. In these, I usually ask, what is on your list? And mentally compare it to what's on my own list. Most of the time, things overlap by 90 per cent. But by letting my direct report lead the discussion, I am automatically putting them more in control of the session.

Recently, a talented manager came to me with feedback on another colleague's performance in a meeting where I was not present. The manager said that several other senior managers had sought her out to say that her colleague's behaviour had negatively impacted them. She felt she should just let me know, and that it was up to me to give the person the feedback, or not. I asked her what she thought I should do. She said, tell the other manager about the negative feedback from colleagues. I asked her how she thought her colleague would react. She said she thought the colleague would feel defensive, and that the colleague would probably not trust her or the other senior managers as the CEO was now giving the colleague negative feedback passed on second hand. I asked her what she could do instead. She said she could talk to those who had given her the feedback and persuade them to take their concerns directly to the individual; giving examples and asking the colleague to do it differently next time.

I never had to say anything to achieve this conclusion. By asking questions, I helped her to figure it out.

Be sincere

When you are sharing things about yourself with direct reports, try to keep it sincere and human, and make sure you also ask about them. Otherwise it can come across as arrogant. I once had a new boss who came in on his first day and handed out a one-pager he described as 'The idiot's guide to dealing with *xx*', referring to himself in the third person. I am sure he meant it to be helpful, but because it was one-sided and he never asked about anyone else in his team, it came across as self-serving and insincere.

exercise

> In your next meeting with someone who works for you, try listening without interrupting them for five minutes, except to ask open questions.

GROW: the coaching session

There is a model that is most used by coaches everywhere in the world. It's called GROW.

GROW stands for Goal, Reality, Options, Will, and these form a virtuous circle.

■ **Goal** What would you like to get out of the session together? How does that contribute to your objectives? How will you know you've succeeded?

■ **Reality** Identify the key facts and their context. It's where you explore what is going on with the issue, who is involved, what has happened. What else is relevant?

■ **Options** What could you do to resolve this? What would be the impact of that? What else could you do? What are the pluses/minuses of each?

■ **Will** What will you do? What is your plan? What might get in the way? What other help do you need?

This is a great model to use if you are a newly promoted people manager. You will be very tempted to do things yourself rather than encourage others to think for themselves and guide them.

exercise

Try using this model at first to coach yourself. Then use it one-to-one with your direct reports. Finally, you can also use it with your boss. That is like reverse coaching. It will draw out what your boss sees as your goals, the situation, the options and what you should do. It can be a great way to learn from others.

The limits of GROW

A major retailer adopted this model for its entire staff and trained all the managers in it. One day, an area manager on a store visit was using GROW to help a stressed supervisor who couldn't cope without her manager present when dealing with store staff. The area manager started using the model, only to be interrupted. She said: 'Please don't GROW me right now. Please don't coach me. My mental state can't handle it.' Later when he spoke with HR, he learned that several employees had said the same thing. Coaching conversations were becoming too formulaic. They didn't like being so obviously manipulated, even if the intentions were good. So don't over coach!

Managing your boss – top tips

1 *Identify your boss's leadership style*. The way in which your boss acts or behaves towards you can also be affected by their particular leadership style. Think about what kind of personality they might have in Myers Briggs.[6] Try to figure out if your boss tends to focus on minutiae or the 'big picture', likes or hates change, is a right-brain or left-brain boss.

2 *Understand your boss's key objectives and values*. The key objectives and the support you can give; his or her personal values, and motivation.

3 *Communicate clearly, constructively and often*. Do so in as many different ways as possible – face-to-face, on the phone, and by email, both formally and informally. Always be honest.

4 *Clarify boundaries of responsibility*. If you are clear about your sphere of responsibility you will gain confidence in decision-making. What can you decide on your own with no input from your boss? What can you decide together? What can you decide but need to report? Never go over your boss's head to their boss or behind their back to their peers.

5 *Focus on loyalty and support*. Focus on supporting your boss in any weak areas they may have, without making it too obvious that you are doing so. Make yourself indispensable. Volunteer for opportunities which can increase your visibility, value and aid your longer-term development. Win their trust by achieving things they value.

6 *Develop a good relationship with your boss's personal assistant*. This person acts as the gatekeeper for your boss. If you cultivate a good rapport with him or her it can dramatically improve your relationship with your boss.

Mentors and sponsors

One reason for networking (see Chapter 5) is to find appropriate mentors and sponsors. Mentors are typically people who are not directly in your organisation or business unit. They might not even be a part of your organisation. They help you with guidance, advice and confidential discussion so that you can become more self aware and develop your potential. The mentor/mentee relationship is usually between someone more senior (mentor) and someone more junior. Most organisations, professional bodies and industry associations sponsor or run mentoring groups.

Sometimes there are official programmes in organisations or across sectors that focus on developing the female pipeline. For example, Peninah Thompson has founded The Mentoring Foundation in which

[6] http://www.myersbriggs.org/

FTSE 100 Chairmen mentor each other's talented women; now those talented women are starting to mentor others further down the management chain. The Cherie Blair Foundation for Women uses technology to mentor over 1000 women in developing countries by pairing them with women entrepreneurs in the developed world (I'm really proud to be able to say that I helped to set this up). CMI's Women in Management has a very successful Horizon mentoring programme which links up professional women mentors and mentees all over the UK.

A sponsor, as opposed to a mentor, is a senior person in your organisation who actively helps you become more visible and recognised. Sponsors will invite you to key meetings, have you participate in special courses, and take extra care to ensure you are given the chance to meet the 'movers and shakers' in your organisation. They will also champion you when discussing people 'behind closed doors' and tap you on the shoulder for crucial opportunities and projects. In this way, they add tremendous value and are vital in furthering your career. According to research by the Center for Talent Innovation, having a sponsor increases your chances of promotion by over 20 per cent, and greater access to sponsors is one of the key recommendations for increasing the percentage of women in the talent pipeline. This rings true for me; I was very fortunate to have a senior sponsor early on in my days at P&G and he played an enormous role in my visibility and development. My advice is to cultivate a relationship with someone far more senior in order to encourage them to be your sponsor.

Motivating others

What motivates others? A simple answer is: power and money. But actually that's rarely the case, with the exception of a few individuals with psychopathic tendencies, although some studies indicate that very powerful CEOs are more likely than the normal population to display such characteristics.[7]

How you approach your employees will be coloured by what you believe motivates them. And it may be different for different groups. If you think of a group you like, you are likely to think that they are

[7] Forbes, 11 June 2011.

self-motivated, enjoy their work, and can exercise control. If you think about a group you don't like, you may think they are lazy, looking to slack off at every turn and without coercion will never get the job done. These two theories of motivation are called X and Y. Theory X gives rise to controlling and directive managers, motivating by fear, whereas Theory Y will allow for more coaching and self-direction in setting and achieving objectives. This section is for Theory Y managers. Indeed, over time, it's been established that Theory Y will produce greater results in the long term.[8]

Things do become more complicated: we are complex beings, motivated by many different things. This is where Maslow comes in. Maslow (see Chapter 22 'A guide to the gurus') defined human needs in terms of basic needs (such as food and security) followed by recognition needs and ultimately by self actualisation or fulfilment. This tallies with daily experience, and with research. I like to use an acronym – people want to smell A RAT: Autonomy, Recognition, Achievement and Trust. Studies show that employees are motivated by the ability to make a difference at work.[9]

So assuming that your folks want to smell A RAT, how can you help them?

Look at simple things:

- ■ Trust them until proven otherwise.
- ■ Don't micromanage: delegate, and allow people to fail.
- ■ Set challenging but achievable targets; have consequences for failure.
- ■ Recognise them when they achieve them.

The same study showed the opposite was also true. People were much less motivated in companies with bureaucratic, autocratic and controlling leadership styles. These firms had lower productivity, lower growth and levels of engagement.

---

[8] Theory X and Theory Y: McGregor, Douglas, *The Human Side of Enterprise*, McGraw-Hill Professional, 2006 [1960].

[9] http://www.managers.org.uk/workinglife2012

Twelve secrets of successfully motivating people

Trust and be trusted

Trust is at the heart of motivation. While fear can be a great short-term motivator it is unlikely to bear fruit over time. I will never forget the first day of a new CEO I worked for. He walked in and announced that we were all singing for our supper. The immediate impact was to create an atmosphere of mistrust, which quickly degenerated into people knifing people behind their backs and point scoring; unpleasant, and also unproductive. Start by trusting people. If people lose your trust, make sure they know why and that they need to work to earn it back.

Create meaning

What we really want is to make a difference and to do something meaningful at work. This doesn't mean saving the world, but if we understand how what we do makes a positive difference in people's lives, and how our specific task helps to contribute to that, then we will be more motivated.

Delegate

If you want something done, let others do it and accept that they will do it differently than you. But they will learn. You will never be able to be everywhere at once. And if you spend all your time micro-managing people they will be less successful and so will you.

Set achievable targets

Part of delegating means setting challenging but achievable targets, and then letting your managers figure out how to get there. There is nothing better than being surprised at how people respond to challenges.

Set direction and communicate this clearly

Are you all clear on what success looks like? Because if you're not, it will be very difficult for people to feel motivated. Lack of clear targets is a common reason why people don't perform according to many leading studies of what makes successful organisations.

Have it their way – speak their language

Once the targets are clear, let them get on with it. How they achieve things should be up to them, not you. As long as it is ethical of course. And it's best if you adjust your style to match theirs. If they are using negative language, use negative language. If they are positive optimists, be positive and optimistic. It's surprising how quickly you can build rapport by listening well and tailoring your communication to the style of the person you are coaching.

Give credit for success and make sure you get recognition too

One of the biggest turn-offs for employees is when the boss steals the credit. I know someone who never took their direct report into the board meeting but always used their work. The direct report became very despondent and unmotivated. Similarly, I once had a boss who used to take my team's results and champion them as his own. There was nothing more dispiriting to us. I even wrote a note to correct his version of the truth. But the main thing is it was a waste of time for all parties. Not that you shouldn't credit your boss with success – you should, but you should also insist your contributions are recognised. This is even more important for women, who tend to be shy about claiming recognition.

Give freedom to fail but set your expectations about the consequences of repeat failure

Part of challenging people is letting them fail. On average we will fail about one-third to one-half of the time when launching new initiatives. But we will always learn more from failures. Win big, fail cheap is a great mantra. It is also important for people to know that it is not OK to fail with no consequences – even if the consequence is as simple as learning, in which case ask the employee for a one-pager on the lessons learned. If they fail repeatedly it is important to know that there will be consequences. I have seen many organisations and individuals stuck in a cycle of inertia and mediocrity because there is no incentive to succeed, but, equally, no consequence of, or learning from, failure. Always, however, take the rap for the failure of those who work for you up the line, even if it means you will have to fire them. In fact, not getting rid of under-performers is very de-motivating to those who do perform.

Use recognition and rewards that matter

This is perhaps the most often overlooked piece of the puzzle. When people do well, recognise them. You can do this through rewards, but personal thanks are just as important. Finally, if you spawn those who do better than you, be happy. That is the greatest recognition of your achievement. I am very proud to have managed many people who have gone on to bigger roles. It is immensely satisfying when they acknowledge that my coaching helped them to succeed.

Apply peer pressure

Studies have shown that people perform better when they are actually committed to deliver to specific individuals and so don't want to disappoint the group. That's why peer commitments have become an increasingly popular tool (see Chapter 9).

Encourage benchmarking

One very good aspect is to encourage learning from others who do something well. If, for example, you need your team to improve lead generation, arrange for them to go out and visit those who are good at it. They will learn more, having undertaken that themselves, than if you send all your old papers their way or spend an hour telling them how to do it. I've used this often; people genuinely enjoy it, plus it helps spread best practice. It's also encouraging your folks to build a peer network. Because maybe there is something they are good at that they can help with in return.

Perform performance management often

Try to have a coaching or motivational outcome to every encounter you have with your direct reports. Make the performance review an ongoing discipline, not a once a year tick box exercise (see Chapter 9). And if you encourage them to do the same, you will be amazed at how quickly you can turn around the performance of an organisation.

To help you track progress, try to agree a plan of action. For example:

▦ What will success look like?

▦ How will we know?

- How often will it be discussed?

- Based on that, what will I do to help you achieve your goal?

- What will you do to help you achieve your goal?

Top tips, pitfalls and takeaways

Top tip

- At work, people want to smell A RAT: Achievement, Recognition, Autonomy, and Trust.

Top pitfalls

- Not letting people know where they stand. Not having consequences for poor performance.

- Over-coaching: sometimes you just have to say something, or get something done.

- Managing by fear.

Top takeaways

- Coaching and delegating to your colleagues requires an initial investment of your time, but this gets repaid as they do not need to refer back to you so often.

- Motivation is not just about power and money; people need a sense of achievement and want to have a sense of progress, which is why coaching can be highly effective.

7

Hiring, firing and reshaping talent

What you will learn in this chapter

- How to attract and hire the right people
- How to create clear job descriptions and decisive interviews
- How to fire people
- How to manage downsizings, redundancies and reshapes

When asked about the biggest challenge facing them in 2013, over 700 CEOs from around the world agreed: it was 'human capital'.[1] That term may sound mechanistic to you, but its 'HR-speak' for people. And people are the main asset of any organisation. How to attract talented people, develop their careers, and keep them employed with your organisation through the many reshapes that are a part of our changing times is the subject of this chapter, alongside how to shed those who don't measure up. In each case, keeping your messages clear, consistent and constructive is the key challenge.

---

[1] Conference Board CEO Survey, June 2013.

Using your employer brand with the right audience

The culture you offer is likely to be a key factor in convincing employees to join you. Your employer brand should communicate your values; it will encompass your broader reputation with other stakeholders and the outside world. If you are a start-up firm, you will need to emphasise different attributes than you would if you are a FTSE 100, for example by giving people more meaningful work and an entrepreneurial environment. Conversely, if you are a large organisation, access to a global wealth of talent, resource, benefits and a well-established reputation may be the crucial selling points.

Today, people change jobs frequently and are on and off the job market many times throughout their careers. This means that your talent pool will come from many places: internal, external, social networks, via recruitment agencies, or head-hunters.

Do not overlook internal candidates. Be sure you advertise all vacancies internally before going externally. You might be surprised at how many people started off in different departments where they were unable to fully showcase their skills. Unilever CEO Paul Polman began life in the finance department before switching into brand management. Recently, someone who was in a call centre dealing with customer service had a hobby designing websites in her spare time. Such was her skill that when we were recruiting for a digital designer she very easily met the criteria.

If you do find yourself going externally, be creative. Recruiting via LinkedIn can save time and money and often yield candidates that are in some way connected to your organisation. I recall one head of HR saying at conference how she had reduced the cost of recruitment from £10,000 per person using recruitment agencies to around £11 per person by using LinkedIn, with no compromise in quality – the saving won her team department of the year!

If you are recruiting graduates from a particular university, bring recent alumni along to help you recruit. It's a great combination and one of the real secrets of P&G's recruiting success. When I was at BSI, we beat out a number of bigger, more prestigious companies in terms of attracting interns from the London Business School because while many of the larger companies sent their HR recruiter on 'road shows', we sent real managers who talked about how the interns would be given projects tailored to their skills so that they could make a difference. We ended up with five high fliers.

Job descriptions and interviews: keep them simple, clear and decisive

You always need to have a job description available. There are templates for this. The best include information on the job, the key outcomes expected, the resources available in terms of team and budgets, the reporting lines and the key stakeholders. They should also include a number of desired competencies or experiences – but ensure this is reasonable.

It helps to have some flexibility for the right candidate. The best people will often help shape and add to the job description as they go along. But it is vitally important that you are clear and honest at the outset about the job's responsibilities. Above all, be clear about the people and the money. Blurring the lines of who reports to whom, or who makes major decisions, in the hopes of luring a prime candidate, is something that will come back to bite both you and them. I remember once, because of a lack of clarity between my role and a colleague's role, the colleague effectively took over several of 'my' existing reports in the month between my being hired and the time I turned up to work. Not surprisingly, our relationship always struggled. On another occasion, on my first day my boss asked me and three peers who was responsible for a given business function. I had been led to believe that this was part of my remit. When he asked, all four hands went up. Awkward! If you are the hiring manager avoid these situations by creating clarity between your new hire and your existing direct reports. You will help them to have better relationships and produce better results.

The best interviewing processes involve more than one person, some form of structured competency questioning and a common assessment framework. It can also be very helpful to have the candidate prepare a short presentation. You will learn much from this: Do they prepare? Do they answer the question in a structured way or meander around it? Do they present well? And if you ask for 10 minutes do they deliver 40?

In my experience, the best interviews are structured, but around open questions that probe the person on the companies they have worked for, their motivations and experiences. Probing for examples is also helpful – and do not interrupt, but let the candidate finish. If they never do it's usually a warning sign that they will lack similar clarity on the job. Even if you aren't interviewing in a panel, it's always a good idea to have a series of interviews and a group input. This helps overcome the 'mini-me' problem – the tendency to recruit in one's own image. Giving everyone the same criteria for evaluating, and encouraging people to give a score and justify their remarks, will not only ensure that you get a quality decision that can be backed up, it also provides feedback to the candidates.

Make sure it isn't just HR – take responsibility to ensure that the people in the job area who will work with the candidate are involved in their hiring process. If you are using psychometric tests, then make sure adequate time is given and offer the candidate a debrief.

When it comes to hiring, the best decisions are quick; the very best are made on the day. It may be the case that you cannot do this – especially if you are seeing several candidates over weeks or months. But the worst thing you can do is drag the decision out. It sends a signal of indecisiveness to the candidate, who may have many options. Also, you really should know if someone is suitable after four people have seen them. At P&G, people would be invited in, and interviewed by four different people, who then convened and discussed whether or not to hire the candidate. The candidate was informed on the same day, and often encouraged to accept on the spot.

If job descriptions are clear, and the interview is good, then decisions should be easy. And if you can make a decision quickly, you are more likely to get a yes – everyone likes to be wanted. A very talented and sought-after graduate told me that he had had eleven interviews with a bank and still wasn't sure if he'd be offered the role. How excruciating for all involved!

Paperclip panel

One of the most idiosyncratic but effective methods of recruiting people that I have used is the 'paperclip panel'. After everyone had interviewed candidates individually, using the same structured questionnaire, we would all convene in someone's office. Paperclips would be laid on the table and everyone would put up to three of these in a fist according to the following guide:

0 clips: over my dead body will we hire this person.

1 clip: this person is OK but not strong in my view – I could pass ... or possibly be persuaded.

2 clips: a strong candidate whom we should hire.

3 clips: over my dead body will we NOT hire this person.

Then, on a count of three, the fists would open and the paperclips would drop to the table. They would be counted. After four people had interviewed candidates, at least eight clips would be needed for an offer. If people disagreed, say a zero clip and a three clip, which rarely happened but sometimes did, the two would debate and put forward their cases. Then the process would be repeated, with the more convincing one often having won over their colleagues.

Keeping talent through reshapes

A job for life is a thing of the past. It used to be frowned upon to see tenure of three years or shorter on résumés, but it's now much more common. This means that keeping talent can be a challenge. This is especially true given that it costs much more to recruit and train an employee than it does to retain them. So retaining talent is important. How can you do it? Here are four tips for retaining talent:

1 **Train and develop** Nine out of ten managers say that investing in them makes them feel appreciated and more likely to stay. According to a major study by CMI and Penna, the most effective forms of training and development are professional qualifications such as MBAs and Chartered Manager status. The least effective are one-off events.

2 **Move people up and around** At major multinationals, people are put on developed career tracks where they change job, function and country every two to three years. This helps enormously in retaining talent, as it develops new skills and avoids fatigue.

3 **Create an engaged culture** See Chapters 8 and 14 on how best to do this.

4 **Have great line managers** The biggest impact on people staying is their line manager. Equally this is the biggest single reason people move on. People leave people, not jobs.

In one recent survey, over 80 per cent of managers had experienced downsizing and redundancies in their companies over the past year.[2] Organisations are often looking for smarter ways of working using technology and simplifying processes.

Make sure your change programme links to your strategy and you can explain to people why you need to make these redundancies. Include reference to cultural changes in ways of working, not just cost savings. Again, if you need to move to an outcomes or performance culture, say so, and ensure you change those processes as well and do not just eliminate jobs.

Be open and gain input into new role design; it is always more effective if the people doing the work have input into the roles, and you will end up with a better organisational design. It's best to do this in phases, with each group helping to shape and streamline their work. Communicate quickly and often, and make sure messages are confident. Don't lie – if you know there will be redundancies, say so. This ensures that as few rumours as possible can start. Don't just cut cheaper roles while ring-fencing expensive, and often less needed, senior roles. This is readily seen through and will be viewed cynically. Take the opportunity to even out inequalities in titles, pay and job descriptions. It is amazing how often these differ unnecessarily across departments or countries.

Try to promote some positions from within. Reorganisation can be an opportunity to create bigger roles and allow current employees to apply for them. It is really important that you keep linking back the new roles to the strategy and desired outcome, so people see it not as change for change sake. Get rid of positions that you genuinely do not need, even if it is hard. Too often, roles will be ring-fenced because someone has been there a long time, or people are afraid to tackle a perceived sacred cow. (See also Part 5, 'Managing change', Chapters 14–16.)

[2] http://www.managers.org.uk/workinglife2012

When promoting internally, one of the common ways of managing successions is to ask peers in the organisation who they wouldn't mind working for were that person to be promoted, and, equally, who they would never support. You would certainly want your name coming up on the first list – not the second.

Letting people go (aka: firing)

Most of us have to do this at some point and have also been on the receiving end. It is one of the toughest tasks in management and one that too many managers assiduously avoid. Some managers will think that it reflects badly on them if they need to sack someone, others will be too concerned about the consequences and the reaction of the individual being fired and also the rest of their team. But people are not always rational and ethical, and will not always behave and perform in a way that is acceptable and in line with your company's policies and values.

The key reasons for needing to resort to firing someone are persistent poor performance and failure to deliver, or a disciplinary offence or grievance. Managing somebody out through poor performance needs to be handled carefully, as the manager needs to take steps to ensure that the person being dismissed is fully aware of their own performance issues. There will need to be clear evidence of how they have persistently missed objectives, failed to respond to warnings and failed to improve performance. If there is not clear evidence, then the individual being fired can claim unfair dismissal and sue the company. So investigate your company's performance procedure well in advance and follow it carefully. Document every meeting.

When managed effectively the end result usually benefits the individual concerned. Most likely, they were in the wrong role and unhappy that they couldn't deliver as required. In most cases, the individual will soon be employed elsewhere and much happier. I once had to fire someone who was in their fifties and going through a divorce – it was difficult but necessary. How rewarding it was when he rang me six months later to thank me – he was now doing charity work, which he had always wanted to do, and had found a new partner.

On the day, follow the tips below on letting people go, changing the circumstances accordingly. Even people whom you fire deserve another job somewhere. Don't hold grudges.

Here are some tips on how to approach this difficult conversation.

1 **Keep to the point** state your intent within the first minute. Chances are the person knows and the sooner you can say it the better for all,

2 **Keep it factual** because you did not improve your performance, we are ending your employment; or, because of the restructure we will be eliminating your role and you will be leaving us as a result.

3 **Expect people to get emotional** and have a tissue to hand.

4 **Be clear, but be quick** and have HR there too to handle technical details.

5 **Emphasise that you wish things to be handled constructively and with dignity and respect for both sides** and in a way that will make their finding their next employment easier. Offer recommendations, introductions and outplacement.

6 **Do it on a Thursday** doing things on a Thursday enables the individual to have the weekend to recover, but also one day before the weekend to absorb the news. You can then pick up any remaining questions on Monday.

Settlement agreement

A settlement agreement is a legal agreement where both parties agree to put the past behind them, in exchange for the leaving employee being paid. Neither party may then sue the other, or speak ill of the other. These agreements are really useful when things don't go smoothly. Such as:

■ where there are concerns of unfair dismissal, discrimination or other statutory claim;

■ a failure to follow your own procedures, including consultation requirements;

■ a detrimental change in the employee's terms and conditions;

■ in takeover/merger situations;

■ any form of employee dispute.[3]

Before using a settlement agreement, assess the time required to defend the case. Any potential harmful publicity should be considered in addition. Weigh up all the pros and cons carefully.[4] Settlement agreements are almost always used when senior employees are asked to leave and are considered 'the norm'. Still, make sure you consult an employment lawyer before signing one.

Top tips, pitfalls and takeaways

Top tips

■ When interviewing, involve different people, ask open questions, and request a presentation.

■ Draw up clear job descriptions; they can evolve, but there mustn't be serious ambiguities over the role or the level of decision-making or autonomy.

■ If you have to make redundancies, tell people early; don't waffle or obfuscate. Be decisive, but sensitive; offer outplacement.

Top pitfalls

■ Holding on to a post or department for sentimental reasons.

■ Hiding behind euphemisms when you are cutting costs and posts.

Top takeaways

■ Developing and retaining people is the most cost-effective way of building talent, and helps to strengthen the culture.

■ Be honest in communication on hiring and firing.

---

[3] Business HR, 'Compromise Agreements', 2013. www.businesshr.net/docs/legal/compromise.html
[4] Ibid.

8

How to engage, evaluate and align employees

What you will learn in this chapter

- How to get employees more engaged (with your organisation)
- How to do a performance review that really means something
- How to align employees and figure out who does what

If you engage your employees, use performance reviews to help them develop their contributions and understand how these meet your overall objectives, and keep everyone clear about who does what in achieving these objectives, you will have achieved the management equivalent of walking on water. If this is you, read no further. For the rest of us, here are some ideas to help.

In my view, this is the single biggest management challenge we face. And many would suggest that we aren't very good at it and are getting worse.[1]

Employee engagement

As with any buzzword, most of you will have heard of employee

---

[1] Conference Board CEO Challenge Report, 7 June 2013.

engagement. Many have a vague notion that it's something to do with motivating and gaining employees' commitment. Few actually practise it, and even fewer do it well. So what is it actually? The truth is there is no agreed definition, but employee engagement views the employer–employee relationship as one that is mutually beneficial for both parties. To quote one of the major reports on the topic:

A workplace approach designed to ensure that employees are committed to their organisation's goals and values, motivated to contribute to organisational success, and are able at the same time to enhance their own sense of well-being.[2]

It sounds a bit soft and squidgy, but before you begin your eye-rolling, take a look at some of the evidence the same report presented:

▨ **Performance** A Gallup poll of 2006 found that the earnings per share (EPS) growth rate of organisations with high engagement scores was more than 2.5 times higher than those with below-average engagement scores.[3]

▨ **Innovation** CMI research from 2007 found that employee engagement had a significant association with innovation.[4]

▨ **Absence** Engaged employees take less sick leave, according to another Gallup poll.[5]

▨ **Lower staff turnover** According to the Corporate Leadership Council, engaged employees are 87 per cent less likely to leave the organisation than the disengaged.[6]

Arguably, engagement is even more important in recessionary times, when hiring freezes and cost-cutting make winning the hearts and minds of remaining employees even more vital. Without engagement,

---

[2] Macleod Report, p. 9.
[3] 'Engagement predicts earnings per share', Gallup Organisation, 2006.
[4] Kumar, V. and Wilton, P., 'Briefing note for the Macleod Review', Chartered Management Institute, 2008.
[5] Gallup, 2003, cited in *Employee Engagement: How to Build a High Performance Workforce*, Melcrum Research Report Executive Summary, Melcrum Publishing, 2005.
[6] Corporate Leadership Council, Corporate Executive Board, 'Driving performance and retention through employee engagement: a quantitative analysis of effective engagement strategies', 2004.

strategies cannot be well-executed, values are not brought to life and organisations can suffer from high turnover and inertia.

So how to go about engaging employees, and how is it measured? Here's a simple seven-point checklist:

1 Give staff clear information on the mission, strategy and purpose of the organisation.

2 Help staff understand how their work objectives tie in with the organisation's goals.

3 Involve staff in decision-making (even if they don't always get what they want).

4 Enable people to have a certain amount of control and autonomy over their own work.

5 Promote good relationships with managers, colleagues and a supportive working environment.

6 Offer feedback on a regular basis constructively, including praise and support.

7 Create opportunities for people to progress in their careers.

Other things, like open-plan offices, atriums or other places where employees can gather and communicate informally, and social intranets, can help boost engagement.

Typically, employee engagement is measured by staff questionnaires. Most involve selecting key questions from these questionnaires, using some sort of proprietary algorithm to create an engagement number, and then indexing this number compared with other organisations. If no one really understands the ingredients that make up the index, and nothing is ever done with it, it can become an end in itself rather than a useful means to an end.

Here is an example of the sorts of questions that comprise a typical engagement index:

> I am proud to say that I work for *xxx*.
> I would recommend *xxx* as an employer.
> I am willing to go the extra mile for *xxx*.

I intend to be working for *xxx* in 12 months' time.

Overall I am satisfied working for *xxx*.

Measuring the index is one thing, doing something about it is far more important. One of the pitfalls of taking the questionnaire too seriously is that you pay more attention to getting a high score on the 'right' questions than creating actual engagement. I recall one organisation where the rumours were that every year the survey came round this particular manager locked his employees in a room and said their bonuses would be dependent upon their scores – something they then repeated with their employees. Little wonder the scores were top-notch. But were they real? At the other end of the spectrum, I have seen employees become very disenfranchised with such surveys because year after year they are done, often with mediocre results, and yet nothing ever happens to address the results. I have also seen organisations where the results are 'edited' before being presented to the Board.

None of those behaviours is going to improve engagement. So if you do surveys, take them seriously, share the results openly, and take action to improve the results, preferably by involving those who provided the feedback and committing to measure improvements. Finally, remember that it's better to have a clear idea of what to do better, and that many things that will influence your scores, not least culture. Different cultures score differently when it comes to things like enthusiasm, pride and personal identification with goals.

exercise

Do you measure engagement in your organisation? If so, how? If not, why not? How do you benchmark your results? Why do you think that is, and what's needed to improve? Dig out the last three years of surveys. Has anything moved? If not, why not?

Performance reviews that improve performance

Performance reviews are something that every organisation does, but astoundingly few, in my experience, do well. Indeed, maybe this is one area where technology has let us all down. There is little more disheartening than receiving loads of automated email messages that your annual performance reviews are now overdue. You then log in to a clunky system that administers the review, and makes it hard to see the data, crashes frequently, and makes reviewing people a terrible 'tick-box' chore. Little wonder they are frequently the subject of lots of headlines such as these, from the Management Innovation Exchange (http://www.mixprize.org/tags/performance):

"When Best Practices Aren't Good Enough – Putting the Performance Review on Review"

"Blowing Up Performance Management 1.0 from the Inside: How One Manager Transformed His Company's Approach to the Dreaded Performance Review"

Annual performance reviews are done in most places. However, the best way of managing performance is on an ongoing basis, every time you have a meeting with your employees. Immediate, consistent, specific and positive feedback is likely to be much more effective than a one-off review. Nonetheless, formal systems are required in most organisations so here's how to get the best out of them.

Personally I think old-fashioned written reviews are much better than the online formats. The best performance reviews ask about your contribution to business objectives, to organisational objectives, your ability to interact effectively with others and develop people, your strengths, your development areas, and finish off with a personal development plan. There will usually be a five-point rating scale, with 1 being outstanding and 5 being unacceptable. Other features may be integrity, customer focus, values, exemplifying leadership, setting priorities, ability to collaborate, and so on. The review should also include a section for career goals and aspirations.

Ten steps to better performance reviews

You will have a more effective performance review if you follow these guidelines:

1 Make sure you ask your direct reports to do their own. This ensures that they are thinking about their own contributions.

2 Ask that everyone obtains 360 degree feedback – i.e. feedback not only from you, their boss, but also from people they manage and peers, which can be people they work closely with in other departments.

3 Use the 'Start–Stop–Continue' framework – it is simple and effective: What should *x* continue doing to be more effective? Start doing? Stop doing?

4 Schedule a face-to-face meeting to review what has been written. Start by listening to the employee's own evaluation. What went well? What are they proud of? What went less well? Most people will be honest when they speak, even if they have over- or underrated themselves on the form. Then discuss.

5 Emphasise the positive things, and discuss what they did to achieve these results. Encourage them to apply those behaviours to other areas. Make sure you end on a positive note.

6 Be honest. The most common mistake is to overrate people! Someone who has missed every objective is rated as excellent, then, when it comes time to performance manage the person, they take action because they can cite a slew of glowing performance reviews.

7 Use specific examples, not sweeping statements such as 'you are too emotional'. Discuss how the person might have handled a situation differently. Equally, be specific with positive examples: 'Your presentation to that client really captured their needs and how we could help. I'm sure it was a major factor in our win.'

8 Draw up an action plan to improve the given areas. Make sure you try to draw on the employee's strengths. For example, if someone is a great networker, but has difficulty sticking to priorities, encourage them to check with their colleagues and with you as to whether they are on track.

9 Make sure you contribute to the action plan. What behaviour will they do differently? How will you help them? Draw up a plan to encourage both of you to help each other. Make sure your action plan addresses both performance and career goals.

10 Feedback on progress frequently; weekly is not too often.

exercise

Plan to review your team's performance weekly using the above approach for the next eight weeks. After two months, review the approach with each individual. Are you gaining better performance as a result?

Ideally, performance will affect both pay and promotion opportunities. However, there are some pitfalls. Many organisations used to have forced rankings, such as a certain number of employees in the top 10 per cent and firing those in the bottom 10 per cent. These have moved out of fashion, as it was found that over time the bottom 10 per cent became a political tool used to isolate people for personal rather than performance reasons. However, some sort of calibration on rankings is really important. Otherwise, you will find some departments where everyone is rated outstanding and others where everyone is rated average. If your pay is linked to performance, as it often is, this can be very discouraging.

Most organisations that manage talent well always distinguish between performance and potential. Someone may be a great performer, but be at the top of their level. Others will have loads of potential, but may be too inexperienced to be performing at a high level; so sending them a message that they are great is confusing, and will not help them realise their potential.

All performance reviews should indicate when the individual might be ready for promotion. To avoid creating undue expectations, the section on potential and promotion might be kept confidential.

Although everyone requires some degree of acknowledgement for a job well done, people are motivated by different 'awards': for example a bonus, instant thank-you, certificates or public announcements. Award ceremonies are often a good thing and many companies do these very well. It is especially effective if the employees do the nominating and the leaders judge the awards. They have the added advantage of forming 'case-studies' of success.

Beyond that, make sure you have the ability to recognise people on the job for the little things they do well. This can be by thanking them or with small rewards. In the end, nothing substitutes for a genuine and specific thank-you from managers and, when appropriate, from their managers.

Decision-making clarity

Life used to be simple. You worked for one person, and he or she sat in the office above you. If you were the boss, you had full responsibility for your site or business unit, department or country. Now, organisations are much more complicated, with multiple business units, countries, divisions, customer groups and functions. Departments and responsibilities are often shared by several stakeholders. This can result in lack of clarity over who does what, and who makes decision. Such ambiguity often results in conflict, inertia and poor performance. In my executive career, the 'who decides what' question has often been the major reason behind executive squabbles, power plays and intrigues. Dealing with decision rights is essential. Ultimately, this requires great leadership, because it's about creating a culture where everyone feels that they want to move ahead, on the basis of common objectives and personal accountability rather than maximising their own power base. Poor leaders will ignore these conflicts and let them fester, maintaining that 'big boys and girls' will solve everything themselves. They won't, and the organisation's culture and performance will suffer.

Tools can help, however. A useful one is the RACI model (see below). It is no substitute for a great culture – I once spent a weekend with colleagues trying to sort out a RACI, but no one wanted to collaborate, so it was a waste of time. So don't use this tool until you are all ready to work together. And make sure the boss is there to take the call in the cases where people cannot agree.

The RACI tool

- **Responsible** This is the class of people who are ultimately responsible for getting the work done. This may refer to the individual workers who perform the given task or it could refer to the system if the task is automated.

- **Accountable** This is the class of people who are accountable to oversee that the work gets done. This usually means the immediate manager overseeing the work.

- **Consulted** These may be subject matter experts who need to be consulted when necessary, for example when an unanticipated scenario arises. These are the people who will recommend deviations from the Standard Operating Procedure (SOP).

■ **Informed** This is the class of people who have some interest in the performance of a given task. This may be a manager trying to control the execution of the task at hand. Also this could be an input signal to the other process.

Basically, with the RACI tool, you map the people or functions that decide down one side and the activities or processes that need doing and deciding down the other. The output is shown in Figure 8.1.

Activities	CEO	CFO	Business Executive	CIO	Business Senoir Management	Head Operations	Chief Architect	Head Development	Head IT Administration	PMO	Compliance, Audit, Risk and Security
Determine risk management alignment (e.g. assess risk)	A	R/A	C	C	R/A	I					I
Understand relevant strategic business objectives		C	C	R/A	C	C					I
Understand relevant business process objectives			C	C	R/A						I
Identify internal IT objectives and establish risk content				R/A		C	C	C			I
Identify events associated with objectives some events are business-orientated (business is A); some are IT orientated IT is A, business is C	I			A/C	A	R	R	R	R		C
Assess risk associated with events				A/C	A	R	R	R	R		C
Evaluate risk responses	I	I	A	A/C	A	R	R	R	R		C
Prioritise and plan control activities	C	C	A	A	R	R	C	C	C		C
Approve and ensure funding for risk action plans			A	A		R	I	I	I	I	I
Maintain and monitor a disk action plan	A	C	I	R	R	C	C	C	C	C	R

A RACI chart identifies who is Responsible, Accountable, Consulted and/or Informed.

figure 8.1   **The RACI matrix**

Source: COBIT © 2007, IT Governance Institute. All rights reserved. Used by permission.

Rules for using the RACI matrix

■ **Only one Responsible and Accountable Person** Only one person should be assigned the R/A roles. Having more than one person responsible for the same task increases ambiguity and the chances of the work not being performed, and of duplication. Having more than one accountable person again leads to the same problem. However, having only one person accountable also leads to a problem. If the assigned person is incompetent the whole process fails. For this reason there is often a hierarchy of accountable people.

■ **Responsible-Accountable is mandatory** The consult or inform roles are not mandatory for every activity. It is possible that some activities may not require them at all. But the Responsible-Accountable roles must be assigned.

■ **Communication with the consultant** There must be a two-way channel of communication with the consultant. The important aspect is that the communication be two-way.

■ **Inform the required stakeholders** This is a one-way channel of communication.

When your next big growth initiative or other project comes along, use the RACI model to plot out just exactly who is responsible for what before you begin. Then revisit every two months. Is the group sticking with the initially agreed responsibilities or are they shifting? Discuss as a team, including any adjustments to behaviours or realignments in RACI that need to be done.

The matrix doesn't have to be your enemy

12 September 2012 Forbes.com

By Paul Rogers and Jenny Davis-Peccoud

It's a world of multiple bosses, endless relationships, and – as this example shows – murky accountabilities. It's also a world of frustrated managers and employees, people who feel that they can't take effective action or deal with a customer without running into a series of organisational obstacles.

Some form of matrix – or organisational structure – is essential for running any large company. As companies grow, they become increasingly complex, especially in today's world. When executives talk about crossing organisational boundaries, they usually mean not one or two boundaries but five or six, such as function, geographical region, process, product and customer.

To make this multifaceted system work ... a company needs to focus on its decision-making processes, not its organisational chart.

Here are just a few of the steps your company can take to do that:

1 *Follow the money*. High-performing companies know how each side of the business creates value and which decisions are key to unlocking that value.

That helps them locate critical decisions at the appropriate points in the organisation.

2 *Align people around key priorities and principles.* Most successful companies operate according to a set of core principles and priorities that supersede any matrix. These principles create a context enabling people anywhere in the organisation to make appropriate trade-offs.

3 *Assign clear decision roles.* People can have more than one boss, but decisions can't. The most common problem we find in matrix organisations is confusion over who should play which role in key decisions.

4 *Help leaders set the right tone.* If leaders don't make good decisions quickly, others are likely to dither. If leaders don't collaborate across boundaries, others won't either.

5 *Foster a performance culture.* This is the holy grail of decision effectiveness: an environment in which people naturally take responsibility for cross-boundary cooperation. It's critical for a smoothly functioning matrix as well.

Top tips, pitfalls and takeaways

Top tips

- Always have clarity over who makes the decisions.

- When managing someone, give constant and honest feedback on their performance; don't just save it up for the formal review.

- The RACI tool for defining accountability has stood the test of time. It refers to being: Responsible, Accountable, Consulted and Informed.

Top pitfalls

- Proceeding with a tool for accountability when the culture is weak and people don't trust each other.

- Setting up employee questionnaires, but not acting on the findings.

Top takeaways

- Employee engagement is not a fuzzy thing: it can make a huge contribution to financial returns and better risk management.

- Face-to-face reviews, with regular follow-ups, can be far more effective than online once-a-year box-ticking versions.

9

Performing teams and productive meetings

What you will learn in this chapter

- Assemble, brief and manage effective teams – inputs
- Review team effectiveness and behaviour – processes
- Get better team solutions and decisions – outputs
- Manage productive meetings

Teams and meetings, meetings and teams. These two items account for well over 60 per cent of our at-work activity. So getting these things right is critical. Yet, this is an area that frequently goes wrong – indeed, even CEOs admit that only 40 per cent of their meetings achieve their objectives.[1] Probably everyone has experienced meetings that seemed pointless, where everyone was on their laptops, or teams with minimal contributions and maximum conflicts. This chapter discusses how to make teams tighter and meetings merrier and more meaningful.

When to have teams

Teams should happen when there is something that needs to be discussed and decided by a group of people from different areas of the

---

[1] HBR Blog Network, Anthony J. Tjan, 14 Nov. 2012.

business on a regular basis. This can be because of leadership and governance issues, such as executive or management boards, or because of project issues, such as designing a new product. Teams can also be useful for improving existing business processes, such as transitioning from paper to digital. Now that sharing resources is becoming the norm, and technology makes working across boundaries easier than ever before, teams have become a normal way of working.

Team composition

When choosing teams, it's a very good idea to have different skills and experiences. Try to avoid picking 'placeholders' – people who are there just because they are representing a department. Have the fewest team members necessary for any task. As well as capabilities, consider behaviours. Meredith Belbin did some work on team diagnostics which is widely used. He said that different people serve different roles on teams by virtue of their behaviour in a group and approach to problem-solving. Belbin's team roles are: Resource-investigator, Co-ordinator, Shaper, Monitor-evaluator, Team worker, Implementer, Completer-finisher, Specialist and Plant (creative).[2]

Team charters and briefings

Once you've assembled your team, it is a good idea to get everyone face-to-face for 'KICK-OFF'.

At the kick-off, you should:

- ■ brief the team on why they are there and what they are expected to do;
- ■ cover off your objectives, time frame, and how you will gauge the outputs;
- ■ allow team members to contribute to build a simple charter as to their expectations and the behaviours they would like to see.

---

[2] www.belbin.com

You may also wish to ask them to rate themselves with the Belbin model, and then come back to it four or five meetings later and ask the group to comment on how everyone has rated themselves. On your first meeting, pull together as a group your objectives, behaviours and ways of working in a simple team charter document – this is often called more formally a Terms of Reference, or TOR, but Team Charter sounds friendlier.

It is a good idea to combine this with some sort of ice-breaker, especially if the team don't know each other. Good ice-breaker questions include: who I am, why I'm here and one thing you don't know about me. Or, ask each member to share three things about themselves – two are false; one is true – and ask everyone to guess which is true. The final thing to review as part of your briefing are the resources you think you will need, the time commitment and frequency of meetings, as well as the work required between meetings. Be honest about how much time will be required to work on team matters between meetings, and make sure everyone has the support of their line manager. Finally, you may wish to talk about how you will communicate as a team, both with each other and with the wider group.

Technology and teams: virtual teams

Virtual teams have existed for a decade and are now common. Conference and video calls allow team members to communicate across time zones, countries and sites. Technologies like intranets and Google documents allow team members to share things easily. Here are some tips to help them be effective:

■ If possible, get people face to face first. Meeting once a year in person boosts relationships and effectiveness. This is particularly true with multi-cultural or global teams. For many cultures, such as the Chinese, face-to-face relationship building is very important.

■ Don't skip on the team norms and ways of working. Go through that, even if it is harder to do remotely. If possible do it during your first face-to-face session.

■ Remember that many people will not speak English as their native language. Speak loudly, clearly and use simple words not metaphors or idioms.

▪ Eliminate multi-tasking. It is distracting if people are typing into keyboards during a conference call. If they are not needed for certain sections of the meeting, let them leave.

▪ Muting those not speaking eliminates unnecessary feedback noise. Not everyone needs to hear the cars whizzing past you on the motorway.

▪ Respect time zones. The middle of the day in Europe is often good, as it is early morning in the Americas and mid evening in Asia. But you may have to break sessions into two – one for Europe and Asia and one for Europe and America.

▪ Share presentations in advance. Keep them short. Expect them to be read.

▪ Use intranet sites sparingly. In my experience, sites become far too populated with unnecessary stuff, or not used.

▪ Try meeting more frequently for less time. Encourage people to touch base informally between meetings if you do allow too much time to lapse.

▪ Make sure the leader reviews team progress, motivation, and encourages everyone to participate. The leader should note those who are silent and encourage them to contribute.

exercise

Top team tip: Power Brainstorming

These sessions get everyone working and contributing no matter how introverted or shy they are. I have seen it work across mixed cultures, functions and levels, in groups sized from 10 to 100, and with people who come in disagreeing. It's wonderful to see a group file in anxious or cynical in the morning, and be absolutely buzzing by early afternoon.

You need: ▪ Flipcharts and pens   ▪ A stopwatch

▪ Notepads or large Post-Its   ▪ A timekeeper

Here's how you do it:

1 Pick your top three questions you need to gain input and alignment to. These could be: What are the team objectives? What are our ways of working and behaviours? What are the measurable outcomes and how long will they take? The questions should be open; they should also concern important matters that affect everyone.

2 For each question, divide people into teams of two. The chair, or most senior person, or someone outside, needs to play timekeeper.

3 For two minutes, one person in each pair answers the question. The other person takes notes. The one listening is not allowed to comment or interrupt – just note down what their partner is saying. After two minutes the timekeeper says switch, and roles are reversed. After two minutes, the timekeeper calls time. During the next two minutes, the pairs discuss their answers and come up with their 'Top 3' priority list. After two minutes, the timekeeper calls time. In the final two minutes, the pairs prepare to feed back their answers to the group. Each group then has two minutes to feed back their answers to the broader team.

4 Repeat this process for each question.

NB: If you have more than 10 pairs you may wish to split things into tables. In this case, each table has an extra three minutes to agree their 'Top 3' from those presented to the table.

In the rare event you do have a disagreement over the priorities, you can always allow everyone to choose their 'Top 3' from the list, and go with those.

What results is a list of answers to each question you posed. But you get much more than that. People see how common their answers are, which really adds to bonding and common purpose. People feel a sense of belonging, as everyone has contributed.

Team effectiveness, behaviour and conflict

Reviewing team behaviour is very important. Good leadership will maintain clarity of purpose, allow people to participate, and balance the task focus with constructive behaviour and conflict resolutions. You also need to track progress and know how to change course or even disband.

Give the team time to bond. One description for this is around forming, storming, norming and performing (see below). Teams take time to gel. On average it will take three to six months of working together to form patterns.

The progression is:

■ forming;

■ storming;

■ norming;

■ Performing.

The features of each phase are explained below.

Forming (Stage 1)

High dependence on leader for guidance and direction. Little agreement on team aims other than received from leader. Individual roles and responsibilities are unclear. Leader must be prepared to answer questions about the team's purpose, objectives and external relationships. Processes are often ignored. Members test tolerance of system and leader. Leader directs (similar to Situational Leadership® 'Telling' mode).

Storming (Stage 2)

Decisions don't come easily. Team members vie for position as they attempt to establish themselves in relation to other team members and the leader, who might receive challenges from team members. Clarity of purpose increases but plenty of uncertainties persist. Cliques and factions form and there may be power struggles. The team needs to be focused on its goals to avoid becoming distracted by relationships and emotional issues. Compromises may be required to enable progress. Leader coaches (similar to Situational Leadership® 'Selling' mode).

Norming (Stage 3)

Agreement and consensus is largely formed by the team, who respond well to facilitation by leader. Roles and responsibilities are clear and accepted. Big decisions are made by group agreement. Smaller decisions may be delegated to individuals or small teams within group. Commitment and unity is strong. The team may engage in fun and social activities. The team discusses and develops its processes and working style. There is general respect for the leader and some of leadership is shared more by the team. Leader facilitates and enables (similar to the Situational Leadership® 'Participating' mode).

Performing (Stage 4)

The team is more strategically aware; the team knows clearly why it is doing what it is doing. It has a shared vision and is not reliant on the leader. There is a focus on over-achieving goals. The team has a high degree of autonomy. Disagreements occur but now they are resolved positively, while necessary changes to processes and structure can be made by the team. It attends to relationship, style and process issues along the way. Team members look after each other. The team requires delegated tasks and projects from the leader. Team members might ask for assistance from the leader with personal and interpersonal development. The leader delegates and oversees (similar to the Situational Leadership® 'Delegating' mode).

There are many ways of guiding the team towards the 'Performing' level. One is to ensure that after every team meeting you evaluate your progress. What went well? What went less well? How could you improve? By getting that as a standard part of the team meeting, you will continually encourage awareness. Try having each peer commit to the team what they will add. This will help focus people on their contributions and make them more aware – and everyone else as well – of what they have contracted to bring to the party. It discourages skiving.

The peer commitment process

1   *Purpose*. What is your fundamental commercial purpose within the enterprise.
2   *Activities*. What are the key activities you do to achieve and deliver that purpose?
3   *Milestones*. What metrics let you know where you are in terms of your performance against those activities and your commercial purpose?
4   *Time*. How much time are you willing to commit to achieving your purpose?
5   *To whom*. Who are the colleagues to whom you are making these commitments?

(*Source:* MIX)

Dealing with conflict

Inevitably, teams will come into conflict. This is not always bad. Sometimes, conflict can lead to a better solution – but only if you have an agreed method of conflict resolution. The other aspect of behaviour worth watching is signs of conflict, or indeed of withdrawal, which is a passive form of conflict. If you are the team leader, it's important that you look for the signs: if there is conflict, is it task-based – that is, are people disagreeing on the task at hand? Or is it personality based – are people not getting along? Is the conflict limited to the team or does it involve other line managers or departments?

Once you have identified the source of the conflict, address it openly but in a non-threatening way. If it is task-based, then getting together and using the 80/20 rule – i.e. let's focus on the 80 per cent that is common rather than the 20 per cent that isn't – may be the way forward. Or it may be that you look for a compromise that is win–win, and allows each approach to maintain what's important whilst compromising on something less important. If the conflict involves a lack of support for the team member from their line manager, discuss with the line manager. It may be that they are simply unwilling to 'share' their people with you. If this is the case, try ensuring you stress the benefits that will accrue to them from participating, or allow them to help shape the team's outputs. Equally, with individuals who have ceased to contribute, make them aware of the impact of their behaviour and try to understand the cause. It could be they really aren't right for the team. If so, then ask them to suggest a replacement.

If the conflict is between individuals, then it's best to ask them to meet up in a neutral setting. Perhaps you would like to speak with each person individually and get their perspective before bringing them together. It's important when you do bring people together that you make them aware of the impact their behaviour is having on the rest of the team. Most people when asked supportively will put personal differences behind them. Try to encourage both of them by saying that they add value and complement each other. If this doesn't work, you may need to move one of the members, or risk the team becoming dysfunctional.

The dysfunctional team

There are many different ways of evaluating team performance. If you are leading a team where little gets done, you may wish to call a third party to help you. Methods such as the Ashton Team Performance will look at various questions answered by each individual member around inputs, process and outputs, and will rate them against a benchmark. It can be very useful – but only if you have a good leader.

If you are leading a dysfunctional team, unfortunately you are the problem! Ask why it isn't working, and what you need to do to address this. If it is reminding individuals to improve their behaviour, then do so. If it's about increasing trust or outputs, then agree steps to improve this. If you need to be clearer in decisions then do so. Then ask for feedback after each meeting. If you are a member of a dysfunctional team, try talking with other colleagues. As difficult as it is, you may wish to confront the leader and ask to be better led. If you don't you will likely continue to struggle along, wasting time and being dissatisfied.

Team outputs: better decisions and solutions

Ensuring that you encourage different ways of looking at a problem will often get a better result. One of the popular methods of doing this is called Six Thinking Hats, devised by Edward de Bono. It's a good way of checking out whether you are thoroughly engaging the different ways of looking at a decision. The 'hats' are coloured:

- white – data and information;
- red – feelings and intuition;
- yellow – taking a positive view;
- black – exercising caution;
- green – creative thinking;
- blue – process control.

Monitoring progress: only diamonds are forever

Due to the constant change in organisations, teams will need to adapt, and they have a finite lifespan. Make sure you check progress against your original outputs and if you need to refresh them, do so. In the end, if you are done you are done. Don't be afraid to disband the team and form new ones as your circumstances change.

Make sure you learn from the experience of working together, asking everyone to critique constructively.

If you have achieved your goals, celebrate your success. Being part of high-performing teams is one of the best feelings of belonging to an organisation and you are right to encourage everyone to recognise it. Nominate yourselves for awards.

Productive meetings

Meetings. As few as possible. Asda famously had meetings standing up to keep them short. Meetings are necessary only when they are necessary. So ask yourself: Will a phone call do? If I need the meeting, who really needs to be there? What is it about? What is the expected outcome?

Once you know you need a meeting, have a good process. This is simple:

1 Have an agenda and a timetable – and stick to it! Invite input on the agenda.

2 Clarify the objectives. What do you want to cover? What would you like the meeting to achieve? It's amazing how often this *isn't* clear.

3 If papers are submitted, make sure people have read them beforehand. Avoid items that are only for information sharing. Focus on items that require discussion and decision. If the items are controversial, make sure you have spoken to key people before the meeting, rather than spring it on them at the meeting.

4 Allocate enough time for each item. If you are over-ambitious, you will over-run, and leave people feeling unproductive and dissatisfied.

5 Moderate discussion – have a chair. Even if the chair rotates, someone always needs to lead the meeting and ensure the objective and outcomes are met.

6 Always take minutes and appoint the minute writer before the meeting. Minutes should cover agreed action, timetables and who is responsible.

7 If it's a regular meeting, review the actions of the previous meeting at the next meeting. If they aren't happening, you have an issue.

8 Always practise 'cabinet responsibility' – agree or disagree at the meeting but commit to agreement outside of it.

9 Agree and clarify the main communication points before you all leave.

10 After each meeting, ask what went well and what didn't. Aim to improve.

Top tips, pitfalls and takeaways

Top tips

- Be aware of different personality types and how they act within teams.

- Power brainstorming sessions can be extremely powerful.

Top pitfalls

- With a team, failing to get support of a team member's line manager, so that they cannot contribute fully and have conflicting priorities.

- As a leader, failing to address team conflicts and letting these hijack team performance.

Top takeaways

- Meetings are often wasteful. Look for ways other than meetings to get things done.

- When meetings are necessary, make sure you have a clear purpose for the meeting, an agenda, and the right people there.

part

4

Setting direction and achieving results

10

Setting a strategy

What you will learn in this chapter

- How to identify what a strategy is and importantly what it isn't
- How to set a strategy for your business area
- Tips for refining and improving your strategy
- How to use tools to help you set better strategies
- How to check whether your strategy is right – using stories

What is strategy?

Strategy is one of the most scary and misunderstood words in the management lexicon. People use it to confuse, threaten, condemn and otherwise torture their colleagues. It's often used as a prelude for much complicated analysis and reams of PowerPoint slides and binders labelled 'strictly confidential'. The truth is, strategy is a set of simple choices, and relevant, interrelated and prioritised activities based on those choices. It should be based on evidence, capability, as well as instinct. It should be short. It should be obvious, and expressed in simple language. Amazon's Jeff Bezos has this down to a 't'. He doesn't spend much time on strategy, he says, because it's obvious. Amazon's strategy is to offer the widest range at the lowest price and fastest delivery for every category in which they compete.[1]

---

[1] Kevin Roberts, 2013 talk at P&G reunion.

Yet many smart people and smart companies do not understand this. I have participated in numerous strategic planning sessions that have produced tons of initiatives and charts and resulted in something that was too difficult to understand or communicate. I once sat in a day-long board meeting discussing a strategic plan we had worked on for weeks. At the end of the session, one of the newer non-executive directors, asked: 'Maybe I'm missing something, but what exactly is the strategy here? All I've heard is a long list of initiatives from categories and geographies that don't join up.' She was right.

Equally, sometimes people misjudge obvious strategies because they are looking for something 'deeper' or 'hidden'. For me, a clear example concerned a misunderstanding by analysts and business journalists of the decisions of Marjorie Scardino, the former CEO of the *FT* parent company Pearson. She had declared that sale of the *Financial Times* would only occur 'over her dead body'. When she stepped down, commentators began clamouring for its sale, arguing that it didn't fit the company strategy. Yet the mission of the company is to become the number one learning company globally, for people throughout their lives. As one of the most trusted brands in business education, the *FT* is a natural asset. The strategy had been logical and Scardino's decisions supported it.

There are two more essential rules of successful strategies. These are perhaps the most important of all:

1 No one ever sees the strategy – only the execution.

2 Operational excellence is not a strategy.

Many companies flourish for a long time because they are operationally excellent, even if they don't have clear strategies. Other companies perish, even though they had clear strategies, because they couldn't execute them well; this is the more common.[2] Here are two opposite examples to illustrate the points.

---

[2] Centre for Creative Leadership, Leadership at the Peak Mars training course, 2001.

Good strategy, shame about the execution

Company A was a very successful health and beauty retailer, which had diversified into clothing, food and other areas. The margins on health and beauty were good, so the chain decided to refocus on health and beauty retailing, and to add value by branching out into services, such as beauty care, massage, acupuncture and dentistry. Over thirty different new businesses were launched over two years, each fully staffed with marketing, operations, and so on, as well as a managing director. There were no test markets or milestones that were clearly defined. Executives became uneasy about admitting that they weren't successfully executing the strategy. Long leases were signed, millions were spent on purchasing equipment and expensive staff were hired with advanced health qualifications. All before any business model was proven. The net result? £300 million of shareholder money was spent with no return. The CEO lost his job, and all the new businesses were shut down.

Operational excellence is not a strategy

Once there was a very successful company that sold telephone directories. It was extremely well run and twice won awards for operational excellence. It had successfully expanded into the US and UK. It had also entered the digital and mobile market places with new directory services. The internet began growing much more quickly than the print-based directory services. However, because the company had such operational excellence in sales and distribution of directories, it was reluctant to embrace the internet quickly. Also, because the internet offered such great untapped capabilities, the executives running it were reluctant to be associated with the directories and wanted their own sales forces, marketing, routes to market and product lines. Separate divisions were maintained; there was no integration and no cross-media platforms. The board decided to spend £2 billion buying more directory businesses rather than invest heavily in the internet or mobile. Today, the stock has been as low as 3p, the board and brand names have changed and the company is going bankrupt, with the banks swapping debt for equity.

What strategy is:

- A simple clear set of choices.

- An integrated, relevant set of activities based on those choices.

- Obvious to everyone – you can tell it like a story.

- Based on evidence, instinct and capability.

- Something that constantly helps steer your business and organisation.

- Evolving to new market and environmental conditions.

What strategy isn't:

- A headache.

- Death by PowerPoint, numbers, or binders.

- Too complicated, obscure, and/or not easily articulated in a story.

- A series of plans, initiatives, targets and budgets.

- A substitute for execution (but then nor is great execution a substitute for strategy).

Strategic storytelling[3]

This is a story that Herb Kelleher – one of the founders of Southwest Airlines in the United States and its former CEO and Chairman – used to tell as he visited his operations. He would say:

It's funny; I get letters all the time from shareholders, and they're often angry letters. They say 'America West is flying between Los Angeles and Las Vegas for $149 one way and you, Herb Kelleher at Southwest, are pricing $79 for that same one-way ticket. Don't you have the decency to at least kick your price up to $129? Why are you leaving so much on the table?'

Well, what I do is write back and reply, Thank you so much for your letter. However, you don't really understand who we are, and you really don't understand who our competition is. It's the automobile; it's not other airlines. And $79 is the price to drive, including maintenance, insurance and gasoline, from Los Angeles to Las Vegas. That's how we price our tickets.

---

[3] Conger, Jay, 'The impact of strategic storytelling', http://edls.com/50lessonsdemo/edls/433_ProfessorJayConger_TheImpactOfStrategicStorytelling.pdf

He would use that simple story to drive home what in many ways could be seen as the entire strategy of the organisation, vis-à-vis its competition. It was done in such a way that everyone at Southwest knew who the competitors were and why that ticket was priced the way it was.

So what makes an effective story?[4] Douglas Ready has come up with the following elements. Effective stories are:

- context-specific;

- level appropriate;

- told by respective role models;

- have drama;

- have a high learning value.

More strategic stories

Punica

My first brand was Punica. This was a watery fruit drink – only 20–29% fruit juice. The rest was water. And many of the flavours were sugar free, sweetened with artificial sweetener. My first boss asked me to go away and write an analysis of the brand. I noticed that the segments Punica was in were growing – fruit-based drinks and sugar-free drinks; and it was sold in crates of six 1-litre returnable bottles alongside other soft drinks. But Punica had been promoted as a fruit drink, as it was perceived as a watery orange juice. Because of the wide- mouth 1-litre bottle, the low fruit-juice content, and being sugar free, Punica was a great thirst quencher. So we decided to reposition it as a premium soft drink rather than as a cheap orange juice. We needed to reframe the competitive set away from fruit drinks and towards sodas. We needed to complete the following: Like soft drinks, Punica is _____. Better than soft drinks, Punica is _____. We filled in the blanks thus: Like soft drinks, Punica quenches thirst. Better than soft drinks, Punica is full of fruit and sugar free. Sales doubled, it became a major success in Germany and was ultimately sold to Pepsi.

---

4 Ready, Douglas, 'How storytelling builds next-generation leaders', *MIT Sloan Management Review*, Summer 2002, Vol. 43, Issue 4, pp. 63–9.

Always

Women could either use thin sanitary pads that were more comfortable but often failed, or they could wear thick pads that were uncomfortable but more absorbent, so didn't fail. Always Ultra solved this trade off. A 1mm thin pad that absorbed like a thick pad. The problem was that women didn't believe it. So we needed to turn the rules of the category upside-down to convince them. Instead of subtle imagery we did side-by-side product demos, and showed testimonials of ordinary women amazed at its powers. We sent out samples to over 400 million women in Europe, and even put a cut-out piece of a real pad in the leaflet inviting women to do their own demo at home. It worked, and Always became the market leader everywhere it launched in Europe in Year 1.

Whiskas pouches

The strategy for years had been to expand canned pet food in grocery. One of the owners had a favourite slogan: the profit is in the can. Canned pet food was sold at a premium, but contained a lot of water. Meanwhile, Mars had invented something that had less water, and was much easier to use and store than a can. It was a single-serve pouch, superior in taste, convenient, profitable – and also unique to Mars. So the strategy had to be to convert the market from cans to these new pouches. How to get people to switch? Convince the owners that their cats, notoriously finicky animals, preferred the taste of new pouches to the best of cans. This meant giving away samples and having cat owners compare Whiskas pouches to Whiskas cans. So we did. And Whiskas gained 12 share points.

Six tools to help you develop strategy

1. SWOT

This classic tool stands for Strengths, Weaknesses, Opportunities and Threats. It's a useful way of summarising information. But it's not a strategy. It's more like a frame of reference.

2. Michael Porter's Five Strategic Forces

Working in the 1980s, Michael Porter identified five factors affecting the competitive position of a company. He argued that a company that wishes to improve its performance must take account of these five forces, before it can make a decision as to the best strategy for future success. The five forces identified by Porter are:

1 The entry into the market of new competitors.

2 The threat of substitutes – similar competing products.

3 The bargaining power of buyers or customers.

4 The bargaining power of suppliers.

5 The level of competition from existing competitors.[5]

Porter's model is designed to help companies choose the most promising strategy for their business. It does this by focusing attention on the competitive forces at work in the wider industry scene, not just the company's internal resources and operational efficiency. In the 1980s, Porter identified three generic strategies: competing on price, differentiating products and services by offering something not offered by competitors, or focusing on a niche market; later he went on to consider the role of diversification and the impact of the internet. But he stresses that it is not enough just to gather information. Companies need to ask themselves how they can use competitive forces to their advantage and rewrite the rules of the industry.

3. The Four Cs

1 What is your unique value to Consumers?

2 Advantage over Competitors?

3 Advantage for Customers or those who distribute or sell your products and services?

4 How does your strategy reinforce your Company's core strengths and competencies?

[5] Porter's Five Forces, CMI Management Model.

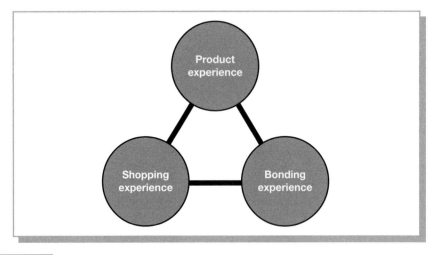

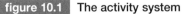 **figure 10.1**   The activity system

4. Activity system

This was developed by Michael Porter of Monitor Consulting and used by a lot of companies.

All customers relate to your product in three ways (see Figure 10.1). They have a bonding experience with your brand based on how you communicate with them. They have a product or service experience of your offer. And they have a procurement, or shopping experience of how they get your offer. The trick is to come up with a set of activities that reinforces your unique proposition across the bonding, product and shopping experiences. Often, if you can reinforce these, you will develop an unassailable competitive position. IKEA does this really well – see an example on p. 132. So do Net a Porter, Lego and Starwood.

5. The Ansoff matrix

It is helpful to prioritise and class innovations and strategies with regard to new markets and new products versus existing ones. Remember it's always hardest to go for new products and new markets simultaneously.

6. One-page strategy picture

A boss of mine at Mars used this – I think he and some others made it up. It's a great tool for keeping strategy simple. See Chapter 11.

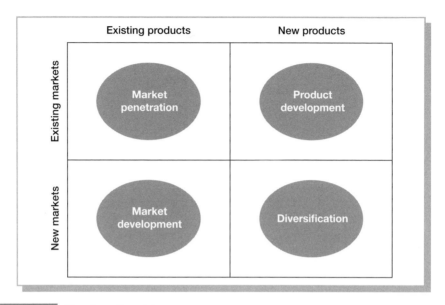

Six tips

1 **Solve a trade-off** This can very often result in a breakthrough strategy, one where you will create a new category. Like Always Ultra, or Spanx or concierge services for busy professionals – or even Wal-Mart, which tries to help you to save money and live better at the same time.

2 **Redefine your competitive set** Like Punica or Southwest Airlines (see above).

3 **Come up with a new creative use for something** The weak glue that should have been a failure at 3M became the Post-It note. All because someone noticed that people were using the weak glue to mark up files.

4 **Don't forget to do a business review** Look at the four Cs, look at your customers, competitors, market and environment. What is it telling you in your gut? Also, what do you need to watch out for?

And do you have the right capabilities to execute? If not, how will you get those?

5 **Invent a new category** Invent an iPod or iPad rather than just another mobile or PC.

6 **Have a strategy day** Often those in the company will have a tacit knowledge of what strategic direction they need to follow. Bring it out using a 'power brainstorming' approach to collective problem solving (see Chapter 9).

At P&G I was lucky enough to work with A.G. Lafley. He was and still is a great strategist. While I was writing this chapter, his new book came out, co-authored with Roger Martin.[6] What they have to say on strategy is priceless: I am reprinting Martin's blog[7] here.

> I must have heard the words 'we need to create a strategic plan' at least an order of magnitude more times than I have heard 'we need to create a strategy'. This is because most people see strategy as an exercise in producing a planning document. In this conception, strategy is manifested as a long list of initiatives with timeframes associated and resources assigned. Somewhat intriguingly, at least to me, the initiatives are themselves often called 'strategies'. That is, each different initiative is a strategy and the plan is an organized list of the strategies. But how does a strategic plan of this sort differ from a budget? Many people with whom I work find it hard to distinguish between the two and wonder why a company needs to have both. And I think they are right to wonder. The vast majority of strategic plans that I have seen over 30 years of working in the strategy realm are simply budgets with lots of explanatory words attached . . . . To make strategy more interesting – and different from a budget – we need to break free of this obsession with planning. Strategy is not planning – it is the making of an integrated set of choices that collectively position the firm in its industry so as to create sustainable advantage relative to competition and deliver superior financial returns. I find that once this is made clear to line managers they recognize that strategy is not just fancily-worded budgeting and they get much more interested in it . . . . That strategy is a singular thing; there is one strategy for a given business – not a set of strategies. It is one integrated set of choices: what is our winning aspiration;

---

[6] Lafley, A.G. and Martin, Roger L., *Playing to Win: How Strategy Really Works*, Harvard Business Review Press, 2013.

[7] http://blogs.hbr.org/cs/2013/02/dont_let_strategy_become_plann.html

where will we play; how will we win; what capabilities need to be in place; and what management systems must be instituted? That strategy tells you what initiatives actually make sense and are likely to produce the result you actually want. Such a strategy actually makes planning easy . . . . This conception of strategy also helps define the length of your strategic plan. The five questions can easily be answered on one page and if they take more than five pages (i.e. one page per question) then your strategy is probably morphing unhelpfully into a more classical strategic plan . . . .

So if you pass the five-page mark it is time to ask: Are we answering the five key questions or are we doing something else and calling it strategy? If it is the latter: eject, eject!

Source: Roger Martin, 'Don't confuse strategy with planning' (HBR Blog Network, 5 February 2013). Roger Martin (www.rogerlmartin.com) is the Dean of the Rotman School of Management at the University of Toronto in Canada. He is the co-author of *Playing to Win: How Strategy Really Works*.

Lafley, A. G and Martin, R., *Playing To Win: How Strategy Really Works*, Harvard University Press, 2013.

Top tips, pitfalls and takeaways

Top tips

- If strategy is difficult to communicate clearly, it's probably not well thought-through, or not really a strategy.

- Try to put your strategy on one page, using the example here – or another one.

- A SWOT analysis and Michael Porter's five forces remain useful tools for deciding strategy.

Top pitfalls

- It is still common to have a good strategy, but be let down by poor execution.

- Lots of plans with budgets attached do not constitute a strategy.

- Don't overcomplicate it!

- It's no use having a strategy that no one understands or is tucked away in a binder marked 'strictly confidential'.

Top takeaways

- Strategy is about clarity of the positioning of a company's services. It should be simple, and clearly communicated.

- Strategies are more likely to fail because of poor implementation than because of poor concept.

- Strategic choice is essential, however; operational excellence is sometimes not enough as it could be in a dying business sector.

11

Making strategy actionable

What you will learn in this chapter

- How to turn strategy into initiatives, business plans and budgets
- How to communicate your strategy
- How to link your strategy to your organisation, systems, processes and what people do
- How to monitor, measure and correct strategy

Congratulations. You've led the creation of a strategy that you are convinced is simple, sound and will enable you to win. But that's the easy part. As I said in Chapter 10: no one ever sees the strategy, only the execution. So if you cannot make the strategy happen, you won't succeed. Executing strategies successfully is one of the top skills managers can have.

To convert strategy into effective execution, you need to have a strategy that can be broken down into a framework of activities that people can understand, and that you can communicate easily. You also need to have an organisational structure that will enable you to deliver, as well as systems and processes in place to support it. Finally, you need to have tools and mechanisms that will help you assess whether you are making progress and when to change course. This has been summarised into six steps by Harvard Business School Professor Robert Kaplan.

1 Develop the strategy.
2 Plan the strategy.

3 Align the organisation.

4 Plan operations.

5 Monitor and learn.

6 Test and adapt.

Although I don't use his framework here, it is useful for thinking about what needs doing and you may want to find out more about it. We'll also talk about Kaplan in the Balanced Scorecard section in Chapter 13.

Turn strategy into business plans and budgets: frameworks for scoping strategic initiatives

Usually it is easiest if you try to articulate your strategy in a series of initiatives. It is very easy to come up with a whole raft of initiatives that don't really address your strategy, but are just convenient, or things you think need doing because you have always done them. So it is key throughout this process that the initiatives you are scoping are relevant to the strategy. Like: Who are we selling to? What will we do to be better than our competitors? How will we use our key competencies to deliver this? What capabilities, processes and systems do we need? And how will we measure our progress? If you aren't sure whether your strategic initiatives are actually addressing these, and are supported by evidence and examples, then refer back to Chapter 10.

A strategy in and of itself is not something that you can do. You need to break it down into a series of initiatives. There will likely be several key themes you will need to address: some of these may involve products, positioning or partnerships you may need to launch or deliver. Some will involve new routes to market or customer insights you may need to create, or digital transformations – moving from paper to online, or from servicing face-to-face to servicing online. Some will also involve organisational redesign – such as combining several functions to reduce costs or reorganising to create a new capability. One of the hardest tasks is to determine just exactly what you will – or won't – need to accomplish to achieve your strategy.

A helpful discipline is to classify these initiatives. Most will fall into one of five types: growth, efficiency, enabling, entrepreneurial and organisational. In addition, you should be aware of risks or potential obstacles and have a plan to overcome these.

1 Growth initiatives May include launching new products through existing channels; targeting existing customers with new propositions; or modifying propositions to target new customers or markets. Always try to tie these back into a discreet target group of customers, and a compelling proposition. You should be able to articulate these initiatives in terms of the number of customers who will buy and how much they will spend, or in terms of additional revenue and number of products sold or in terms of improvement to the delivery of your service as measured by increased customer retention and/or spend.

2 Efficiency initiatives Include cost reduction programmes, sales and marketing realignment, single operating models, lean process redesigns and digital transformation. This is usually about stopping non-value-added work, so you can redeploy resources to value-added work. I look at this further in Chapter 13.

3 Enabling initiatives Include better data, customer insight, boosting digital capability, better targeting and positioning. The most important of these will always be about understanding what your customers are buying and why they are buying from you. I discuss this further in Chapter 19.

4 Development or entrepreneurial initiatives Include things that are going to create new revenue streams in new markets or small things that are currently insignificant but might become very big in the future. They are inherently higher-risk and higher reward.

5 Organisational Your structure must follow your strategy and you will need to have the capability and culture to execute. For example, you might need to consider how your various departments are going to work together to achieve your strategy. Is that clear? If it is not, you will need to address this. You may need to create new capabilities. For example, if you have no current way to understand the customer, you may need to create a customer insight capability.

6 **Obstacles and risks** Things that may get in your way that you need
to be cognisant of overcoming – that is, key risks that could derail
you. These can be, and usually are, both internal and external.

Try breaking down your strategy into initiatives, categorised under the
five headings above. Most likely you will require at least one or two of
the first three, plus one of the fourth to keep focused on innovation
and the future. You will also need to identify your two greatest risks
or obstacles and have plans to overcome them. This means you will
end up with a maximum of ten initiatives, or a minimum of five. You
may end up combining the initiatives. Or varying the time frame. You
cannot do them all at once, so you need to sequence them.

Once you have broken down your strategy into a series of initiatives it
becomes more doable. Be careful not to have too many, and to think
about the interdependencies of each. For example, you may not be
able to attract new customers without better data or digital capacity.
You will also need to prioritise. It may be that partnering and fixing
your route to market is essential before you can realistically develop and
launch new products. Try creating an overall roadmap with each initiative on it. An example of a roadmap is given in Figure 11.1.

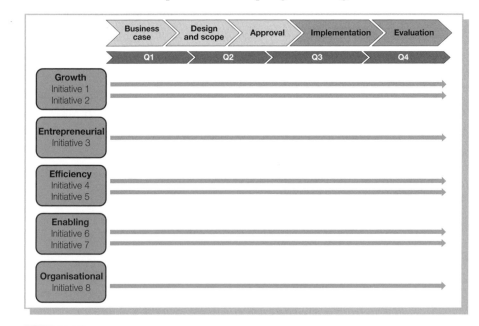

figure 11.1 Strategy implementation roadmap

Once you have identified your key initiatives, and set priorities, it will be useful to have a framework for flushing out and communicating. Table 11.1 shows an example of a one-page framework.

table 11.1   **Strategy framework**

1. Name of project/initiative	Customer Insight
2. Brief description	To support the growth strategy, specifically: ■ xxx ■ xxx
3. Strategic objectives supported	Growth in sales to employers
4. Measurable outcomes	Identified significant opportunities with respect to: ■ xxx ■ yyy ■ zzz
5. Sponsors	xxx
6. Project manager	xxx
7. Key dependencies	Availability of resource to support the activity Activities fall within budget and timescale
8. Key milestones	Quarter 2 budget review Launch of new ecommerce system
9. Business Case available	By 1 November 1 xxxx
10. Business Case approved by xx	By 31 December xxxx

Once you have completed this document you can shorten it to fit on a single PowerPoint slide.

exercise

Develop a strategy roadmap for your top initiatives and a series of one-pagers for each. Do they correlate well? Can you identify the different kinds of strategic priorities and sequencing? Are they joined up?

You should also have a framework to express all your initiatives and see whether they fit together. Visualising or mapping the strategy is an important process that will help you to understand how all the initiatives are interrelated. Think of the strategy as an activity system (this builds on the visual framework identified in Chapter 10). Activity systems or maps are a tool first created by strategy guru Michael Porter and now widely used to identify in a visual way the interconnected activities that your organisation, brand or company is using to create value and focus on outcomes for your customers. They help to prioritise and show how things are interconnected.

Figure 11.2 is an example of an activity system for IKEA – which is a great example of a strategy well executed.

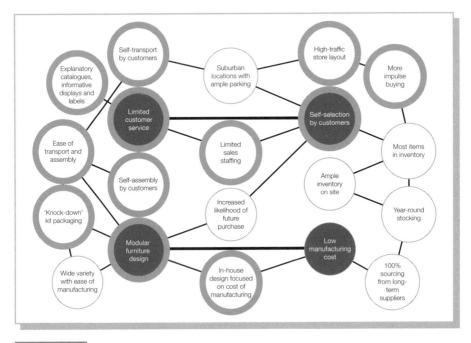

figure 11.2   **IKEA's activity system**

Source: Adapted and reprinted with permission of *Harvard Business Review*, from 'What is Strategy?' by Porter, M. E., 1996. Copyright © 1996, by the Harvard Business School Publishing Corporation; all rights reserved.

Activity systems are easy to understand and communicate. They can help you to have a great reference point, prioritisation and mapping of your strategy for all to see. However, sometimes, we can get far too caught up in defining the map and lose sight of the overall outcome. I remember once being locked away with an executive team for two days and producing a horrendously complicated activity system that ended up being of little use.

Another approach is to use a one-page diagram to draw out your business model. This should focus on the key customers, propositions, channels, activities and partners you use to create value. See www. businessmodelgeneration.com/downloads/business_model_canvas_ poster.pdf

exercise

Can you visualise your strategy initiatives and how they can build your business or organisational plan? Using some of the tools above, gather your key reports into a room. Discuss, debate and design your key strategic initiatives.

Communicating your strategy

There is little point in keeping strategies top secret, because they will only happen if people in the organisation understand them well enough to be able to execute them. You would be surprised how often lengthy strategy documents end up filed away in a drawer and never used. A great deal of time needs to be invested by the leadership to communicate how people's work fits with the overall objectives. These sorts of frameworks are more and more difficult with large multinational companies and multiple business units. But basically everyone has a role at every level within the organisation.

Of course it's best if the CEO communicates the overall strategy to everyone at the same time in an open session followed by a Q&A. In small companies this may well be possible. In large or dispersed organisations this may happen in a video or other format. But all managers need to know what the strategy means for them and their people at various levels. They should be given summaries and there needs to be a plan to communicate the specific messages to the various groups in an organisation as well as the overall 'big message' from the CEO. And the two should work in partnership.

One major retailer uses what they call balcony briefings. These are monthly updates on key priorities. They are then recorded and shared with thousands of stores. These are followed up with individual pocket-size cards that every store manager can place in their shirt pocket, so that they can refer to them when they are walking around the shop floor. These cards change regularly. Another organisation, a global business services business, followed up the message from the CEO with presentations on what the strategy meant for their region or business unit. But they all used the same slides, so that there was visual and verbal consistency.

Strategies often work well as pictures, or simple cards (as described above). If you can depict your strategy on one page using simple visuals it will help to communicate it. Try drawing a one-pager. Here is a version we use at CMI. It makes you think about things differently and understand how they are interrelated.

figure 11.3 One-page growth strategy using visuals

Linking strategy to initiatives that are then reflected in everyone's work is often the missing piece of the strategy puzzle. Even companies that are reasonably good at communicating strategies often don't do a decent job showing how everyone's work is linked to the overall strategy of the company. But the best companies do this.

When you set your team's objectives you should understand how your work and their work will contribute to the overall strategy and the different initiatives. If you do not understand this it is very important that you sit with your line manager and review. In a big company it will be the case that your work may only touch on one or two of these. In a smaller company you may be responsible for many of them. But your objectives and your activities should be contributing. It is vital you understand the critical success factors which will deliver your strategy.

Budgeting the numbers: top–down versus bottom–up

At some point, all strategy gets translated into numbers. The trick is not to rush into the numbers; a mistake that is often made. Remember, a strategy is NOT a series of numbers. However, all strategies can be translated to numbers eventually.

Typically, strategy frameworks last for three years. Some companies use five-year frameworks, but given the world keeps changing faster it seems wiser to stick to shorter time frames. For your three-year time frame, you will need to put forward an overall financial shape and framework that you expect to achieve by the end of the three years in terms of revenue, costs and profits. If you work backwards from Year 3 in this way, you will end up with Year 1 of your strategy being next year's budget. Almost every strategy I've been involved with, whether for big multinationals, FTSE 100s or small charities, has worked in this way.

Later, I'll explore more about how to prepare budgets (in Chapter 18).

The other approach to strategy is to Win Big and Fail Cheap. In this approach you may set a BHAG (Big Hairy Audacious Goal) that you really don't yet know how to achieve, but you want to focus the organisation on doing it. A great example of this is Unilever's Sustainable

Living Plan, which seeks to double the size of the company whilst halving its environmental impact. CEO Paul Polman didn't know how to achieve this but by announcing it he set the company on the way. As he has said, if he achieves 48 out of 50 initiatives in this endeavour, isn't that still a great result? Similarly, Peter Ayliffe at Visa set a BHAG of taking over a 50 per cent share of debit payment transactions in Continental Europe when he became CEO (they were starting from zero). He had no idea of how to achieve it but over the next several strategic planning periods he led his teams to craft initiatives that delivered against this strategic objective.

Whether you set your strategy top–down in an incremental or breakthrough fashion, it is always a very good idea to benchmark it with a bottom–up approach to the numbers. This means asking your folks what exactly they are going to do in terms of outputs and revenue, and what it is going to cost, and the profit it will contribute. Remember to break it down into specific activities. And then review the top–down and bottom–up approaches. Do they align or are there huge gaps? The bigger the gaps, the more important it is to clearly communicate the strategy and ensure that everyone's objectives are aligned.

Monitoring your strategy

You will need to think about how you will monitor the success of your strategy (see also Chapter 13). You should look at four sets of KPIs:

1 **Customer** Market share, customer satisfaction, number of customers, average value

2 **Employee** Employee engagement, productivity per employee

3 **Brand** Brand equity versus competition, effectiveness of communication and marketing mix

4 **Financial** Incremental revenue, contribution, cash

It's very important to realise that a strategy is not engraved in stone. Have milestones where you check whether it is working and correct or change course if it is not. If it is a new strategy, or an entrepreneurial initiative, make sure you consider doing pilots before launching something broad scale. Once a month go back to your key strategic initiatives roadmap and one-page tracking document. Take a look at what's working, and what's not, and make the necessary adjustment. I suggest a format for this in Chapter 13 on measuring.

Strategies are living documents. They will change. They must change in response to changing environments, competition, or because the initiatives aren't working as well as you hoped. Make sure you agree with your organisation to review strategy at set intervals and adjust. The idea is to win big and fail cheap. Said differently, feed your success and starve your failures.

Top tips, pitfalls and takeaways

Top tips

- Illustrate your strategy on one page and use this in communicating.
- Draw a one-page diagram of your business plan, including customers, propositions, channels, activities and partners.
- If you're going to be ambitious, be really ambitious: a 'Big Hairy Audacious Goal' can lead to transformational benefits.
- Continually monitor success of the strategy.

Top pitfalls

- Don't confuse a financial objective with a strategy. If you say you want to double your business size that's fine, but it's not a strategy and people will not understand how to do it.
- It can be unhelpful to use a mission statement or catchphrases. They can become empty slogans. I once worked in an organisation that had a global strategic initiative called SGE – Strengthening Global Effectiveness. But it involved consolidating divisions and shutting factories. It was quickly dubbed 'Say Goodbye Everybody'.
- Don't have too many strategic initiatives. People will get confused.

Top takeaways

■ A strategy in and of itself is not something that you can do. You need to break it down into a series of tangible initiatives.

■ Most initiatives fall into one of five types: growth, efficiency, enabling, entrepreneurial and organisational.

■ Make sure you can turn your strategy into a series of initiatives or projects that people can deliver to achieve the strategy.

12

Creating a culture

What you will learn in this chapter

- What culture is and why it matters
- How different kinds of culture influence success and failure
- How to set missions, visions and values
- The link between risk, reputation and culture
- How you can monitor and 'fix' culture

Many of the problems surrounding management today – lack of trust, lack of performance, increased stress, bad ethics, bullying, tax evasion and declining job security – can be traced back to poor organisational cultures. Equally, most of the leading lights, from corporate bellwethers WL Gore to new sensations like Zappos, have achieved their success and cult status on account of the consistency and greatness of their cultures. Culture matters hugely, yet too many managers still dismiss it as 'soft stuff'. This chapter takes a look at what culture is – and why it matters.

What culture is, and why it matters

Culture is the personality and character of the organisation. It consists of the shared values, beliefs, behaviours and basic assumptions of the people who work there. It shapes how they think, defines their expectations, and guides how they interact within the boundaries of the company as well as externally. It shapes an organisation's moral code.

In the LIBOR (London Inter-Bank Offered Rate) scandal, everyone fiddling the interest rate did so because it was simply the way things were done. Similarly, in the UK's NHS Mid-Staffordshire crises, a culture of 'looking up' at whether or not targets were being hit superseded a culture of 'looking out' to provide the best standards of patient care.

Organisational culture also plays a big part in determining employee morale, shaping strategy and enabling organisations to achieve goals and results. It also determines how they go about doing these things, and gives employees a sense of community and purpose. As a manager, it is really vital that you understand your organisation's culture. If you embrace and share the values of your company you will have a much easier time. Famously, Wal-Mart requires all of its managers to hold pep rallies prior to the beginning of each sales day. That's a really tiring daily ritual if you don't get some sort of buzz and sense of belonging from it.

---

case study Culture

When I was a newly promoted marketing director at P&G in the UK I got a visit from the head of HR in Cincinnati. The reason was I had one of the most diverse and highest performing departments in those days. It was 55 per cent female. And we had the highest market shares and profit margins on our brands. Even then, I instituted flexible working. It suited my employees, and not all of them were mothers. One was a very talented guy who left early a few days a week to play cello in an orchestra. He is now CEO of a FTSE 250 company. Another young guy liked to go out and hear music in clubs, so started later. He's now an award-winning and successful entrepreneur. The point is, by allowing them to work in ways that suited them, they were able to develop and deliver their best.

In contrast with the flexibility in the team cited above, I remember another very successful company I worked for that had a much less flexible culture. Every week managers were expected to travel on their own time, leaving the house Sunday evening or 5 a.m. Monday morning to visit remote sites until they arrived home Friday evening. That really didn't suit my schedule. So I managed by often flying out in the very early morning and flying back in the evening on the same day. I did that for most major European cities. But then a new boss took over and banned that – he wanted everyone to stay overnight everywhere, to encourage 'bonding' over team dinners. I tried that for a time – I recall sneaking to the Ladies during the team dinners, getting out my mobile and reading *Anne of Green Gables* to my eight-year-old before she went to bed – but when her father fell ill, I couldn't countenance that way of working. It didn't work for me, and eventually I left the company.

When you move from one company to another you will experience different cultures. My advice is to lie low, observe and adapt to the new culture. Do not assume they are similar, or attempt to import your previous culture into your new organisation. You will fail. I once made a huge mistake by referencing my previous company on my first day at my new company in a large gathering. I alienated a lot of people that day and really got off on the wrong foot.

Generally speaking, 'values-based' cultures are regarded as more successful than 'rule-based' cultures. Sharing common values is a strong way of getting employees to do the right thing; plus, it's nigh on impossible to have rules for every situation. Unfortunately, values-based cultures are in the minority, according to major reports. UK studies show that organisations that have trusting, collaborative, purposeful and positive cultures are much more likely to be growing and to have happier, healthier more productive employees.[1] Nonetheless, the top three organisational management styles are still bureaucratic, authoritarian and reactive. Similarly, a 2011 study of thousands of American employees found that 43 per cent of the firms surveyed had 'blind obedience' cultures. In these cultures, almost half of those surveyed had observed unethical behaviour. Only 3 per cent of organisations fell into the enlightened 'self-governance' category.[2]

Companies have launched programmes where they are trying to move towards more collaborative, trusting and ethical cultures. However, senior executives are far more likely to believe that their cultures are ethical and collaborative than middle and junior managers. So those at the top usually don't recognise the scale of the problem.

[1] Cooper, Cary and Worrall, Les, 'The quality of working life', CMI Management Article of the Year, 2013.

[2] 'Bosses think their firms are caring: their minions disagree', *The Economist*, 11 Sept. 2011. The study cited is by LRN, a corporate culture advisory firm.

What does good company culture look like?

One helpful tool has been created by Best Companies in conjunction with the London *Sunday Times* to come up with the 100 Best Companies to Work For. The rating systems look at eight different areas which help to drive a good organisational culture:

1 **Leadership** – how well the people at the top are performing.

2 **My manager** – the relationship with the immediate line manager.

3 **My company** – what their company stands for and whether it inspires pride; would they recommend others to work there?

4 **My team** – their relationship with peers.

5 **Giving something back** – does the company support and encourage charity participation?

6 **Wellbeing** – what, if any, health programmes, gym discounts, etc. are offered?

7 **Fair deal** – equitable pay and benefits and opportunities for promotion.

8 **Personal growth** – career development, training and qualifications.

> **exercise**
>
> Describe your organisation's culture. Then ask the people you work for and your boss. Then check what you've found versus the official company or organisation's mission, vision and values statement. Do they match? If not, why not? What can you do differently? What can your leaders do differently?

They also take a look at what the companies offer in terms of holidays, pensions, health insurance, flexible working arrangements, as well as their overall female–male ratio, average age, and staff turnover.[3] Similar surveys, such as 'Great Places to Work' exist in America and in many other places.

---

[3] *Sunday Times*, 3 Mar. 2013, separate section.

The power of diversity

Diverse cultures, especially in terms of gender diversity, outperform those that aren't in terms of growth, return on sales and other performance metrics. A myriad of evidence supports this.[4] Diverse cultures are also more likely to outperform on 'softer' measures such as customer satisfaction, and be more ethical, with higher employee engagement. Yet progress is still too slow. Women, on average, are paid up to £500,000 less than men over the course of their careers.[5] And despite the majority of junior managers being female, only 40 per cent are department heads and less than one in four are directors or CEOs, whilst in America only 45 of the S&P 500 are female. The good news is that measures to encourage diversity benefit everyone, both female and male. More flexible working, more inclusive and meritocratic cultures, and greater access to sponsorship and mentoring programmes, benefit all employees. These measures also boost brand reputation, revenues per employee, and engagement.[6]

Here are five simple things to create a more diverse workplace:

1 Set a target for the number of women. Publish your statistics in your department on the ratio of women to men and what they are paid (anonymously).

2 Set up sponsoring and mentoring networks and encourage talented women to apply for promotions. Make sure they are included in important networking events.

3 Be a sponsor or a mentor yourself.

4 Encourage flexible working, making sure you are focused primarily on outcomes and outputs not face time.

5 Train leaders and managers early – go into your local school to build their exposure to business, and send your female managers to talk to the girls to encourage role models.

[4] Curtis, Mary, Schmid, Christine and Struber, Marion, Credit Suisse Gender Diversity and Corporate Performance, 13 July 2012; 'Women matter' by McKinsey (2007, 2008, 2009, 2010, 2012); the Catalyst reference is 'The bottom line: connecting corporate performance and gender diversity', by Catalyst (2004).

[5] http://womeninleadership.managers.org.uk/women-in-management

[6] Devi, Sharmila and Bothwick, Fleur, 'Working for progress in a firm with global reach', *Financial Times*, 20 Feb. 2013.

Missions, visions and values: the backbone of culture

Culture is fundamentally shaped by an organisation's missions, visions and values – but unless these are truly brought to life they aren't meaningful. And many organisations don't do a good job of 'walking the talk'; which means that many cultures can actually contradict and undermine the missions, visions and values. This leads to cynicism at best and poor morale, reputation and results at worst.

The vision statement should outline how the organisation will know when it is delivering its mission. It should be positive and inspiring. It might be about providing the best product or service for your customers, but it will need to say who they are and what your product or service is. If possible you should involve your employees in creating the mission and vision statements or refining them, as then they will feel more engaged with them.

Many mission statements are vague and unhelpful. Lucy Kellaway, the *FT* columnist and author, lambasts most as cringe-inducing guff.[7] However, one that she did like – and I agree with her – has been around for many years. It is from J&J and an excerpt follows:

We believe our first responsibility is to the doctors, nurses and patients, to mothers and fathers and all others who use our products and services. We are responsible to our employees, the men and women who work with us throughout the world. Everyone must be considered as an individual. We are responsible to the communities in which we live and work and to the world community as well. We must be good citizens. Our final responsibility is to our stockholders. Business must make a sound profit.

exercise

Rewrite your organisation's mission and vision statements. Then compare it with the current one. How is it different or better? Show it around the office. Do people agree with you? Have a discussion on your company's core purpose and vision, and discuss ideas on how to bring it alive, or highlight the areas where you've gone off mission and need to take corrective action.

---

[7] http://www.ft.com/comment/lucy-kellaway

Core values

Core values or principles are arguably the most important aspect of creating a culture. Equally, when values go awry and are not practised is when companies and organisations get into trouble. My favourite illustration of good values comes from Tony Hsieh, the CEO of Zappos.com, the company that put customer service at the heart of its success and grew to $1 billion in revenues via repeat business and word of mouth. He wrote about his experience on the importance of core values in a blog.

Even though our core values guide us in everything we do today, we didn't actually have any formal core values for the first six or seven years of the company's history. It's my fault that we didn't do it in the early years, because it was something I'd always thought of as a very 'corporate' thing to do. I resisted doing it for as long as possible.

I'm just glad that an employee finally convinced me that it was necessary ... I only wish we had done it sooner ....

I thought about all the employees I wanted to clone because they represented the Zappos culture well, and tried to figure out what values they personified. I also thought about all the employees and ex-employees who were not culture fits, and tried to figure out where there was values disconnect ....

We eventually came up with our final list of 10 core values, which we still use today:

1   Deliver WOW through Service
2   Embrace and Drive Change
3   Create Fun and A Little Weirdness
4   Be Adventurous, Creative, and Open-Minded
5   Pursue Growth and Learning
6   Build Open and Honest Relationships with Communication
7   Build a Positive Team and Family Spirit
8   Do More With Less
9   Be Passionate and Determined
10 Be Humble

... Be Humble is probably the core value that ends up affecting our hiring decisions the most.

Source: Hsieh, Tony, HBR Blog Network, 'How Zappos infuses culture using core values', 24 May 2010.

The link between risk, reputation and culture: the Road to Ruin

In 2011 the Institute of Risk Management Airmic commissioned a study by CASS Business School that examined twenty major corporate crises after 2000 involving over $6 trillion of assets. Their report, with the catchy title *Roads to Ruin*, revealed the link between culture and corporate downfall. Once they went beyond the initial triggers, they uncovered many factors that they described as deep-set, underlying risks. These were often the most dangerous, as they posed threats to the organisation's business model, caused serious uninsurable losses to the business, and destroyed reputations, careers and shareholder value. Many of these risks are cultural.

In particular, the 'Underlying Risks' they identified included:

- **Board risk blindness** – failure of the board to recognise and engage with risks inherent in the business.

- **Inadequate leadership on ethos and culture** – failure of board leadership and implementation on ethos and culture.

- **Risk 'glass ceiling'** – arising from the inability of auditors and risk managers to sufficiently challenge the C-suite leaders regarding risks emanating from this level – including risks from ethics and behaviour.

Predisposition to 'groupthink'

To quote the report:

A number of the risks we identified concern the so-called 'soft skills' (staff, style and shared values) as opposed to the 'hard skills' (technical know-how strategy, structures and systems). A valuable question for further investigation in this area is whether there is a causal link between the weaknesses in leaders and board composition with respect to the so-called 'soft skills' and the propensity to suffer major reputational crises. More controversially, there is the question of whether there is a statistical or causal link with the much-discussed gender balance on boards.[8]

---

[8] *Roads to Ruin*, a report by Cass Business School on behalf of Airmic, sponsored by Crawford and Lockton, 2011, p. 5.

The report serves as a stark reminder that not getting culture right has far more sinister implications than 'merely' missing out on growth and employee engagement.

A separate initiative, the Well Managed Organisation Index, developed by Mettle Consulting together with CMI, has identified six predictors of strong cultures:

1 Corporate Culture

2 Internal Controls

3 Critical Self Analysis

4 Organisational Agility

5 Disclosure and Transparency

6 Quality of Management

In almost every case where a company meltdown occurs, one or more of these areas is 'broken'. For example, bad news is not escalated quickly enough, or is ignored. Critical self analysis is absent, as managers are arrogant, as in the LIBOR scandal. Or, people don't accept responsibility for things, and don't communicate.

Business continuity

Business continuity is all about having a contingency for when things go wrong, and is very important, given that eight out of ten companies will experience an unplanned disruption in any given year.[9] Business continuity plans help companies to recover faster, understand business exposure and aid the overall preparedness of the organisation to respond to crises.

The reason I've included this under culture is that it is remarkable how ill-prepared some companies can be when cultural and reputational risk explode – often with disastrous consequences. Recall the ill-judged remark of former BP CEO Tony Hayward that he 'wanted his life back' just after the Horizon explosion and Gulf of Mexico oil spill. Thinking

---

[9] BSI, CMI, Cabinet Office, 2011 survey on business continuity.

about how to handle crises, and in particular the media, gracefully under pressure is very important to bear in mind.

Whistle blowing

Many of the recent examples of business and reputational meltdowns occurred because no one communicated bad news clearly and truthfully up the line. Any good company should enable employees to blow the whistle on unethical conduct. A good organisation will have a whistle-blowing service to enable employees to register concerns anonymously outside of their line management. Recently, the NHS was heavily criticised for penalising those who spoke out that targets and a bullying culture were getting in the way of proper care. Whistle blowing is becoming more and more important as a means to expose systematic corporate or organisational bad behaviour. If your organisation doesn't have a whistle-blowing service, you should ask why not.

Equally, if you are leaving and asked to sign that you will never speak negatively about the organisation, then you should question whether you accept that. Take legal advice as to whether or not you should sign away any rights. See also the section on settlement agreements (in Chapter 3).

Monitoring and fixing culture

There are no widely accepted and applied tools for measuring and predicting good culture, though some professional bodies are trying to develop indices of the good outcomes of investing in people.

So, if your culture is broken, can it be fixed? Usually, fixing the culture will require lots of change at the top – as in the cases of Toyota, the BBC, BP and Barclays. It also takes a lot of time and some fairly decisive action. You also need to be quite specific about what you are changing from to what you are changing to.

Barclays Bank is an interesting case study. In 2012 the bank fired its Chairman, CEO and CFO in the wake of the LIBOR scandal. The new CEO Antony Jenkins has resolved to fix the culture. Here is what he has done so far:

■ Refused a bonus of £2.75m for 2012.

■ Appointed the former head of the Financial Regulator as his Head of Compliance.

■ Dressed deliberately conservatively – off-the-peg suits, no brash ties or belts.

■ Reviewed 75 business units and shut down the ones that ran tax avoidance schemes.

■ Launched a change programme which specifies cultural change as the key part of the agenda.

■ Created a new mission: helping people to achieve their ambitions – in the right way.

■ Introduced new core values: staff will receive bonuses and be measured on matters such as respect, integrity, service, excellence and stewardship – in addition to financial targets.

■ Written to all staff inviting them to leave if they can't live up to the values.

■ Announced all this publicly and asked for five years' time to deliver.

So, he's been quite busy, but the jury is still out.

Top tips, pitfalls and takeaways

Top tips

■ Write a mission statement that declares what you will do, how, and for whom – and make sure you live up to it.

■ Make sure you have effective whistle-blowing procedures to help root out poor practice.

■ The J&J mission statement has stood the test of time. It pledges commitment to all stakeholders

Top pitfalls

■ Planning only for things going well, and not building in contingency for crisis.

■ Groupthink: lack of diversity in outlook, experience or behaviour at the top.

Top takeaways

■ Organisational culture is of fundamental importance to strategy, performance and risk management; it's not 'the soft stuff'.

■ Many of the recent crises can be traced back to poor organisational cultures.

■ Think carefully about the culture of any organisation and whether or not you can agree with its values personally before you join.

13

Getting results and how to measure them

What you will learn in this chapter

- Why monitoring and benchmarking matter
- The importance of getting results by building brands
- How to identify brand essence and brand equity
- Why customer satisfaction metrics are pivotal to improving your organisation's strategy and execution
- Tools and techniques for measuring performance
- Why consistent monthly reports work better
- Feedback formats for continuing learning and success

I was fortunate enough to spend the first seventeen years of my career at two marketing powerhouses, with an enviable record of sustained commercial success: P&G and Mars. Both have brand-building at the centre of business development; both are highly advanced in understanding their customers; both are dedicated to measuring performance, and make intelligent use of performance data available. It was only when I left these companies that I realised that they are the exceptions. In many companies, marketing is little more than logos and communications. When it comes to monitoring and measuring performance, too many companies measure too little, or too much, or the wrong things.

In earlier sections, I covered managing yourself, and managing others. In later sections I will cover aspects of change management, such as handling stakeholders, especially customers, and innovation. Here, the focus is the commercial core of developing a business: building brands, delivering services, measuring to check you've achieved what you intended and learning from the results.

Why monitoring and benchmarking matter

You've got the strategy, the plan, the budget and the team. But six months into your plan, you are 20 per cent down on income and profit against your budget. Morale is down. Hours worked are up. Your boss and your board are asking big questions. If you have ever been in a situation like this, then you'll know the feeling. The problem is, by that time, it's almost always too late.

In well-managed organisations there's a real 'hunger' for knowing results and monitoring the trends. At P&G, the highlight of the day for many brand managers was when the daily shipment report came in, so they could check where their brand was compared with other brands and the target. The reverse is also true. Organisations in trouble often don't measure, measure the wrong things or too many things. Many of the recent crises in the UK's NHS hospitals were caused by measuring the number of patients processed rather than employee engagement and quality of patient care. When employee engagement was measured and correlated with mortality rates, patient care and cost targets, all headed in a positive direction.[1]

As well as measuring your own results, it helps to 'benchmark' – compare with others. With the internet, this is much simpler. If you're in sales and marketing, you can benchmark your open rates, click-through rates and conversion and closing rates. Just be sure you are genuinely comparing like with like.

In this chapter, I am going to share ways of measuring that I have seen work over the years. I am also going to encourage you to feed your measurements back into your strategy, understand and probe them,

---

[1] Michael West, 2012.

and encourage ongoing improvement. You will get better results from doing this. You will become curious. You will help set yourself and your team on a path of continual discovery. In short, you'll be a much more successful manager.

Getting results by building brands

The most high-performing companies understand that everything is connected: the brand is a reflection of how you do business collectively, not just a task on a checklist for the marketing department. Companies that build leading brands reap many rewards, including: more loyal customers, more market share, category-leading innovation, a positional priority in stores and media, higher prices, better-quality job applicants, lower borrowing costs and higher shareholder value. Interbrand, which has pioneered the valuation brands in the market place, estimates that the top 100 global brands are worth US$1,384,644,000,000.[2]

When building a brand, the first thing to define is its essence, or equity: the brand's personality and values, the relationship the brand has with the target consumer, and the benefit it delivers. It is important to understand your target consumer(s) (and here, I mean consumer as customer). For example, if you run a convenience store and your target consumer is an urban, savvy, 20-something single person, then stocking your store full of baby-care items is inappropriate. Finally, always be aware of the competitive context. How is your brand really different from and better than the main alternatives from your customer's point of view?

There are many frameworks for articulating this. In my view, the simpler ones are the best. The most common is the pyramid, which describes functional attributes at the bottom, and the emotional benefits and brand personality at the top (see Figure 13.1).

I strongly recommend that you turn this into a brand strategy – a simple set of words and/or pictures. It will force you to simplify and get to the heart of your brand. Try addressing the key dimensions in your brand strategy as follows:

---

[2] Jez Frampton, Interbrand CEO.

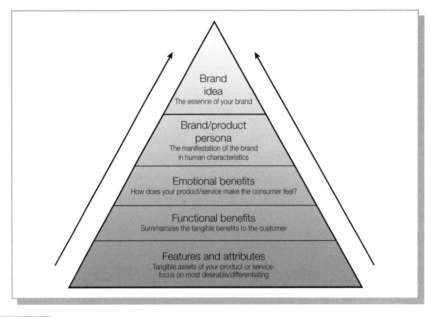

figure 13.1   Brand pyramid template

Source: Noesis Marketing.

- ▪ **Benefit** What need are you satisfying for the consumer or customer?

- ▪ **Emotional benefit** What emotional need are you fulfilling?

- ▪ **Reason why** Functional attribute that supports this benefit (proven by research).

- ▪ **Brand personality** Values of brand that also reflect values of user.

If you are dealing in highly emotional categories such as beauty care, pictures can often express these values better than words. It's important that you develop a consistent visual style and look for your brand. A clearly articulated brand essence gives everyone a guideline for the brand strategy and execution, including distribution, media, innovation and product development. In well-run companies, brand strategy or pyramid is based on consumer research and mapping in order to identify the target market and values. The emotional benefits are well understood and functional benefits are tested against the competition to ensure they are superior. And the innovation and routes to market and communications are kept in line with the brand personality. This approach is rigorous, and makes it easier to replicate globally. Although these brands' pyramids and essences are updated, they are rarely changed. Consistency is a key attribute. The brand pyramid transcends particular campaigns. It is the DNA of the brand.

It is best to make the choices on the basis of market analysis and data. If the brand's features do not have this foundation, recognise that they are aspirational and be prepared to go through these steps. For example, if you are a skincare brand aimed at outperforming prestige brands for a fraction of the cost but your packaging looks cheap and nasty then your brand will not deliver on the promise and will quickly be in trouble.

Some pitfalls to watch out for in setting brand essences and pyramids:

■ Too complicated

■ Too generic

■ Too ambiguous

■ Not relevant

■ Not proven

■ Not distinctive versus competition.

Brand equity: shaping the customer experience consistently

Once you have defined your brand essence, it is time to shape what your brand stands for in the hearts and minds of the target consumers. This is your brand equity. To shape this, you need to be aware of what you want your customers to feel and think about your product or service, and what you want them to experience. Brand equity should be specific, positive and create thoughts and feelings. It helps to use an activity system, as advocated by The Monitor Company. This looks at the different ways the consumer experiences your brands. There are generally three ways:

1 **The shopping experience** How the consumer experiences your channels to market (stores, sales visits, check-ins, etc.).

2 **The product experience** How the consumer experiences your product or service when they are using it.

3 The bonding experience How your consumer experiences how you communicate with them (advertisements, customer service and so on).

Different aspects of your brand experience should be mutually reinforcing. Apple does a brilliant job of this (see also Chapter 11). The stores, the communicating channels and packaging and the products themselves are impeccably designed, user-centric, clean and consistent.

case study   The make-up of the make-up artist

> Max Factor was the original make-up artist in Hollywood. When we repositioned the brand as 'the make-up of make-up artists', we translated the in-store look to focus on make-up artist tips, and made the counters look like a make-up artist's box. We linked up with Hollywood make-up artists and used them for testimonials, advertising and in store events. We used product names like 'Lasting performance foundation', and featured the make-up in situ in demanding movie situations. The brand doubled sales in Europe and attracted a younger target audience without alienating its core older user.

By ensuring the shopping, product and bonding experiences are 'on equity' you strengthen the likelihood that the consumer will remain loyal. It helps if you prioritise the customer experience that is most likely to shape his or her impressions of you. For example, Pampers are used by parents several times a day, seven days a week. If the product isn't working, the parent knows about it. You could have the world's best shopping experience; it still wouldn't help. Conversely, in make-up, over 90 per cent of purchase decisions are made in-store. Companies like Estée Lauder devote meticulous effort and attention and measurement to the in-store shopping experience as a result. Finally, with 'cool' brands like b headphones, they may not be the best, but the bonding experience of knowing these are the brainchild of Dr Dre, the rapper, makes them a must-have for many.

You can and should measure your brand equity annually, benchmarked against your competition. If it increases, it is very likely your sales and profits have increased as well. You can measure your brand equity many different ways. The most widely used is an annual tracking study, which measures awareness, advertising awareness, consideration, trial, purchase, repeat purchase. It also measures specific attributes you want your brand to stand for and the degree to which you do compared with your competition.

exercise

Try to develop an 'activity system' for your brand. Do your product, bonding and shopping experiences reinforce each other or contradict each other? Think about where your purchase decisions are made. This will help you to identify the key focus area for your brand and prioritise getting that right.

Value propositions and messaging

An insight is something that will change the way people think about your brand, and ultimately has the power to change their behaviour. Effective ads have some sort of insight which convinces us to behave differently and choose the brand being advertised. You can think about insights in any market. For example, furniture giant IKEA urged UK consumers to 'chuck out their chintz' because they needed to get people to break with their traditional interior decorating habits in order to switch them to IKEA's modern, functional look.

If you have your brand pyramid and your insight that you will use to change behaviour, you are ready to form your value proposition. The best value propositions are based on an insight that will help consumers understand and appreciate the value of your brand. Often you will work with an agency on this. The main thing is to be convincing, distinctive and credible. When we launched Always (at Procter & Gamble), we knew that women didn't trust a pad so thin, so we needed to confront that scepticism directly (see 'More strategic stories', in Chapter 10).

Think of a target group that is not buying your brand. Why? What are they thinking and feeling? What would you need to overcome if you were to change what they think and feel? What insight would do that? Once you understand these barriers you can build an insightful campaign which will convince him or her to try it. Insights are vital to effective campaigns.

It is always best to test your propositions and insights before spending a lot of money to develop an ad campaign. This has become easier in the digital age, as you can use online research. When you test your proposition, you are looking for the purchase intent – the likelihood that people will try; and relevance – whether it matters to them and helps them to deal with an issue; and the credibility – whether they believe your promise. Measure these on a five-point scale. You will want to score higher than the competition or higher than your current proposition, which you can use as a control.

Integrating your messages

There are many different media: television, print and radio advertising, digital banner, pay-per-click, email marketing, social media, event marketing, sampling, in-store advertising, sponsorship and many more. You should choose media depending on your target audience, their media habits, and what you want to achieve.

Selection is usually the job of the ad agency. The best media plans have an integrated approach, where similar messaging is delivered across many formats consistently, exploiting the advantages of each particular platform. Make sure your messages join up. The media weight of these campaigns is measured in something called GRP, or gross rating point. This is about the reach and frequency. A GRP = reach × frequency. What percentage of your target audience are you reaching how many times? You can compare this against your competition in a measurement known as SOV or Share of Voice.

Typically, digital media will be cheaper. They can also be up to four times more effective than other forms of media. However, they are still not the majority of spend, because there is more glory, and profitability (for the agencies!), in TV commercials. If you are just starting out, it pays to use lower-cost means of communicating, provided you can reach your target audience. Always measure the effectiveness of campaigns. This can be more precise with the web and data analytics.

If you are launching a new product as an extension to your brand, then linking up the brand essence and equity of the new product with that of the 'mother brand' is very important. This is because doing so will stimulate sales of the 'mother brand'. This is known as the 'halo effect', and it can be very important to building a successful 'power brand' that spans several categories. For example, when we launched Olay body wash, Olay skincare sales increased by several percentage points. But you will only achieve this if your equity and messaging is consistent.

exercise

Measure your campaign effectiveness: map your campaigns across different media. Are the messages, tone, look and feel integrated? Or are they different? Plan your media so things join up in terms of message, tone, visual and verbal style.

Business-to-Business campaigns

B2B campaigns are much more likely to rely on content marketing than Business-to-Consumer. The B2B role is about creating content, capturing leads, and developing compelling stories for the sales force. Much of this is likely to be measurable and benchmarked and should be. It's very important that you have a consistent lead classification and nurturing process, as well as a clearly defined handover point from marketing to sales. Otherwise, many leads get lost in the middle. Make sure you have tracking systems that enable you to figure out how many leads you are getting from content marketing from your website, and from your emails, and what is happening to these leads. Measure your open and click-through rates on emails and websites. And always, always, benchmark. Test different emails, subject lines and content formats. Which works better? Why?

Campaigns can always be measured and should be. How much did the campaign cost? How many click-throughs did it generate? You may also want to set KPIs around how many leads you need to generate, given the average closing rate of the leads, in order to hit your sales targets.

The sales force

The sales force is vital in Business-to-Business, because they are the route to market, unlike in business-to-consumer, where you can influence purchase behaviour more directly. Sales may be categorised as 'hunters' – new business specialists, whose job it is to get new customers; and 'farmers', or account executives, whose job it is to up-sell and cross-sell customers and penetrate further into an account. Both are very important.

These five key steps are a useful outline of sales excellence:

1 Plan and prepare for customer visits.

2 Conduct a business review to gain and retain the client interest.

3 Test intention – does the customer recognise that you have appreciated his or her needs?

4 Propose and provide solutions – does the customer agree that the solution provided meets his or her needs? Is the price right?

5 Agree service requirements.

Nowadays there is more 'solution selling', and less product-based selling, because solutions are increasingly specific and complex. They may require a package of certain products and service that is unique to the customer. However, selling remains basically a numbers game. Good sales people are numeric, inherently targets-oriented and like to be measured. It is one of the few functions where KPIs are very easy to measure.

When you distribute accounts you should ideally use customer insight and analytics in order to target those accounts most likely to convert, lapse or up-trade.

Six tips for handling the sales force:

1 Make it easy to prepare for visits and ensure you give good access to account history and reasons to buy.

2 Make sure all metrics are clear and tracked: number of leads, appointments and visits per week; lead to close ratios, etc.

3 Reward and rank frequently – sales people enjoy healthy competition.

4 Feed the producers – it's easier to feed the top performers than to move the bottom third up.

5 Avoid sales versus marketing blame by having one director responsible for both.

6 Customer service is a valuable source of leads. Make sure you partner sales with customer service.

Customer satisfaction – and how to measure it

Measuring customer satisfaction is something that all companies do. When it's done well, it can be a great source of customer insight. You can figure out which customers are advocates or fans, and which customers are about to lapse, and install efforts to retain them. You can look at the impact of different products, sales people, or geographies on customer service. You can even link messaging that customers have received to their response, or what interventions have impacted satisfaction either positively or negatively. But in order to get all this information, customer service systems must be integrated with the rest of your systems so you can look at the data end to end. This is where it becomes really valuable and important to have a single view of the customer.

There are many different ways to measure customer satisfaction. Too often it is on a five-point scale, and comes in between 4 and 4.5 – and has stayed at this level for years. This offers little insight. Even worse is when companies ask, would you recommend us? And give responders two choices: yes or no. Typically 93–95 per cent say yes, but this rosy picture could be misleading.

A much better measure is the Net Promoter Score (NPS). This is a customer focus measure developed by Fred Reichheld of Bain and Company, based on research that investigated the correlation between customer survey responses and actual customer behaviour. They determined that the top-ranking question (on a ten-point scale) was far and away the most effective across industries:

■ How likely is it that you would recommend [company X] to a friend or colleague?

They determined that customers can be either Promoters or Detractors. You can calculate the percentage of customers who respond with nine or ten (these are 'Promoters') and the percentage who respond between zero and six ('Detractors'). Subtract the percentage of detractors from the percentage of promoters to arrive at your Net Promoter Score. Compare these scores from different regions, branches, sales reps and customer segments, and how you compare against the competition. This often reveals causes of differences as well as best practices.

Companies that use NPS find that the rigorous implementation of a simple customer feedback system has had a clear impact on their business. To be effective NPS must become a prominent metric known throughout the organisation, and also linked to KPIs for employees.

Other tools and techniques for performance measurement

The customer experience should always be measured, and should find its place in a range of organisational measurement approaches. There are many other tools. Some get highly technical and we won't cover those here. The main point is to put the effort into deciding what to measure rather than which framework you use.

Balanced scorecard

This was created in the 1990s by Robert Kaplan and David Norton (see Chapter 22). Its origins were to wean people away from over-reliance on financial measures, as this tended to produce short-term thinking and also didn't provide any insights as to why the results were as they were. The balanced scorecard looks at four key areas:

1 How do we look to our customers?

2 How do we look to our owners?

3 What do we need to excel at?

4 How do we innovate and learn?

All of these are linked. The idea is to set concrete objectives, measures and targets for each area, and to then reflect these in your overall initiative plans.

table 13.1   An example of a balanced scorecard

Our business		Our customers	
Primary KPIs	Secondary KPIs (examples)	Primary KPIs	Secondary KPIs (examples)
Income	Debtor days	Net customers	Sales by product group
Operating profit	Creditor days	Retention	Sales by channel
Cashflow		ARPA	Lead generation
EBIT		Satisfaction – net promoter	Lead conversion
EPS			Campaign outcomes
Our people		**Our brand**	
Primary KPIs	Secondary KPIs (examples)	Primary KPIs	Secondary KPIs (examples)
Engagement	Staff turnover	Awareness	PR reach
Productivity	Attendance ratios	GRP – reach and frequency	
	Training delivery	Brand equity	
		Content downloads	

The priority should be to focus on what matters. Take call centres for instance: if the main measure is the number of calls per hour, then you will have customer service reps not resolving issues and keeping calls short so they can be 'productive'. If the main measure is to resolve the customer complaint in a single call, they will have a much more positive impact on customer satisfaction.

Companies often add perspectives to the scorecard, such as community or brand. But if you have too many they will become meaningless or misleading. One company I worked for had an entire page in the central management accounts devoted to KPIs – there must have been sixty of them. No one in the business units even looked at them, but because they were required reporting, everyone just stuck numbers in to comply. The result was meaningless data. The company ended up with no common performance measures across the units, and much unnecessary conflict and mistrust among senior management.

> **exercise**
>
> Try creating a balanced scorecard from your strategy. Debate and discuss what really will matter to your organisation. Try to come up with no more than one objective and three primary measures and targets for each area. Any more and people will get lost and it will become too complicated.

KPIs

KPIs are the Key Performance Indicators that will enable to you to track and hit your targets. For example, if your target is to have 500,000 customers overall, one key performance measure might be around customer retention.

For each measure, you should ask a series of simple questions:

- What is the measure?
- Why are we measuring this?
- Who measures this?
- How often is it measured?

■ Where does the data come from to measure it?

■ Who acts on the data?

■ What do they do?

Notice how often the simple: who, what, when, where and why and how are used in setting these measures. If you cannot answer these questions they may be the wrong targets.[3]

Drilling down and linking primary KPIs and secondary KPIs and deciding which initiatives are critical to achieve your objectives and KPIs is an essential part of measuring: 'In order to achieve this we need to achieve that.' It's really important that everyone in your team, and ultimately organisation, understands how their work is linked together to deliver the KPIs.

Example

The sales department needs to achieve 100 sales per month of a product or service. In order to achieve this, they need 300 appointments, since one in three visits 'converts' to a sale. In order to achieve the 300 appointments, they need the marketing department to generate 3,000 qualified leads per month, because one in ten converts to an appointment.

In order to generate the leads, the marketing department looks to three sources; email marketing, Google ad words and PR. Each of these has a different conversion rate and is done by a different team. So each of the teams looks at how many emails they need to send, how many Google ad words they need to run and how many PR articles should be generated to hit the target. Secondary KPIs are set accordingly so everyone is working towards achieving the same objectives, and they nest within each other in the same way as a Russian stacking doll.

In reality, of course, customers may do more than one of these activities, so it can be difficult to measure interactions between these things without sophisticated tools, which I will discuss later (in Chapter 19).

---

[3] Adapted from *Balanced Scorecard*, Bourne, Mike and Bourne, Pippa, Chartered Management Institute Instant Manager Series, Hodder, 2007, p. 64.

But it's a good way of getting you started in thinking about how your work links into the overall KPIs of your organisation.

Suppose you have now set your KPI for customer retention and customer satisfaction. What do you do now? This is where Critical Success Factors (CSFs) come in. In order for you to achieve your KPI, you will need to deliver certain things that will help to retain and satisfy your customers. It could be they will need certain levels of performance from your product or service, or a swift resolution of a complaint or a competitive price point. If you analyse the relative proportion of those people who have left because of dissatisfaction in each of these areas you will be able to prioritise which requires attention. These are your CSFs. Often, they will not be your or your team's job, but the job of another department. This is why it is so important to work together.

■ KPI = number of new customers. For example, 1,000 per year, or 20 per week. (Measurable, quantifiable.)

■ CSF = a website where customers can buy online and could be a critical success factor enabling you to achieve your number of new customers. It is a key enabler of your strategy.

■ It's important to agree your reported KPIs – it is also worth investing time in narrowing this down to the top 10.

exercise

Look at you and your team's objectives and KPIs. Do you understand how they link to the overall KPIs of your organisation? Will what you are doing help the organisation to achieve those objectives, targets, and KPIs? If not, why not? Have a chat with your boss – you may not have the right KPIs.

table 13.2	An example of a KPI report

Proposed primary KPIs 2013/14	Frequency	Measure 2012/13	Budget 2013/14	Stretch 2013/14
Our business				
Income	Monthly	££	££	££
Net contribution	Monthly	££	££	££
Cash flow and reserves	Monthly	££	££	££
Our customers				
Net customers (existing + new – losses) Members (fee payers) Learning organisations Employers	Monthly	#	#	#
Customer retention Members (fee payers) Learning organisations Employers	Monthly	%	%	%
Net promoter score Members Learning organisations Employers	Monthly	#	#	#
ARPA Members (fee payers) Learning organisations Employers	Monthly	#	#	#
Our brand/reputation				
Brand awareness Spontaneous Prompted	Annual	%	%	%
GRP – overall PR activity	Monthly	#	#	#
Brand equity	Annual	%	%	%
Content downloads	Monthly	#	#	#
Our people				
Employee engagement survey score	Quarterly	%	%	%

Monthly reports and briefings: consistency of format is best

Now that you have your scorecard and KPIs, talk about them! Initiate monthly reports from your entire department and for your staff on how you are doing. Do this routinely, and use the same format. In one company I worked for each of the regional managing directors had their own monthly report format. Often the MDs would try to justify these differences on the basis of cultural variations.

Cultural variations may explain why an outcome is different, but they should not be used to justify different metrics. In this case the behaviour was political: each regional managing director was trying to window-dress their results. This is the worst kind of reporting, as it hides problems that need fixing.

If you have a standard format, you can quickly benchmark and see where you are good and where you might need to improve. Table 13.3 shows one example of a standard format that I like.

Briefings for all employees are a very good idea. If you expect employees to deliver the strategy, inform them on a monthly basis how your organisation is doing. The best way to do this is to have a simple version of the monthly report shared at each briefing, and encourage different people to share what they are doing. I encourage you to be very open about financial and performance information. Why keep it secret? If you expect your employees to achieve things, they need to know what, why and how. Don't hide it away in a desk drawer or a top management meeting. It may also be that your employees have some great ideas on how to improve performance.

Don't be afraid to escalate bad news. One CEO told me a story of how, in his first managing director position, he used to report to his board on all the bad things that were happening. One day his Chairman took him aside and told him not to do that, as it made a bad impression, but he carried on. So he got fired. He went on to found Berkeley Homes – a very successful FTSE 250 company.

| table 13.3 | Performance dashboard |

Financial*	Result	Budget	Variance	Year-to-date	Variance to prior YTD month	R-A-G rating
Income (£k)						
Contribution (£k)						
Cash/Reserves (£k)						

Customers*	Result	Budget	Variance	Year-to-date	Variance to prior YTD month	R-A-G rating
Net number (new – lost) (#)						
Proportion retained (%)						
Net promoter score (#)						
Average revenue per account (£k)						

Our projects	RoI	Status This period	Status Last period	R-A-G rating

Our risks		Net Risk Score This period	Net Risk Score Last period	R-A-G rating

Comments on Performance Dashboard Variance

Highs and Lows

Sharing and Discussion

The annual 'business review'

It bears repeating that all measurement tools are a means to an end: to challenge and improve your strategy, execution and results. It helps to complete a thorough analysis of the business and the KPIs once a year. This is called a business review: it looks at the overall objective and targets, which were met and which not, and then drills down into each of the measures and initiatives to look at why that is.

Begin with detailed findings for each area. For example, you might look at pricing, product performance, customer satisfaction, campaign performance or communication effectiveness, employee engagement and manufacturing efficiency. Do so systematically, using the available data in each case. For each area you explore, identify specific actions for improvement. A picture will emerge, which can be translated into overall conclusions: Which were the most important areas that explained the over- or under-performance? Which actions will make the biggest difference?

These methods might not work for disruptive innovations that are about inventing totally new business models, but they are very effective for most organisations that need to undergo change and improvement. Organisations are like managers – the more aware they are of their strengths and shortcomings, and the more committed they are to learning to correct them, the better and more successful they will be!

Top tips, pitfalls and takeaways

Top tips

- Understand your brand's 'essence' or equity, and always make sure the product lives up to the promise.

- Measure your open and click-through rates on promotional emails and websites. And always benchmark.

- Use a 'Net Promoter Score' (NPS) to determine the likelihood that customers would recommend your product or service.

- Reports for different departments, such as monthly performance reports, should always be to the same format, testing the same things.

■ Use Key Performance Indicators to support Critical Success Factors – those matters absolutely essential for achieving your goals.

Top pitfalls

■ A brand pyramid that is too complicated, too generic, too ambiguous, not relevant, not proven, or not distinctive.

■ Setting too many KPIs, such that no one is able properly to understand and use them.

■ Relying too heavily on data without checking its accuracy and validity.

Top takeaways

■ Marketing is not just about logos and communication; the heart of the discipline concerns understanding customers and customer behaviour.

■ You can measure your brand equity, benchmarked against competitors, in many different ways.

■ Measurement is an essential part of ensuring you are on target to reach strategic goals.

■ Measurement of inappropriate targets can create perverse incentives and lead to serious operational problems: for example, tracking activity but not checking quality of service.

■ Any measurement is no more than a means to an end, so indicators should be relevant and proportionate.

■ A balanced scorecard can help prevent too much reliance on financial data.

part

5

Managing change

14

How to manage change

What you will learn in this chapter

- How to identify when change is needed and anticipate its impact
- How to plan the different types and steps of change
- How to implement change in your organisation
- How to help people understand the impact of change

'Be the change you want to see.'

Mahatma Gandhi

In 2012, over nine out of ten managers experienced change programmes in their organisation,[1] yet only 30 per cent said that senior managers managed change well.[2] We also know that it makes employees uncomfortable, with 70 per cent of managers saying that change decreased morale in their organisations.

Here are some of the reasons changes fail:

- **Fad of the day** Doing it because it's in vogue rather than because it's right for your organisation.

- **Lacking in authenticity** An autocratic leader sends everyone on an empowerment course but doesn't go – or change their own style.

---

[1] http://www.managers.org.uk/workinglife2012, exec summary, p. 6.
[2] http://www.managers.org.uk/workinglife2012, pp. 13 and 21.

▪ **Losing sight of the end-goal** Becoming so obsessed with the process you forget what the output was supposed to be, as long as it's on time and on budget.

▪ **Cutting costs without changing culture** Saying you want to flatten things to improve decision-making but really you are just cutting costs without changing the way you work to compensate.

▪ **Systems/user gap** Spending a lot of money installing new systems but not asking users for their input or training them on how to use them correctly.

All these elements are within the control of senior managers. I have been through major organisational changes in every single company I've worked for, and have led them as well as been led by them. Those that actually succeeded combined the approaches discussed in this chapter.

Spotting signs of change and anticipating their impact

The first thing to do is to recognise when change is required, and why. The top five reasons in 2012, according to one study, were:

1 Organisational restructuring

2 Cost reduction

3 Voluntary redundancy

4 Culture change programmes

5 Changed employee terms and conditions

Change can also happen for external reasons, like changes in legislation or markets, but the most common reasons have negative consequences for employees. These can include decreased motivation, morale, loyalty, job security and well-being. Most employees see change as forcing them to work harder, faster and longer – especially when the change is driven by cost reduction. Many managers are also sceptical: over half thought decision-making wasn't any faster and 45 per cent said their organisations were no more flexible as a result of change – nor did the majority think that profitability or productivity had increased.[3]

Planning change

Most changes today are evolutionary, rather than revolutionary. And most involve strategy as well as operations, and transformation as well as transactions. For all types of change, however, you need to plan. And given that most people will have inherently negative views on change, it pays to involve them in the process.

When planning change, think about the different forces at work. There will be forces for and against the change. Try to picture these – list the top three things that are driving the change, and the top three things that will get in the way. Don't forget behavioural issues when you are considering your change programme. Often those will be the things most difficult to change!

Plan for change in the way you would for any major programme. Cover:

1 **Vision** What is the 'big idea' behind the change? What is the organisation striving to achieve? This must be clear and compelling.

2 **Scope** What needs to change to realise the vision? What processes and departments are involved and what outputs, products and services will be different when you are done? What ways of working and attitudes need to change?

3 **Time frame** What will change when, and in what order? Radical change takes time, especially if attitude change is involved.

4 **People** Who will be most affected by change and how? Who will play prominent roles in implementing change (the change agents)?

5 **Resources** How much will the change cost? Will there be offsetting benefits?

6 **Communications** Will you need new mechanisms and structures to communicate with employees, customers, suppliers and other stakeholders?

---

[3] http://www.managers.org.uk/workinglife2012, pp. 12, 13, 15.

g Training have you allowed for the training of managers and front-line employees in both hard and soft skills associated with change?

It's best to do this in a group. Try the power brainstorming technique described earlier in Chapter 9.

Look at change programmes in your organisation. Do you understand why the change is needed? Do you have a clear change plan? Do you understand the forces that are working in favour of, as well as those that are working against the change? Make sure you and your team are comfortable with all of these elements before you proceed to implement.

Implementing change

The best-known model for implementing change comes from John Kotter of the Harvard Business School. It involves an eight-step programme, illustrated in Figure 14.1, which builds on three phases: create

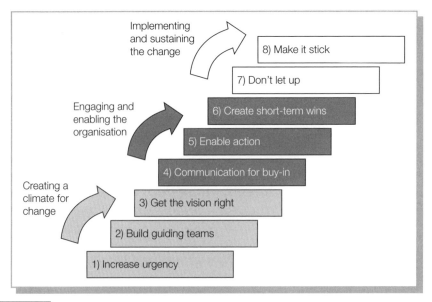

figure 14.1 Kotter's eight-step programme for implementing change

Source: Kotter International (www.kotterinternational.com).

a climate where change can occur; engage and enable your organisation; and implement and sustain the change.

It is difficult in practice, although it works very well when you do it well. Most people fall down on the people aspects of change, rather than the business aspects. Here are some tips for how you can best engage people when it comes to implementing change.

Make sure you make a clear case for change that includes both business and cultural aspects. Why should you change? Are your costs growing faster than your income? Do you have a pension deficit to service? Is your business model under threat from new technologies? Thinking about tangible business reasons that everyone can grasp will help your case. But you'll also need to think about cultural reasons. For example, if employees are not engaged, and the main reason is that they think directors don't work together, then you can use the change to drive a more collaborative and participative culture.

The most difficult part of any change programme is convincing people of the need to do things differently. People will often take recommendations as a personal criticism, or have come to have very ingrained ways of doing things. Often people leave this task to outside consultants, but it is best owned by people within the organisation. Try getting a group together and asking them about things they do that could be done better. If the business isn't growing, ask people what they think needs to be done differently. Most people understand that things need to change, but they are still fearful of it. Involving them lessens that.

About 80 per cent of changes involve organisational redesigns and restructurings. The best way to do this is to involve the people affected in the process, rather than leave it to HR and senior managers to draw up organisational charts behind closed doors. Even if you are making redundancies, you will get a much better organisation if you engage those who do the work in the design. Besides, it is virtually impossible for leaders to sit and design an entire organisation, from top to bottom. Involving people at the level of the changes and above in designing that part of the organisation will result in a better structure with fewer overlaps and greater ownership. Plus, involving people will help gain their commitment to the new roles, as well as stimulate their interest in applying for them.

Maximising your chances of making change successful: the change equation

Sometimes it can be helpful to consider change as an equation: $C = A \times B \times D > X + Y$

C = the probability of change being successful

A = the dissatisfaction with the status quo

B = a clear statement of the desired future state

D = concrete first steps towards achieving the desired future state

X = the cost (not just financial) of the change

Y = the inertia to be overcome

If you are dealing with organisations that have been doing things the same way for a long time, it may be easier to focus on B and D than on A, as it's unlikely they will be keen to change the way things are done.

Source: Gateshead Council, *Understanding and Managing Reactions to Change*, 2009, p. 10

Ten tips for driving organisational and cultural change

Remember that attention to organisational design and culture (see Chapter 12) is necessary. Here are ten disciplines that help:

1 Share information as widely as possible. If information is limited to top management, this will generate rumours and resentment.

2 Allow for suggestions, input and differences from widespread participation. If possible have a cross-departmental representation and consultation committee.

3 Break the change into manageable phases. Encourage the relevant people to be involved in each.

4 Minimise surprises: make standards and requirements clear. If you don't know the answer to something, say you don't know. But try to say when you think you will know.

5 Recognise prevalent value systems may need changing too. If people's primary motivator is who they sit next to rather than their work contribution, try mixing things up so that everyone is sitting next to someone new.

6 Expect – and deal positively with – conflict. Explain why decisions are made: even if they are not popular, most people will respect that you listened and explained.

7 Create a blame-free culture of empowerment and push down decision-making – but clarify decision boundaries.

8 Break down departmental barriers – make sure change teams are cross-departmental and functional. Involve many different people across the business in redesigning LEAN processes for example. Make it fun.

9 Design better, more meaningful jobs, and ensure that some people are promoted internally as a result of the changes. Try to introduce popular policies like flexible working, or reward and recognition programmes alongside the new roles.

10 Make sure you have a feedback system in place that monitors how well your change programme is being implemented. Celebrate every early success, and also admit it when you don't get everything right.

The voice of the customer

'Town hall' type sessions that get customer-facing employees to contribute to better ways of doing things can often encourage change. In one organisation I worked in, the people manning the customer service lines knew that their time was not being well spent. They said they often spent time on the telephone with retired people who were no longer relevant for the services offered, and that they were mailing letters because we weren't capturing email addresses. Listening to these examples informed and encouraged my grasp of the need for change by underpinning it with real examples. It also made them part of the programme. They became 'front-line' advocates for change.

Communicating change

This is the thing that most often goes wrong when managing change. People forget the very high and constant need for communication. It's really not enough to announce a change programme and then expect everyone to 'get on with it'. You will need to constantly repeat and position the reasons for change, and address people's concerns.

Here are seven tips for managing the communication process:[4]

1 **Create a sense of urgency** In a situation where employees are mistakenly feeling 'fat and happy' they need to be re-educated. Or when you are changing a strategy they will need to see how and why that needs to be done in order for you to keep the organisation sustainable. A shared sense of urgency comes from shared understanding of the threats as well as missed opportunities.

2 **Communicate the big picture** Employees need to understand the business environment they are operating in. They will then understand the implications for themselves and their job and will be better equipped to make decisions. Try to link the communication to observations that employees have made themselves (see 'The voice of the customer' box).

3 **Share the thinking as openly as possible** Change will not be properly implemented unless people understand why it is necessary. Commitment comes from a sense of ownership, and ownership comes from participation and engagement. Use this engagement to encourage more examples but also to raise concerns. Be as open as you can. In my experience, open change processes are much healthier than closed ones.

4 **Maximise the sense of continuity and stability** If change is sold as 'revolution', employees may see it as violating their values and will resist. It helps to understand how people are feeling. What they really want is to maintain continuity where possible, and quickly re-establish equilibrium. Positioning change as evolutionary will reassure people and help the organisation retain existing strengths.

5 **Do not wait – communicate!** Even in the most uncertain of situations, there is always something that can be communicated. Managers often mistakenly assume that they are in control of communication and can turn it on and off like a tap. Unfortunately, if management does not communicate, the grapevine will.

6 **Communicate probabilities and scenarios – but be honest** Be truthful – don't say no one will lose their job if it's not true. While you cannot predict the future, you can talk about what might

---

[4] Lucas, Erica, *Riding the Change Roller-Coaster*, Professional Manager, 2002.

happen. People will speculate anyway, so you may as well give them real possibilities to think about. It is also helpful to give people a timescale of when you expect to be able to communicate specific information. This allows you to say something while you are still analysing and debating the way forward.

7 **Make face-to-face the main communication channel** Research has shown that people prefer to receive information about change from their immediate manager, face-to-face. Line managers are often perceived as being 'in the same boat' as their teams. They can help their people 'unpack' information and link it to their own roles. If you communicate in this way, you will be better able to assess people's concerns, correct misconceptions, gather feedback and minimise the chances of sensitive details leaking out. Combine the face-to-face with bigger sessions wherever possible so that messaging is consistent. And be sure managers are trained to emphasise the same key points in their communications.

exercise

What is your ongoing communication plan for your change?
Ask people in different departments and different levels in your organisation about the change – are their answers consistent? If not, address. Also ask them to give you ideas of what's going well, what's going 'OK', and what is going badly in the change process and adjust your communication and plan accordingly.

Understanding resistance to change and the stages of change

Despite your best efforts to do everything right, you will always be faced with blockers. According to research, the way people respond to change is fairly consistent:

■ 5% will champion change;

■ 20% will be early adopters of it;

■ 50% will adopt a 'wait and see' approach;

■ 20% will resist until they have no choice but to change;

■ 5% will never change.

The bottom 25 per cent are often referred to as the blockers or terrorists. They may actually actively try to sabotage the change efforts, or indeed pay lip service to them while undermining them in their own behaviours. Every organisation has these. When you are leading change, it is important to understand who is in which group. You will need to create a coalition of champions and early adopters at all levels. It's important to recognise them and encourage them to be proactive, both in big groups but also back in their departments.

Equally, understanding the motivations of the wait and see types and the cynics is important. They are likely to be this way because of their own fears of disruption to the status quo. Understanding that people respond to change at different speeds is very important. The champions go through the process very quickly, while the cynics and blockers take much more time.

> **Tip**
>
> You will probably never change blockers and may want to give them an exit strategy.

People go through common reactions and stages when dealing with change (Figure 14.2). These stages are as follows:[5]

■ Denial

■ Anger

■ Bargaining

■ Fear

■ Resignation/acceptance.

Often, the blockers and cynics will be behind the curve, to the left of the champions, who have moved very swiftly to the right. Understanding the issues people are facing at each stage of the change process will help you to manage them better.

---

[5] Kübler-Ross, Elizabeth, *On Death and Dying*, Routledge, 1969.

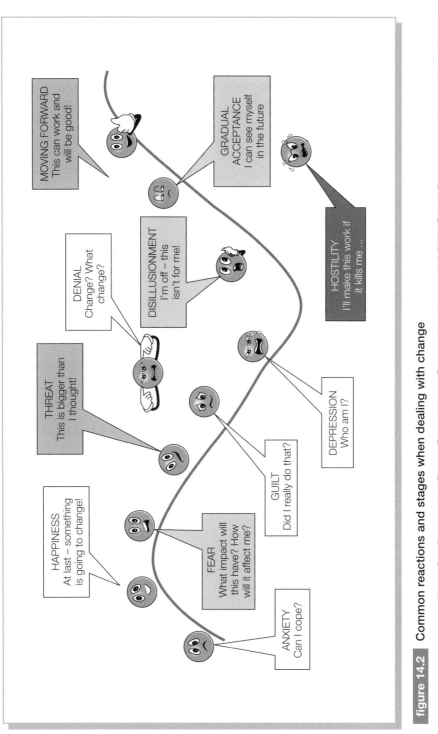

figure 14.2 Common reactions and stages when dealing with change

For your area, plot out where you think everyone is on the path of change. Identify the champions and the blockers. Can you encourage the champions to help move people along and coach the blockers? If not, understand what the blockers' concerns are and recognise how you might deal with them. Understanding and talking through their concerns will help them. By the end of the change we want people to reach a state of hope that this will be better in the future, and enthusiasm for the new way of working.

Top tips, pitfalls and takeaways

Top tips

■ List the top three things that are driving the change, and the top three things that will get in the way.

■ You need momentum, but don't move too quickly. Involve people. Communicate constantly, honestly and specifically. Refer back to the consistent themes. Celebrate early successes. Get stuff wrong and correct quickly. Remember there will always be a rumour mill. Remember people value small stuff.

Top pitfalls

■ Forgetting that cultural change underpins organisational and strategic change.

■ Moving too fast or too slow.

■ Keeping the reasons for change unclear or secret.

Top takeaways

■ Most employees have negative experiences and expectations of change, but some of the key success factors are within the control of managers.

■ Planning for change is a major undertaking and has to be treated as such.

15

Designing and delivering innovation

What you will learn in this chapter

- The power of innovation
- Different types of innovation and innovation portfolio
- How to use Product Life Cycle to manage innovation in your organisation
- The innovation process: funnel versus agile
- Which behaviours encourage (and discourage) innovation

Innovation is something every organisation hankers after but few actually master. I have often been responsible for innovation in my various business roles. There is nothing more exciting than the feeling of creating something new and successful with a team of people – be that a new product launch, or a new way of measuring customer benefits. Equally, there is nothing more frustrating than 'stymied' innovation – as when the CEO cancels something on the eve of a test market because he's decided innovation is simply too risky. Most organisations say they are innovative, but few actually are, because many traditional ways of managing discourage the risk-taking that innovation needs to thrive.

You cannot have successful innovation without failure. I encourage you to focus on the common characteristics that make innovation successful, and accept that these same characteristics can and will cause innovation to fail. Only when you acknowledge that innovation fails more than it succeeds will you begin to get somewhere with it.

Different types of innovation

'Innovate or die.'

Tom Peters

No organisation can survive without innovation. This is especially true in today's world, where technology is changing so rapidly. There are many stories where failure to embrace new technologies quickly enough has resulted in the demise of previous market leaders: Encyclopaedia Britannica, Kodak, Yell and HMV all failed to adapt to the digital revolution. That's why so many leading innovation authors, like Clayton M. Christensen in *The Innovator's Dilemma*[1] and USC's Gerard Tellis in *Unrelenting Innovation*,[2] advocate setting up units that will aim to cannibalise existing products before the competition does. Apple did this with the iPad (cannibalising the iPod). And Toyota did this with Prius, which was conceived by a separate unit to avoid being swamped by the demands of keeping the best-selling Camry going strong.[3]

Usually when people talk about innovation they assume you are talking about a breakthrough product or service. But there are many different types of innovation. As you think about innovation, consider: is the degree of change in what you are offering big or small? And second, is the thing you are changing an input or process, a product or service, or a positioning or channel? Think about the degree to which you are innovating as well as what you are innovating.

[1] Christensen, Clayton M., *The Innovator's Dilemma*, HarperCollins, first Harper Business edn, 2000.

[2] Tellis, Gerard, *Unrelenting Innovation: How to Create a Culture for Market Dominance*, J-B Warren Bennis Series, Jossey Bass, 2013.

[3] http://business.time.com/2013/01/29/innovate-or-die-wisdom-from-apple-google-and-toyota/#ixzz2PITckoVb

The degree of innovation: low, medium or high?

Low: sustaining or incremental innovation

These are small improvements to existing products, services and processes. Making your broadband faster, your packages easier to open, or your bills easier to pay online, getting your seats allocated on budget airlines, or improving the seat comfort on the aircraft are all examples. Sometimes you can join up a series of these small advantages to build a big advantage.

Medium: category or broadening innovation

This is extending the impact of what you are doing by launching new products, processes or services in adjacent categories or to adjacent customer groups. For example: this might be about launching a new form of diet Coke – Coke Zero – to appeal to men and young people; or extending your skincare brand into shampoo or deodorant.

High: transformational, disruptive or breakthrough innovation

Creating something new that changes the rules of the game. Fast fashion is one example: Zara translates fashions from the catwalk to the masses in weeks. Disruptive innovation can literally reinvent entire categories of goods and services through harnessing technology to create new opportunities and ways of doing things. Technology has completely disrupted the way we produce and consume so many things like music and news information.

What you are innovating?

Are you innovating:

■ A product or service?

■ A system, process or organisational way of working – for example, by going directly to your customers instead of through a retail channel?

■ The way in which your existing products or services reach the external market – for example, targeting a new group of customers?

It is important to understand where innovation will make a difference to the value of what you are doing and where it won't. For example, if you are a newspaper owner and you have the best possible content, that wins more prizes than any other paper, that's great. But if the channel to market is shifting drastically from paid-for newspapers to online and free, then it won't help you, as many newspapers have found.

Equally, you need to understand the impact of the positioning of your brand. For example, you might think that Special K Cereal is just a cereal, but by positioning Special K as a female 'healthy indulgence' weight loss brand, the cereal has been able to expand into crackers, bars and other snacks.

When you analyse your innovation portfolio you should aim to have projects in every area of the matrix, as remember, many of them will fail. The higher the degree of change they involve, the more likely they are to do so. Have one or two projects in the high degree of change area, but don't overlook the other areas.

Incremental innovation has a high degree of success, and encourages high participation. It's also likely that the rewards achieved from many small improvements can be substantial when added up. Similarly, category innovation may require extending into new markets or targeting new customers but it's also essential for growth and can build your brand and enable you to boost your margins as well by offering more profitable products and services.

Don't overlook the potential of positioning innovation. Offering pet food in vets' offices, for example, comes with an implied endorsement, so people will pay more. Similarly, skincare sold only in pharmacies has a higher price point and margin than skincare sold in drugstores. The *Harvard Business Review* can take its case studies and course contents online and monetise them to a brand new audience who may never set foot on Harvard's college campus. Selling bundled services such as broadband, TV and telephone is a practice widely used by communications companies to boost customer loyalty and spend with their service.

Process innovation can also be important. Zara dramatically reduced the lead times in designing and producing its clothes, and this advantage enabled it to copy trends much faster than its rivals.

Managing innovation

It is helpful to think about innovation in terms of managing a portfolio. You will need to have examples of most kinds of innovation to be successful. You do need to encourage people to innovate existing products and services, processes and positioning. You should also plan for new emerging services and processes to continue to grow and build your presence in your category. And finally, you should probably have one or two more radical approaches going on. We could try to visualise this using a matrix, or innovation map.

	System/Process	Product/Service	Position/Channel
High: Transforming			
Medium: Broadening			
Low: Sustaining			

Sometimes it can also be helpful to plot your innovations in a matrix, looking at which areas are existing and which are new. Ansoff is often used see Chapter 10 on Strategy. You want to look at innovating within existing as well as new products and markets – but not all at once. It helps you think about your innovation portfolio and the various strategic aspects of it. Where it says markets, think about customers, channels or positioning. Where it says products, think about products, services or processes.

exercise

Think about innovation in your organisation. Try to come up with two examples of each innovation described above. Can you identify them? If not, why not? If you can, think about which have worked and which haven't. What can you learn from that?

Once you have built your innovation map, map it onto Ansoff's matrix. Are you reflecting the various innovation strategies you can use? If not, why not?

Product Life Cycle and innovation rhythm

Consider the innovation rhythm in a particular category. How often do you need to come up with something new? How often do successful businesses bring out new products or services? In online media, the answer is many times a day. In cosmetics, you need to launch a new product every month and cover eyes, lips, nails and face. But in other areas, the pace may be slower – bicycles or bank accounts, for example.

Understanding the rhythm can prevent 'over-innovating' where you are moving on to the next big thing before you have properly exploited your existing portfolio. This is a common problem: imagine a sales force trying to sell over twenty different products to a small business in one half-hour visit, or asking a supermarket to stock some 6,000 pet food items which turn over less than £5K – and add to that the cost of manufacturing, warehousing and distributing all those products. You also need to manage your product portfolio, so that you review and kill products as well as launch new ones. 'One in, one out' is a helpful principle. In businesses with a fast pace of innovation, the items replaced annually by new ones will exceed 30 per cent. In fashion this is even higher. On the internet, the cost of maintaining the 'long tail' will be very low, but may still lead to suboptimal results. With websites, people often add in new content without replacing current content and it becomes cluttered.

The Product Life Cycle is a concept that helps manage your innovation and product portfolio. New products require innovation; they then become adopted by the trendsetters. Then you need to make the transition into the mass market – this may mean broadening distribution, investing in sales and marketing capability and channel innovation. You then move to the late mass market and finally the laggards – here you may wish to look at process innovations that will offer your product more cheaply, or morph it by extending into adjacent areas. Finally, the product or service needs replacing, to start the life cycle anew.

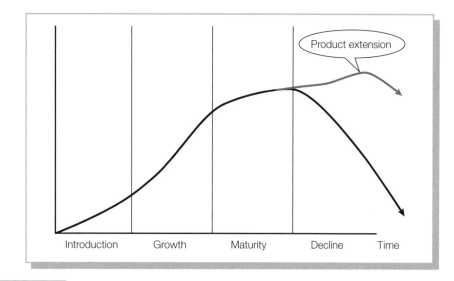

 **Product life cycle**

Source: Courtesy of Jim Riley (www.tutor2u.net).

exercise

Map your product or service portfolio. Where are your products in the life cycle? What does this tell you about what you should be thinking about in terms of innovation?

Innovation process: funnel versus agile

There are many different processes for managing innovation, but generally speaking they fall into two different types: the funnel and the agile. The innovation funnel, or pipeline, starts with a lot of ideas and whittles these down to a few that are actually launched (Figure 15.2). It is typically used in large corporations but can also be valuable for smaller organisations that have many different departments, functions or stakeholders. Agile innovation has grown in popularity with the rise of the entrepreneurial techno community and is typically used in software development. It uses frequent, informal sessions to get to a prototype as quickly as possible, put it to test in the market with customers, and then carry on iterating it or modifying it according to user acceptance until it either succeeds or fails. Both types are valuable.

The funnel

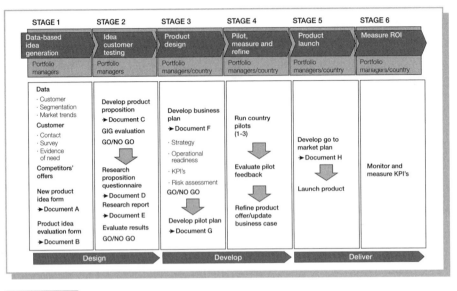

Stage 1   The funnel starts with a stage that is about looking at customers, markets, research and competitors to generate ideas. It may also come from many people involved in the work who have ideas on how to improve goods or services or processes.

Stage 2   The ideas are evaluated. Quickly. This can be done by a group of employees or by management, but it should be an objective and transparent process. There have been really successful examples where databases of ideas have been created for evaluation by employee task forces and not just management or money.

Stage 3   The ideas that are successful move to a fuller design of a prototype and a business case to go along with it. This is where you start to spend money. The strategy, risks and rewards are documented to try to get an idea of the size of the prize and to add greater rigour and focus to the idea. The success factors are defined.

Stage 4 The successful ideas go to a pilot in market where they are put to the test, typically for six months. This is also known as a test market or a proof of concept. Do people take up the new offer? Does the new process lower cost or improve productively? Research is often carried out. Importantly, the KPIs are measured – is the project achieving its agreed measurements of success?

Stage 5 New successful pilots are expanded and launched more broadly into other markets, taking the learning from the pilots and shaping them to refine the launch plans.

Stage 6 The results are further monitored and fed back into the beginning of Stage 1, creating a continuous feedback loop.

Most big organisations will use a funnel. The upside is that it is a visible process that can be tracked and objectively managed, and is transparent and measured. The downside is it is very difficult to do well unless your organisation is very schooled and skilled in innovation. There can be a tendency to over-manage the stage gate process so that nothing gets through. Or under-manage it so that everything gets through. It can also become very complicated. See also the behaviours that encourage innovation later in this chapter.

Agile

Agile innovation has become very popular with the rise of the digital economy. Because it doesn't cost much to try out in digital innovation, people often just put ideas out there and see if they catch on, and modify them until they do. Agile came from a way of doing software development project management and incorporates aspects of lean management. Agile focuses on outputs, not process, and on quick prototyping and continuous feedback, frequent product iteration and adjustment. 'Trial and Error' or pilots are other forms of this approach. The main point is to get it out there quickly so customers and users can interact with it and you can respond to this in an iterative manner.

Agile has its fans and can help companies produce products and services more quickly; however, it is best suited for discrete projects as it can be difficult to approach the entire portfolio in this manner. It is also easily misunderstood; when poorly executed it can lead to higher costs and less success. And it is obviously less suitable for products and services that have long supply chains and require heavy capital investment in plants and equipment.

> Which process are you using to manage innovation? Why? If you don't have a process, try implementing one of the above.

Behaviours that encourage and discourage innovation

Behaviours and cultural characteristics are as important as processes and strategy. Recently, a group called Management Innovation Exchange sponsored a contest for companies to share their case studies of successful innovation. The ten winning examples (from over 140 entries, chosen by judges from McKinsey and the Harvard Business School[4]) are striking in their similarities of what worked – and chime closely with my own experiences.

1 **Innovation starts with innovating culture and behaviour** You have to encourage employees who want to get involved. Many employees don't do this because they feel they don't have time, or that they will not be listened to, or their suggestions will fail and they will get fired. So you need to make clear that you welcome their participation – perhaps have some sort of kick-off event, and a clear output and reward programme.

2 **Innovation is more successful the closer people involved are to customers** This is one of the principles of agile innovation that really also applies to the funnel approach. Many of the big companies like P&G and Unilever institutionalise this. (See also Chapter 16.)

3 **Collaborative, diverse and cross functional beats hierarchical, similar and siloed** Getting departments and different areas of the

---

[4] http://www.mixprize.org/blog/announcing-innovating-innovation-challenge-winners

business to work together collaboratively is key to producing better results. It also helps to have a diversity of backgrounds, functions and views. In one example where people were competing for funding, they learned to peer review and peer judge the ventures that obtained funding. And apparently got returns as good as other more traditional methods where the money men make the calls.

4 **Celebrate failure not just success – this is fundamental** Many more innovations will fail than be successful. Even in the biggest companies success rates will rarely rise above 50 per cent. A.G. Lafley, the P&G CEO famed for stimulating innovation, said that if the success rate rose above 60 per cent it meant that the company wasn't taking enough risks. The trick is to fail fast, cheap and often. And to learn from your failures. One organisation even published a failure report![5]

5 **Learn by doing. Keep doing, keep learning** Innovative active companies accept that innovation is a continuous process and encourage everyone to share their experiences and learn from them. Often this can spark new ideas that will turn into innovations in their own right.

Top tips, pitfalls and takeaways

Top tips

- Win big, fail fast, cheap and often.
- Fake it 'til you make it.
- Innovation is 1 per cent inspiration, 9 per cent evaluation and 90 per cent perspiration.
- Get close to customers.
- Be diverse, argue and have fun.

Top pitfalls

- Over-managing innovation.

---

[5] http://www.mixprize.org/m-prize/innovating-innovation

■ Risk aversion: stopping stuff because you don't like it.

■ Innovating too many things at once.

Top takeaways

■ Everyone needs to innovate.

■ Build and manage a portfolio of innovation.

■ Encourage a culture of innovation.

16

Managing stakeholders, with customers at the centre

What you will learn in this chapter

- To understand the importance of managing all stakeholders
- To become more customer-focused in your organisation and strategy
- To understand the importance of customer insight, value and segmentation
- To treat suppliers as partners to increase value and quality
- To grasp the basics of better buying
- To identify different stakeholders and understand why they're important
- To use simple techniques to help analyse and manage stakeholders
- To encourage collaborative partnerships and other strategic alliances

'The consumer is the boss.'

A.G. Lafley

Successful companies, and successful managers, adapt continually. They have an understanding of the contribution of all stakeholders – and, moreover, they continually monitor and manage their relationships with key stakeholders. This chapter explains how this discipline is essential for effective change management, with a deliberate emphasis on the ultimate stakeholder: the customer.

A 'stakeholder' is anyone who is affected by your work. Stakeholder management is therefore essential, but it must retain a commercial focus, and not become simply an end in itself. I once held a performance review with a member of my team who was responsible for stakeholder management. When I asked him what he'd accomplished, he proudly told me that he was in forty conversations with stakeholders. When I asked him what the outcomes and objectives of these 'conversations' were, he looked at me blankly. He hadn't really thought about that bit. So, I mused, I'm paying you £2,000 per conversation? We ended up making his position redundant.

At the other end of the scale, failing to manage stakeholder relationships can be disastrous. I recall when the environmental debate started happening on disposable diapers (nappies in the UK) when I was a young brand assistant. Suddenly, there was a European-wide call for a boycott and many key environmental and women's groups were saying that the bleach used represented a health risk. Prior to this, P&G had been largely reactive to such pressure groups. Following this incident the company began to engage with them. We switched the formulae to unbleached pulp, and began dialogues and environmental projects and partnerships. Pampers survived this difficult period. Another manufacturer that refused to engage with these stakeholders ended up going bankrupt. The concept of 'critical friend' – of engaging with people who have very different, often opposing views and values, regularly inviting them to critique policy and practice, and acting on their observations – is now a common practice in multinational firms.

Identifying different stakeholders

As a stakeholder is anyone who is affected by your work, it can end up being many people. There are the obvious ones – your boss, your employees, your colleagues, your customers and your suppliers. But there are also many more removed external stakeholders. These include shareholders, investors, lenders, government groups, activist groups, partners, the media, volunteers, donors, trade associations, unions, national interest groups and the local community.

Sometimes it helps to show stakeholders in a diagram (figure 16.1). You

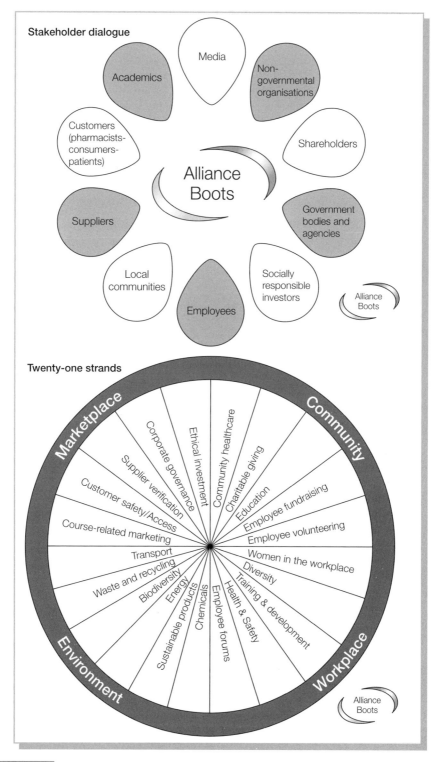

figure 16.1 Stakeholder mapping

Source: Richard Ellis, Corporate CSR Director, Alliance Boots, used by permission.

can then map out how you will approach them for certain activities such as CSR. Alliance Boots, which has an outstanding CSR programme, uses this method very successfully. It uses stakeholder mapping to identify twenty-one different CSR work streams across the four major CSR areas of community, workplace, marketplace and environment. It then sets up programmes, sponsors and quarterly KPIs for each. One of the reasons it is so successful is that delivering CSR for stakeholders is everyone's job – not just the CSR department! Figure 16.1 shows Alliance Boots' approach to stakeholders, stakeholder mapping and CSR work streams.

exercise

Identify the different stakeholders for your organisation, your most important project, and your work. Make sure that you know the person to contact in each stakeholder. How many are common to all three? These are likely to be the most influential stakeholders for you.

Managing stakeholders

Once you have identified who your stakeholders are, it is important to analyse their relative positions and understand how best to engage with them. One widely used way of doing this is to group stakeholders according to their degree of interest in your project or work, and their degree of influence over your project or work. This matrix also gives you the main strategic challenge of how to manage the various stakeholders. For example, those who hold a lot of influence over your work and have a high degree of interest in it are the stakeholders you need to manage closely (see Figure 16.2).

■ **High Interest, High Influence** These are the ones you need to manage closely and ensure they are onboard, engaged and supportive. Frequent involvement and communication with them, as well as reflecting their needs, is important.

■ **High Interest, Low Influence** These people can be very useful advisers as they have a good degree of knowledge and are likely to give honest opinions and help, as they have little influence over outcomes. You should consult regularly with them.

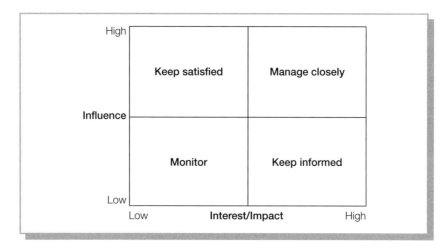

figure 16.2   Matrix for managing the various shareholders

Source: Cambridge Technology Partners (CTP).

■ **High Influence, Low Interest** These people can be important in helping to win over others as they have influence, but they aren't particularly interested and are therefore viewed as non-biased. They make good ambassadors in the external world as they are likely to be well connected. Keep them informed, but not overly so, as they aren't that into you.

■ **Low Influence, Low Interest** Keep abreast of their activities, but don't over-communicate or over-manage them. However, if they suddenly target your project or work, their influence could change, rapidly, so don't ignore them.

exercise

Map the stakeholders you identified in the first exercise on this matrix. What does it tell you about how you should be approaching different stakeholders?

Once you've identified and mapped your stakeholders you need to figure out where they stand on your work. Label your supporters in green and your opponents in red. Put the neutral ones in blue. You'll end up with a map that looks like Figure 16.3 (called the Southbeach Notation Model).

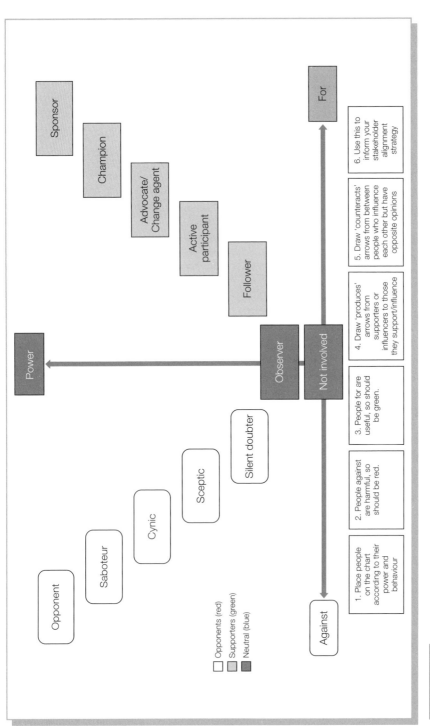

figure 16.3 **Stakeholder map**

Ask yourself: how can you engage your sponsor to help gain broader support for your work? How can advocates and champions be used to successfully lobby others who may be opposed? Who influences your opponents and cynics? How can you work with them to ensure they have good information about your work? How can you manage opposition to your proposal if you cannot win them around to support your work? How can you limit or prevent the impact of saboteurs?

For each of the main stakeholder groups, set a plan to manage them. Assign a member of your team to be responsible for keeping them informed. If all of this sounds incredibly calculated and political, that's because it is! It's part of management.

The fundamental principles of stakeholder management concern anticipation, understanding and then engagement with people who will be affected by your work – beyond the obvious ones. Being taken by surprise by disappointed stakeholders can stymie the best of plans.

The ultimate stakeholder: becoming a customer-centric organisation

Most organisations claim they put their customer at the heart of what they do. In my executive career, I have often been surprised at how little many businesses, including large successful firms, have understood about their customers. I have often had to lobby hard to create customer intelligence functions. Many senior executives comment that the sales force's feedback is enough for them, alongside financial metrics. But the best success stories include an understanding of the customer, linked to strategy development.

There are three elements of a customer-driven strategy: understanding the customer; responsiveness to customer needs; and value for money. Customer strategy should be linked to competitor strategy: Why might they prefer your company or service?

This focus on the customer will require time and effort, as well as financial investment. But remember that being a customer-focused organisation is almost always the key to success.

Who owns the customer?

Everyone throughout your organisation needs to take responsibility for the customer experience. But what does this mean? In many organisations, departments are based on products, technologies, business units, geographies or other internal needs of the organisation, rather than the external needs of the customer. A customer-led organisation:

- encourages boundary spanning efforts and cooperation – reward staff for cooperating between departments and creating customer-centric solutions;

- makes sure that people in departments such as accounts or HR which are not normally customer-facing get to interact with customers;

- invests in training that aims to break through silos and gives people information on different kinds of customers rather than just product-based training. Trains sales people how to recognise and 'spot' different customer types;

- joins forces with suppliers or other companies to share information or offer higher-value propositions for certain desirable customer groups that will engender loyalty;

- restructures the organisation with the customer in mind, sweeping away traditional silos.[1] Consider organising your business by customer segment.

If you and your colleagues engage with customers it is much easier to value their importance than it is if they remain abstract invoices or research reports. Customer engagement is everyone's responsibility, and it is now a lot easier to do with online tools.

The following actions are good starting points:

- **Hold a customer engagement summit** This should involve people at all levels of the organisation. Unilever India did this, requiring everyone in the organisation to spend 50 hours with customers, put their ideas in a database and then discuss how to act on them.[2]

---

[1] Based on Gulati, R., 'Silo busting: how to execute on the promise of customer focus', *Harvard Business Review,* Vol. 85, no. 5, May 2007.

[2] http://www.managementexchange.com/story/project-bushfire-focussing-might-entire-organization-consumer

■ **Create a customer engagement council** This should act as an ongoing forum for focusing the attention of management on customer engagement. At Yell, such a body reduced customer complaints by 70 per cent over 18 months.

■ **Create a listening centre** You can monitor, and respond, where appropriate. At O2, the CEO met with customer-facing call centre staff weekly to hear directly what customers were saying.

Customer insight and value

Customer insight means that you understand who your customers are, how they behave, and increasingly why they behave as they do. It consists of both qualitative and quantitative intelligence. It is also in some degree predictive as well as prescriptive: good customer insight helps to understand and define customer patterns so that you can better predict how they will behave, what will influence their behaviour, and how you might get them to change their behaviour in your favour.

There are many different ways you can increase your customer insight. Start by understanding the basics.

exercise

Try analysing your customer data with your sales transactions to understand the following:

■ Who are your customers?

■ How many do you have?

■ Is your customer base growing or declining?

■ How many do you gain each year?

■ Lose each year?

■ What is the retention rate?

■ What is the average revenue per customer?

■ Is it growing?

Repeat the analysis by product line and geography. Then look at the data by product, by industry sector, by size of customer. Identify those who buy more than one product. You will see some behaviours emerging.

It is very likely the behaviours will look like this:

■ If your total customer numbers aren't growing, you may be losing more customers out the back door, who are more valuable, than you are gaining through the front door.

■ Your retention rates and average spends will improve the more products customers purchase from you – retention will be up to 10 points higher and customers will spend up to 10 times more!

■ You will have a small number of high-value customers and a large number of low-value customers. Typically the high-value customers will buy more than one product, may buy in more than one geography, and will be with you longer.

■ There will be certain industry sectors where you are more popular than others – the top three may be over half your business; equally, other metrics such as size of business or location may be important as drivers of customer value.

■ Products will also have differing take-ups, values and retention rates, with many likely to be very low.

There are likely to be some uncomfortable truths when you delve into customer data. At least one 'sacred cow' will be challenged. That's why the trick is to make it look and feel as simple as possible. Even if the underlying data is complicated – the insight shouldn't be! In fact, insights need to be actionable as well as relevant. It's best to overlay any quantitative data with stories about the relevant customer groups.

Once you have customer intelligence, certain patterns emerge. Finding real-life stories can help to uncover the potential meaning and use for your insights. Many organisations are very sophisticated at using customer insights well – P&G, Tesco and O2, for example:

> **Tesco Clubcard** Tesco former CEO Terry Leahy rightly credits Tesco's Clubcard for its meteoric rise from also-ran UK supermarket to global retailing powerhouse. Tesco collected, analysed and gained insights from their customer database, so that they were able to understand and influence customer behaviour to guide their stores' selection

and managers' behaviours. If you are a regular online shopper and suddenly stop, they will send you a huge incentive to rejoin.

O2 Customer Reward Mobile phone companies typically focused on acquisition rather than retention. O2 realised this and rewarded customers for staying, building their affinity for the brand and identifying customers who might lapse and preventing them from doing so. It was a bold gamble that paid off, as they gained up to sixty times more in value by not losing the customers than they spent in rewarding their loyalty.[3]

P&G Says P&G North American President Melanie Healey: 'Our mantra in North America is "just one more and a healthy core". If I take the 8 to 9 per cent of households in North America that have 10 or 11 P&G brands, what if I got the 8 to 9 per cent to 10 to 11 per cent or I got that 10 or 11 brands to grow to 12 to 13 brands in those households? That "just one more" is equivalent to about $7 billon in growth.'[4]

Come up with similar examples from businesses and organisations you know that have grown by focusing on customer value. Use these to convince your team and boss to do the same.

Customer lifetime value

Collecting the right kind of customer insight will help you calculate a key metric – customer lifetime value. There are different ways to calculate this, but all are aimed at helping you decide how much resource to devote to each customer. Customer lifetime value should be a key consideration in your acquisition and retention strategies (see below).

A great example concerns the Pampers brand. Pampers invests a lot of time and money reaching mothers in hospitals. Although the Pampers hospital product might not make money in itself, it introduces the

---

[3] Talk by Matthew Key, O2 CEO.
[4] Melanie Healey interview, 30 Sept. 2011, AP interview.

brand to mothers in an environment they trust, at a time when they are prone to accepting advice. Similarly, banks target students, as once bank accounts are chosen, consumers are often sluggish about switching. All these companies typically have sophisticated means for tracking when customers are likely to switch. Other measures are valuable. The extra business certain customers give you via referrals may be worth more than the customer lifetime value of some of your most prized clients. Using a 'Net Promoter Score' (discussed in Chapter 13) will help you to define your brand advocates.

In recent years, many companies have invested a significant amount in customer relationship management (CRM) marketing and systems. It can go wrong, however.

Specifically:

■ Poor use of CRM systems can lead to targeting the wrong customers or driving people away with over-done marketing campaigns.

■ There is a limit to the amount of sophistication that CRM databases can provide – and they are often not used correctly, leading to 'bad data'.

■ Are customer relationships in themselves worthwhile? Manage customer value not relationship; sometimes CRM can become an excuse to do the latter with very little impact on the former.

It is perhaps the last point which is the most important. Whilst it is true that there are a number of examples of businesses which rely upon close relationships with their customers, equally, there are a large number of organisations where a strong relationship *per se* with the customer does not lead to better customer retention or sales. For example, supermarket shoppers are likely to be far more interested in price, selection and a convenient location than developing a 'good relationship' with a superstore. [5]

The net lesson here is focus on managing your customer value and not just your customer relationship.

---

[5] Abram, J. and Hawkes, P., *Seven Myths of Customer Management: How to be Customer Driven without being Customer Led*, John Wiley, 2003.

Customer acquisition, retention and segmentation

Many businesses spend too much time and money acquiring new customers and not enough retaining existing customers. Obviously new firms have to acquire many customers, but it is important to remember that it is usually cheaper to retain a customer than acquire a new one. There are several advantages:

■ Lower customer management costs over time.

■ Purchases increasing in value as the customer buys more from you over time – and becomes less price sensitive.

■ Higher retention rates and more recommendations.[6]

Often, up to 75 per cent of marketing budgets are earmarked for customer acquisition. Try reversing this and spend 75 per cent on retention.[7] Many organisations also neglect cross-selling opportunities. If you understand your customer needs you can identify related products they will benefit from. You can see examples of this in the insurance market, where companies who give you car insurance are more than happy to discount their home insurance offer to you.

It is also important to think about different customer groups and how you target and message them. For example, two customers are buying management and leadership training. One is a managing director of a small business; another is a university student studying business. Their reasons for purchase, and expectations, will be very different. Your efforts should be based on the customers' perspective rather than your own internal perspective. In other words, don't make it about you, make it about them.

Don't over-complicate. When I was at Yell we focused on three groups – gold, silver and bronze, based on the return on investment certain customers got from their ads in the directory. At Mars, we created three segments which looked at the relationship between the pet and the

---

[6] Buttle, F., *Customer Relationship Management: Concepts and Technologies*, 2nd edn, Butterworth Heinemann, 2009, p. 261.

[7] Ibid., p. 257.

owner as a determinant of feeding habits and positioned our brands accordingly. Keep the number of segments to a minimum – three to five is about right.

Sometimes you define segments in terms of where you want to gain business. Often it will help to target a group of users with a specific message to encourage them to switch – this is what happens when you buy one brand at the grocery store and they give you a coupon for money off a competitive brand.

exercise

Who are your key customer segments? How do you tailor your message and benefits to meet their needs? Who are your key future customers? What might you need to do to encourage them to become users of your product or service?

Suppliers

In a similar way to customer management, when suppliers are treated as partners they can also become important assets, whereas managing suppliers solely to get the best price can lead to highly negative consequences.

Begin with one particular supplier with whom you already have a good relationship, or an emerging, forward-looking supplier. Identify a partnering champion within your organisation – someone at senior level who will become responsible for laying the foundation of the partnership and making it work in the start-up phase. Partnerships allow organisations to work together to take advantage of market opportunities and to respond to customer needs more effectively than they could in isolation. Partnering means:

■ sharing risk with others and trusting them to act in joint best interests;

■ a 'strategic fit' between partners so that objectives match and action plans show synergy;

- finding complementary skills, competences and resources in partners;
- sharing information which may previously have been considered privileged or confidential;
- involving suppliers at the earliest stages in the design of a new product;
- inviting participation to improve relationships and find mutual cost benefits;
- encouraging partners to put forward ideas that will benefit both parties.

You could also consider starting a supply-chain network. This involves broadening these partnerships to include your suppliers' suppliers and your customers. Take a look at your supply chain. Are there any areas of waste or duplication? Are there any steps you can simplify or that aren't necessary?

Do not forget that everyone in the supply chain needs to generate profits in order to sustain their businesses. Exercising pressure on suppliers to reduce prices, rather than seeking to share the gains of cost reduction, can ultimately be counter-productive (indeed, many blame the horsemeat scandal in Europe on relentless pressure on suppliers to cut corners on cost).

Gaining real commitment from all members of the supply chain means that total costs can be kept to a minimum to the benefit of everyone. Trust takes time to develop and can be quickly lost, but it is worth it. This is especially true as more supply chains are becoming transparent, and more customers are concerned that their product's supply chains are safe, ethical and sustainable. (There is an app that scans a code and immediately reveals whether a supply chain measures up to these criteria or whether there are gaps.)

Measuring supplier quality

It is important to monitor the quality of your suppliers. There is an almost infinite number of ways of doing this, but some of the most common are:

■ **Inspection** – whilst this is not a value-added activity, it is a useful and basic way of gauging quality.

■ **Statistical quality control** – this is based upon sampling and saves time and money which would go on inspecting every single item or product.

■ **Six Sigma** – this is a way of improving the satisfaction of customers by reducing defects. The main method used is Define, Measure, Analyse, Improve and Control (DMAIC), which employs a number of statistical tools, with the overall aim of driving up quality.[8]

There are a huge number of quality control methods, and the one most suitable for your organisation will vary according to a number of factors, such as organisation size. Remember, if you don't monitor the value and quality in your supply chain you may be exposing yourself to significant risk – as the recent horsemeat scandal in Europe demonstrated.

Of course, you also need to buy well from your suppliers. In order to facilitate better buying, make sure you understand your own organisation – what is important to each department in terms of the supply of goods and services? Compile a purchase history, and use this to become a proactive buyer. A clear understanding of the purchase history will enable you to negotiate better deals with suppliers by giving them an indication of the volumes they can expect over the year.

Also, understand the number of suppliers you have in a given area. I once had more marketing services suppliers than people in the marketing department! Obviously this wasn't very efficient or effective.

Here are four tips:

1 Evaluate potential suppliers by finding out what you can about them, such as their turnover and profitability and who their major customers are.

2 Maintain good relationships with suppliers. Keep meetings rather than constantly rescheduling. If you have budget limits, share them.

---

[8] Lysons, K. and Farrington, B., *Purchasing and Supply Chain Management*, Pearson, 2006, pp. 286–9.

3 Compare them with competitors. Try to get at least three quotes for every major purchase decision. You'll be surprised at how much costs vary. But compare offers carefully, as the cheapest is not always the best.

4 Finally, keep records. It may be that your auditors will need to see transactions. This is especially important in light of the recent legislation in many countries on bribery.[9]

Strategic alliance and partnerships

The rise of the internet and the democracy of information have made collaborating much easier, and more international. It is redefining how companies work together. This has given rise to the concept of the 'frenemy' – an enemy with whom you collaborate. A great example is Amazon and authors. Whilst Amazon has often been referred to as the enemy of book publishers, it has, through Kindle, enabled authors to bypass publishers and self publish. Ditto Apple and apps, or You Tube and music. Open source technologies mean it is easier than ever to collaborate. So how can you take advantage of the new age of collaboration?

Identifying potential partners

Use the stakeholder exercise described earlier. Those with high interest and high influence are likely to be sources of strategic partners for your organisation or project. Consider, too, if there is a way of empowering those with high interest but low influence by giving them more power. A great example of this was P&G opening up innovation to external partners through establishing a 'Connect & Develop' function. Crowd sourcing is also a way of enabling individuals interested in a given development to band together and fund good ideas. Sites like Kick-starter are growing in influence and have funded new ventures. Finally, partnering with small independent retailers and giving them more clout has been fundamental to the success of sites like Zulily, notonthehighstreet.com and Tsonga.com. All of these bypass normal business models to offer products and services direct to customers.

---

[9] Based on *Effective Purchasing*, CMI Checklist Series, no. 146, 2011.

Equally, industries banding together and working side by side have established new and more collaborative ways of working. Silicon Roundabout in London is a famous example. Some 800 technology start-ups exist side by side, sharing problems and supporting each other. They have attracted £50 million in funding from the government to build more public spaces in the area. The innovation is fuelled by informal encounters over coffee, where a chance interaction can lead to deals being done, or productive business relationships. There is a sense of community, and people will often share approaches to problems rather than keep things secret. Such informality can lead to a highly creative environment.

exercise

> Using your stakeholder map above, identify potential partners for your key project from a set of potential competitors or opponents. Understand their motivations and how best to approach them. Then make a plan to do so, to see if you could partner in a way that's beneficial to you both.

Managing the Board of Directors

One of the stakeholder groups many managers know least about is their board of directors. Boards are there for fundamentally two reasons: one is governance, and the other is guidance, also known as stewardship. Governance is about ensuring the company complies with principles of how it is run, is well-managed, legal and ethical and has a good approach to risk management. Guidance, or stewardship, is about offering support and encouraging ideas, as well as challenging assumptions to bring out the best thinking. Run by the Chairman, the best boards offer both. What they don't do is management.

Boards typically meet between six and twelve times per year for a day. Directors are not hands-on and will not know the day-to-day details – nor should they. However they will usually be asked to approve strategy as well as major investment decisions such as new capital programmes or takeovers.

Therefore, if you are asked to present to the board, or need to attend board meetings, here are some tips.

1 Recognise the board's role is governance and stewardship.

2 Decide if your presentation is addressing one or the other and craft it accordingly. Always clear the presentation with your executive colleagues – don't surprise them at the board.

3 Ask for input and expect questions, guidance and advice. Make sure you can give the reasons for your view and that they are documented and well founded.

4 Don't draw the board down into detail and endless papers. Make sure you stick to the relevant risk you are describing or the overarching decision, or advice you need.

5 Be professional and discreet. It's not the best idea to divulge what you think about everyone to a board member. That said, they can offer great insights into the thinking of the CEO.

I once learned from a non-executive director that the CEO was thinking of getting rid of my role. While it didn't prevent him from doing so, at least it gave me a 'heads up'!

Top tips, pitfalls and takeaways

Top tips

- Have a plan for every stakeholder group; it's not political, it's part of management.

- Draw up a stakeholder matrix, plotting interest against degree of influence, and use it to shape your stakeholder management.

- Take the trouble to understand customer value, not just customer relationships – in some sectors, the 'relationship' is never going to be deep.

- Create a listening centre and a customer engagement council.

- Maintain continual attention to the quality of suppliers.

- Maintain real engagement with the supply chain – this can result in savings and benefits for everyone, including customers.

Top pitfalls

- Too much engagement in stakeholder relationships as an end in itself, neglecting the commercial objectives.

- Over-complicating customer segmentation – between three and five categories is about right.

- Over-promoting yourself to stakeholders with high influence, but little interest.

- Completely ignoring the low-influence, low-interest stakeholders; their impact may grow suddenly and unexpectedly – for example, through a new lobbying group.

Top takeaways

■ Managing stakeholders, including external stakeholders, is a fundamental part of management.

■ Managing stakeholders can be overdone, but if it is neglected, this can be disastrous.

■ A customer-centred business is going to be the most successful, but it may require a cultural and organisational transformation.

■ Customers should be a key input in any strategy development. In a commercial organisation, customers are the people who provide the revenue to keep the business going.

Managing money, resources and technology

17

Project management basics

What you will learn in this chapter

- The A-B-Cs of good project and initiative management
- Techniques for tracking projects and setting milestones
- How to create a master plan

Project management is something every manager has to do. Projects can be big or small, strategic or operational, aimed at cost-cutting, growth or process improvement. They typically involve people, technology and money. Managing projects is about prioritising, defining an objective, establishing a process and roadmap to achieve the objective using defined resources, timescales and success measures. It is not enough to deliver a project on time and on budget – although this is essential. It is also important to deliver the outcome the project intended. I have seen many projects managed on time and on budget that do not deliver their intended outcomes. For this reason, I like to refer to projects as initiatives rather than projects.

An initiative implies proactively taking steps towards a new or better way of doing something. It also implies an outcome. Whether you are managing projects or initiatives it is vital that you focus on the business reasons for doing something before you do it, and compile a business case with defined benefits and costs in numeric terms. Make sure, too, that your projects are linked to the overall strategy of your organisation.

There are many frameworks for successful project or initiative management. One popular model is based on studying failed projects. It identifies ten factors that contribute to a project's success:

1 Clearly defined objectives.

2 Good planning and control methods.

3 Good-quality project managers.

4 Good management support.

5 Enough time and resources.

6 Commitment by all.

7 High user involvement.

8 Good communication.

9 Good project organisation and structure.

10 Being able to stop a project.[1]

`case study`   A project managed well: The London Olympics

There is a good reason for the success of the London 2012 Olympic and Paralympic Games. I've heard the leaders of the Olympics, like Sir John Armitt, head of the ODA, talking about the great project management. From forward planning, to shared and clear objectives and structures, to inclusive communication and training, to spotting key issues like transport and having excellent contingency planning, such as the British Armed forces stepping in to help with security; everything was well thought through, linked and planned as part of a larger 'legacy-led' Olympics. Behind the success were years of great and hard work by lots of stakeholders. But because they all shared the same objectives, and stuck to good project management practice, they all delivered. In fact, it was voted one of the best-run organisations in a recent poll.[2]

---

[1] Chartered Management Institute, Elbeik and Thomas's successful project requirements, Management Models Series.

[2] 2012 CMI poll of best-run organisations.

A project managed poorly

One company I know spent several hundred thousand pounds and loads of global project and IT team time installing an LMS (Learning Management System). The LMS was supposed to enable customers to book directly online. But it wasn't really needed by this business because over 90 per cent of the learning was done offline. Moreover, online booking and payment wasn't the core function of the LMS so much time and money was spent adapting the system to enable online booking and payment. The hybrid LMS was clunky and didn't perform very well, so almost no one in the company used it – instead, they found workarounds and invented new 'hybrid' procedures as they weren't supposed to use the old system. So there were no standard processes; hence reading the business around the world became almost impossible as everyone did things differently.

This project suffered from a fundamental mismatch between the objective (online booking) and the 'solution' (online learning) from the outset. Everyone knew that, but no one wanted to stop the project because several hundred thousand pounds had been spent already. Finally, a new manager came in and stopped the project. But it was a difficult time for all.

exercise

Look at your projects. Are you clear on the link to your organisation's strategy? Is there a measurable benefit and awareness of costs? Is there a clear outcome and business case? Do you fulfil the ten criteria of successful project management?

Managing projects for outcomes

It helps if you take an outcome-focused approach to managing your projects. Doing this means you start with the 'end in mind' and set your activities and goals accordingly. The six steps listed here will help you to ensure you don't get swallowed up in process management and keep your outcomes in mind.

Prioritise objectives, and stick to them

Many projects don't succeed because of poorly set objectives, or objectives that alter – also known as 'scope creep'. In order to track a project successfully for outcomes you have to be quite rigorous in setting these early on. You also have to ensure you don't have too many, and guard against changing them at whim.

Plan backwards to set a critical path

It is often useful to work backwards in order to create good timing and a roadmap. Once you know what your outcome is, and by when you need to achieve it, you can identify the steps that need to happen and in what order: a critical path schedule.

Not all activities are equal. Some are essential to the success of the project. For example, if you are launching a new product, you cannot do it without a pack to put it in. If that pack takes 18 months to produce, then even if the product only takes 12 months, you cannot launch it. Similarly, in software projects, upgrades are often timed to releases. If your upgrade is not on the schedule of releases, then you won't be able to launch it until it is.

Communicate a clear plan with clear accountabilities

Projects need to be broken down into tasks – your critical path schedule will help you identify them. All of the tasks need to be assigned to people in the project team. Everyone involved needs to know what they are expected to do and by when for a project to succeed. That's why clear communication and clear expectations are essential for success.

Allow for contingencies and risks

You should also build extra time into your plan to allow for unexpected events. The best approach is to identify risks up front, and incorporate contingency planning. It is typically a few extra weeks or months to compensate for the unexpected and keep things on track.

To prevent running over time and budget, it is important to keep track of the project throughout its life cycle. Irrespective of the scale of the project, it typically goes through four stages: initiation/start-up; planning and organisation; implementation with monitoring; and completion and evaluation.[3] It is helpful to understand this project life cycle. The project manager should oversee the entire process.

Agree milestones

You should mark key milestones in your project plan: moments when you review the project with your boss or other key stakeholders before proceeding to the next phase. Examples are when you are moving to a test market or proof of concept, or when you later move to a phased implementation. The last phase is the review and evaluation – one that most often gets left out, but it can be very valuable.

It's always a good idea to review your team's progress at each milestone to ensure you're still adhering to your objectives and that you have the right people in place. It may be a good idea to switch team members in different phases, for example from developing, where customer insight and product development will be key, to launching, where sales and marketing will be important, to monitoring and evaluation, where finance may have more of a leading role. If you are way off track at your key milestone it's really important to communicate that. Equally, if you are ahead of schedule, then celebrate. If you need help, ask for it! It's also a great time to review how the team is working and whether or not the project is still meeting its objectives. If you plough on despite not being sure of these things, there is a high chance of failure. If the project continues to miss its milestones, is not meeting its objectives, or is unclear, it may be time to stop it, and launch a critical review. Too many projects develop their own lives and carry on regardless.

Monitor

An essential part of project management is monitoring the status of projects. The Gantt chart is a commonly used project scheduling tool, which provides a visual representation of the project plan.[4]

1 List all your activities. You may want to start from the endpoint and work backwards, especially if you have a non-missable deadline, like

[3] Chartered Management Institute, Project life cycle, Management Models Series.
[4] Chartered Management Institute, Gantt chart, Management Models Series.

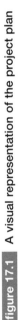

ID	●	Task Name	Duration	Start	Finish
1		PHASE 2 - CMI CRM PROJECT - PRO IMPLEMENTATION PLAN	614 days?	Mon 20/04/09	Mon 12/09/11
2	■		1 day?	Mon 20/04/09	Mon 20/04/09
3	■	Contracts signed	1 day	Wed 02/06/10	Wed 02/06/10
4					
5		Project setup	10 days	Thu 03/06/10	Wed 16/06/10
6		Create environments (at ProTech)	1 day	Thu 03/06/10	Thu 03/06/10
7		Create DBs	1 day	Fri 04/06/10	Fri 04/06/10
8		Base configuration	5 days	Mon 07/06/10	Fri 11/06/10
9		Test base configuration	3 days	Mon 14/06/10	Wed 16/06/10
10		STAGE 1: PROJECT DELIVERY	117 days	Wed 16/06/10	Fri 26/11/10
11	■	Start date	0 days	Wed 16/06/10	Wed 16/06/10
12	■	Data migration - General employer data	14 days	Tue 27/07/10	Fri 13/08/10
13		Data migration meetings	1 day	Tue 27/07/10	Tue 27/07/10
14		Data migration coding	10 days	Wed 28/07/10	Tue 10/08/10
15		Data migration testing (at ProTech)	3 days	Wed 11/08/10	Fri 13/08/10
16		Part 1: Sales and marketing	22.5 days	Wed 16/06/10	Fri 16/07/10
17		Configuration	10 days	Wed 16/06/10	Tue 29/06/10
18		Development	7.5 days	Wed 30/06/10	Fri 09/07/10
19		Testing	5 days	Fri 09/07/10	Fri 16/07/10
20		Part 2: Marketing London	15.5 days	Fri 16/07/10	Fri 06/08/10
21		Configuration	3 days	Fri 16/07/10	Wed 21/07/10
22		Development	6 days	Wed 21/07/10	Thu 29/07/10
23		Data migration	1.5 days	Thu 29/07/10	Fri 30/07/10
24		Testing	5 days	Mon 02/08/10	Fri 16/08/10
25		Part 3: Regional support	16.5 days	Fri 02/07/10	Mon 26/07/10
26		Configuration	6 days	Fri 02/07/10	Mon 12/07/10
27		Development	3 days	Mon 12/07/10	Thu 15/07/10
28		Data migration	2.5 days	Thu 15/07/10	Mon 19/07/10
29		Testing	5 days	Tue 20/07/10	Mon 26/07/10
30		Part 4: Regional managers (excluding remote events)	14 days	Tue 27/07/10	Fri 13/08/10
31		Configuration	6 days	Tue 27/07/10	Tue 03/08/10
32		Development	4 days	Wed 04/08/10	Mon 09/08/10
33		Testing	4 days	Tue 10/08/10	Fri 13/08/10
34		Part 5: Membership marketing	1.5 days	Mon 16/08/10	Tue 17/08/10
35		Configuration	1 days	Mon 16/08/10	Mon 16/08/10
36		Development	0 days	Mon 16/08/10	Mon 16/08/10
37		Testing	0.5 days	Tue 17/08/10	Tue 17/08/10
38		Testing	5 days	Tue 17/08/10	Tue 24/08/10
39		System test	5 days	Tue 17/08/10	Tue 24/08/10
40	■	Delivery	5 days	Fri 10/09/10	Fri 17/09/10

June 2010 | 30 | 02 | 05 | 08 | 11 | 14 | 17 | 20 | 23 | 26 | 29

16/06

figure 17.1   A visual representation of the project plan

the Olympics Opening Ceremony. So start with your endpoint, then list the activities that you need to do in order to achieve that project.

2 Estimate the amount of time each activity will take. Be realistic. If your project involves lots of sign-offs and agreements with others then build in a lot of time for coordinating diaries, or else find a more efficient method. If you have very long lead-time items, pay special attention to these. Always make contingency plans.

3 Put the activities in order. Where things can happen simultaneously note that. However, pay special attention to dependencies. For example, if you cannot install the new packaging line until you have hired and trained the crew to run it, then factor that in. It's best to try to eliminate as many dependencies as possible, or at least have risk mitigation plans for them. In the example – can you identify another short-term personnel solution if your crew isn't recruited in time? Could other part-time workers be trained just in case?

4 Chunk the activities into sections and highlight the critical milestones where you wish to pause and review. Equally, you may wish to highlight those activities on the critical path, such as key management reviews, test results and research.

5 Draw a picture using Excel, Microsoft or other software. When finished it will look like Figure 17.1.

Other methods

The Red, Amber, Green 'traffic light' approach adopted by the RAG Reporting project management model is another useful tool for project management. To use this, simply add in green for on-track, amber for off-track on one parameter but on-track on others, and red for off-track on critical parameters or off-track on the majority of the items. Then list your plan to get the project back on track. Here is an example:

Project   Status/Progress/Issues   R-A-G Rating   Steps to resolve[5]

Additional common techniques include Programme Evaluation and Review Techniques (PERT) and Critical Path Analysis (CPA). [6]

---

[5] Chartered Management Institute, RAG reporting, Management Models Series.
[6] *Managing Projects*, CMI Checklist Series, no. 35, rev. Nov. 2011, p. 3.

The overriding point is to have a method for visualising and tracking project progress. If you are having to oversee many different projects, then you will also wish to have an initiative master plan, which will track all the key projects in terms of their timing, revenue, cost, profit and other critical path items, such as supply chain.

How to create a master plan

Initiative master plans are often very detailed and require keen eyesight to read, but they are rigorously used to provide a single-page overview. They should basically be the same as your Strategy Implementation Roadmap (see Chapter 11) but mapped in more detail. You put time across the top and the various initiatives and their milestones down the side.

Pulling together all your projects or initiatives in one place is a powerful exercise. It allows you and your team to take a look at what people are doing, and what they will deliver when. If you also classify each project by of the amount of revenue or profit delivered, or benefits if you are in the public sector (you can do this on a scale of Low–Medium–High) as well as the amount of time and resource required (again using a scale of Low–Medium–High), you will end up with an overall Initiative Master Plan that you can prioritise.

Mapping out projects in this way will also help you to spot opportunities to combine or streamline initiatives that overlap, and pull together activities that should be linked but aren't. For example, if you are doing research into healthcare, running a healthcare seminar and launching a healthcare LinkedIn group, all at different times, it would be more sensible to pull these projects together into a single 'healthcare launch' rather than do them separately as a series of stand-alone projects.

These plans help to ensure that major projects don't conflict with one another for timings or the deployment of critical resources. It's also important to ensure your initiative master plan has enough in it to achieve your revenue, cost and profit targets. If not, you may have an identified 'gap' which you will need to fill. But at least if it's identified and visible you can try to close the gap by generating more revenue or cutting your costs.

Finally, you can review these plans regularly to ensure everything is on track or take action if it isn't. Adding in an R-A-G rating, described earlier, for projects on your master plan allows you to do this easily.

Ask your team to identify the top three to five projects. Make certain you have a visual method for tracking them, such as a Gantt chart. Pull together an initiative master plan of all your top projects to see how they all stack up in terms of outcomes, timings and deliverables. Do they make sense or can you eliminate, combine or simplify some of these? How do they fit with your overall strategy?

Top tips, pitfalls and takeaways

Top tips

■ Always be very clear about who is doing what by when if you are managing a project. Giving people clarity will save a lot of time, trouble, money and rework.

■ Always make contingency plans.

Top pitfall

■ Project management can become all about updating the Gantt charts and the R-A-G review and not about the outcomes or the steps truly necessary to make the project successful. Sometimes these steps include stopping the project, or switching the team or the project manager.

Top takeaway

■ Having some sort of system to track key milestones and visualise the steps is a good way to plan projects. If you have multiple projects you will also need to keep track of all of them in a master plan.

18

Managing budgets and other financials

What you will learn in this chapter

- ■ The basics of good budgeting and forecasting
- ■ How to read a P&L in management accounts
- ■ Popular financial measures you need to know
- ■ Balance sheet basics

Unless you are a technology or design genius, you are unlikely to progress too far in management without a firm grasp of finance. The fact that 52 out of 100 FTSE CEOs are ex-CFOs or accountants should tell you something. (By the way, arguably this is why we have too much focus on cost cutting and short-term profits and not enough on growth, job creation and innovation – but that is another story.) My advice is to always lobby for 'P&L' (profit and loss) responsibility at some point in your career if you aspire to run something one day.

There are many great short courses and books on finance for non-financial managers – get one. This chapter cannot cover all aspects, but it describes some important disciplines, and explains why they matter. Remember: finance is your friend! It helps you to argue your case in terms that everyone understands and respects. My advice is to partner with your finance manager early in your career. You will benefit from his or her wisdom, and your partnership will help the finance colleague become more connected to the commercial and operational aspects of the organisation. It is win–win!

Budgets and forecasts

Managing a budget, like managing people and projects, is one of the fundamental tasks of management. A budget is a clear statement of income or revenue and expense for a given period, usually a year, broken down by month and quarter-years into targets and activity, such as projects or organisational departments. Learning how to forecast the income, keep track of the costs and project the margins are all key management skills.

One of the very first tasks a new brand assistant is given at P&G is managing the budget. You are told not to overspend under any circumstances. It creates a very good discipline early on about the need to set a realistic budget, and track expenditure against it. It also makes you feel responsible for the money being spent.

A basic budget looks like the example in Figure 18.1.

Review the budget on a monthly basis to identify the discrepancy between the forecast and the actual income and expenditure. When

The Good Banana Company	Period			Year to date					Full year	
Financial year 2012/13	Actual	Budget	Var	Actual	Budget	Var	Prior Yr	Var	Budget	Prior Yr
Gross sales	0.83	0.75	0.08	9.17	9.33	(0.17)	8.43	0.73	10.83	9.20
Trade expenditure	(0.04)	(0.03)	(0.01)	(0.46)	(0.48)	0.02	(0.46)	0.00	(0.54)	(0.50)
Net sales	0.79	0.72	0.07	8.71	8.85	(0.14)	7.98	0.73	10.29	8.70
COGS	(0.29)	(0.25)	(0.04)	(3.21)	(3.29)	0.08	(3.39)	0.18	(3.79)	(3.70)
Gross margin	0.50	0.47	0.03	5.50	5.56	(0.08)	5.04	0.46	6.50	5.50
Advertising and promotion	(0.04)	(0.03)	(0.01)	(0.46)	(0.48)	0.02	(0.46)	0.00	(0.54)	(.050)
Net contribution	0.46	0.44	0.02	5.04	5.08	(0.04)	4.58	0.46	5.96	5.00
Staff costs	(0.27)	(0.25)	(0.02)	(2.93)	(2.97)	0.03	(2.75)	(0.18)	(3.47)	(3.00)
Property costs	(0.05)	(0.05)	0.00	(0.55)	(0.55)	0.00	(0.55)	0.00	(0.65)	(0.80)
Admin & other overheads	(0.04)	(0.03)	(0.01)	(0.46)	(0.48)	0.02	(0.92)	0.46	(0.54)	(1.00)
Net profit	0.08	0.11	(0.03)	0.92	0.86	0.05	0.83	0.09	1.08	0.90

figure 18.1 **A basic budget sheet**

setting a budget, ensure you base it on a solid understanding of the facts when you are linking it to your strategy. Again, the SMART acronym is useful (Specific, Measurable, Achievable, Relevant and Time). For example, it is no use having a strategy that says you are going to double the sales of a particular product that is in a declining market segment, with no investment in innovation or sales; and even with such investment, it may not be feasible. Doing a thorough review of the business prior to budgeting allows you to analyse sales patterns and other dynamics. That is much better than arbitrarily setting numerical targets. Understanding how your budget can be broken down into market share, distribution points, number of customers and average value for customer gives you solid ground to stand upon and will boost your confidence and that of your team in your ability to deliver.

The typical method for preparing budgets is to look at last year and add or subtract something for expected growth or increase in costs or revenues. This is called incremental budgeting. Once you have prepared a base budget based on the trends of last year, it's time to identify the initiatives you have to change those trends. You will need enough new projects to deliver more income. In the example in Figure 18.1, the base business is projected to decline by 2%, to £10 million, in line with the trend of the last five years. So in order to prevent that, the team has added in £500,000-worth of new initiatives which will deliver growth and take the budget to £10.5m. The same is true of costs. If the team decides they need to save £100,000, they will need a slate of projects in order to achieve the savings.

Usually it's best to use a zero-base budgeting process, which means looking at what you actually need rather than what you currently spend. Sometimes it's best to do the whole budget on this basis – expenditure that isn't adding value can be diverted to new projects.

Forecasts

Financial forecasts help a business to budget for the year ahead. Make sure that you only have 'one version of the truth'. It is important to understand who is responsible for a revenue or cost target and that this is transparent and agreed. I have witnessed unscrupulous managers deliberately obfuscate their forecasts so that their colleagues didn't really know what was going on.

I have never been in a company that hit its forecast exactly; don't let forecasting become an end in itself. In order to respond quickly to unforeseen events, you will need to introduce interim forecasts rather than relying on a yearly forecast. Most businesses will re-forecast two to four times a year, sometimes more.

The ten basics of good budgeting

1   **Link budgets to strategy** Focus on the organisation's objectives to consider how your budget needs to be changed. If you have a clear strategy, your budget should fall out of it as year one. In other words, the revenue, costs, profit and cash you generate in year one should be the annual budget plan. Equally, if your initiatives and projects are the right ones, your master plan will contain the main drivers of your budget in terms of changes to costs and revenues, and profits.

2   **Analyse and use data: the budget review** Every year at P&G and Mars each brand and business unit did a thorough business review of what worked and what didn't, based on a thorough analysis of past data; not just financial but market share, consumer research and other metrics. This analysis was expressed as a series of conclusions and recommendations for the coming year. This document was widely circulated. It forced everyone to use the same data in analysing and setting next year's budget. It is a valuable discipline.

3   **Ensure you have growth or change initiatives to address the findings and recommendations of your budget review** Analyse the trends. If segments have been declining at 10 per cent per year, it is unrealistic to expect them to suddenly turn around without a programme. It is best to forecast a continuation of trends in the market – perhaps even an acceleration of those trends if you are dealing with something systemic, like the switch from print to digital. Make sure your plans are tangible and credible: don't set a budget that says we'll double the product sales but do nothing differently. It may be necessary to spend today in order to make cost savings later – for example, by increasing your online presence.

4 **Line up revenue and costs** It is vital that you can link revenues and costs in order to understand profit. Too often the revenues are set in one area and the costs in another department or area. Work with your business team to fully understand the linkages between the two. In the case of costs that cannot be clearly allocated, such as personnel working on different projects, agree a way of tracking them, such as percentage of sales. But look too at the activities of the people to ensure they are adding value. Your revenue should always equal more than your costs and grow at a higher rate than your costs. This simple rule is typically ignored in companies in trouble. It can help to set a financial shape – such as growing your revenues at twice the rate of your costs. For example, if your revenue, or topline, is growing at 6 per cent and your costs are growing at 3 per cent you will make more money. Conversely, if your revenue is growing at 3 per cent and your costs are growing at 6 per cent you will make less money. Simple!

5 **Focus on value-added spending** Carefully examine the processes and practices which provide value for the organisation and the end user of your product or service. Only support projects and initiatives that can demonstrate a return on investment, either in monetary terms or in benefits. What adds value? Which elements of your business bring in more than they take out?

6 **Cut costs that don't add value** Once you have determined which areas create value and which don't, you should then be in a position to see which areas are suitable to downscale or even eliminate. Take a strict approach to budgetary control and take hard decisions as to what can be cut. Identify the areas which are operating at a loss or don't add value to the organisation or end user. Prioritise those things which are essential and consider whether the 'nice-to-haves' are viable to continue with. Ask for evidence that expenditures are efficient, deliver a return, are used by customers or add value in some way.

7 **Keep reserves for the unexpected** No matter how carefully you plan your budget there will always be an event that is unplanned or even unprecedented. This could be an over-estimation of income or suppliers/clients failing to pay on time. Make allowances by allocating a reserve. Building a reserve or retained profit is imperative

if you want the business to grow, re-investing it in order to move the company forward.

8 **Set a stretch target: fuel success and cap failure** It's good to encourage your colleagues to over-achieve without penalising them for missing their budget. If you set a realistic budget, make sure you also set a 'stretch' target. It is typically measured in extra income and/or profit. People often feel freer to get excited about a stretch target, as they know they won't be penalised if they miss it, but rewarded if they achieve even half of it. In order to achieve your stretch, make sure you fuel the projects or initiatives that are working and starve those that are not. Too often people will try to fix everything.

9 **Set and measure Key Performance Indicators (KPIs)** (see also Chapter 13). Understand and measure the key drivers of your business to see if you are on track. For example, in a media or membership business, retention rates – number of renewals – are a KPI. In a food business, it may be the market share and the return on assets, as factories are capital intensive. In a retail business, it may be the average transaction value, and the number of customers who actually buy something once they enter the store. Set your KPIs according to the truly make-or-break aspects of your business, and focus on those.

10 **Don't turn budgeting into a cottage industry** It is futile to engage in endless debates over numbers with nothing underpinning them. Challenge finance directors who are re-forecasting so frequently that everyone loses track of what the original commitment was. It results in employees spending their days re-calculating and reporting budgets rather than acting to deliver them. This is a very common mistake – especially in declining companies. It is a symptom of poor strategy and execution. (See Chapters 10–11.)

Profit and loss

The P&L, or profit and loss statement, shows the summarised trading activity during a stated period. Profit and loss statements are usually prepared monthly or quarterly for internal management purposes, and we are focusing on that version here rather than the annual report or accounting version. Figure 18.2 shows a typical P&L, alongside a series

The Good Banana Company Financial year 2012/13	YTD Actual £m	% of gross sales	Prior Year £m	Variance £m
Gross sales	10.0		9.2	0.8
Trade expenditure	(0.5)	5%	(0.5)	0.0
Net sales	9.5	95%	8.7	(0.5)
COGS	(3.5)	35%	(3.7)	(0.3)
Gross margin	6.0	60%	5.5	0.5
Advertising and promotion	(0.5)	5%	(0.5)	(0.5)
Net contribution	5.5	55%	5.0	(0.5)
Staff costs	(3.2)	32%	(3.0)	(0.2)
Property	(0.6)	6%	(0.6)	0.0
Admin & other overheads	(0.5)	5%	(1.0)	(0.2)
Net profit	1.0	10%	0.9	0.1

figure 18.2   A typical profit and loss statement

of measures to look at. It's the same company whose budget we showed earlier.

1 **Look at the trends** In most profit and loss statements, figures for the current and previous year are given. Key figures for additional periods may be elsewhere in the accounts – for example three-year trends. Compare the last three years. Are sales up or down? Are costs up or down? If you compare the results figures to the budget for those years, you can see whether the targets set are being achieved.

2 **Operating profit – the profit/revenue or sales** This is the fundamental profitability of the business without considering items like interest payments, sales of businesses or plant closures. It is profit on ordinary activities expressed as a percentage of turnover. It is useful to see how attractive the margins are in a certain category. For example, the margins in food and construction are generally lower than in beauty and technology companies. If it is done pre-interest tax and depreciation it is also called EBITDA (earnings before interest, taxes, depreciation and amortisation), or EBIT (earnings before interest and tax). EBITDA is commonly used to value a company that is for sale: the purchase price is expressed as a multiple of EBITDA.

3 **Cost of sales percentage** This reveals the gross margin, which is the difference between turnover (and income) and the cost of goods or services produced or purchased (this is also called Cost of Goods Sold or Total Delivered Cost). Gross margins are affected by two things: the net sales price and the cost of producing or procuring the goods or services. If gross margins are low, it may mean that prices are being cut, or the costs of raw materials are rising, or manufacturing is inefficient. Gross margins also give you an idea of the attractiveness of a particular category. Technology companies typically have very high gross margins, as it costs little incrementally to produce the product once it is built. Conversely, if you are producing goods such as bread, gross margins are slim because raw material prices fluctuate and there is limited ability to charge more.

4 **Understand the difference between gross and net sales** Often companies sell their goods and services through distribution channels. These channels get payments or deals for listing the products. It is important to understand how much a company is paying retailers or other distributors to list and promote its products. This can be a significant factor in reducing the value of gross sales. If the trade expenses are very high it could be a sign that there is more push (promotion) than pull (consumer or business demand).

5 **Check the discretionary amount spent on advertising, promotion and selling costs** This will vary by category. In FMCG it will be in the double digits – between 10 and 20 per cent or higher; in business-to-business it will be much less – more like 2 to 5 per cent. Strong brands will invest more in advertising and promotion, and use this to drive growth, alongside constant innovation. In the digital world, many strong brands have emerged using much lower-cost marketing and selling techniques based on social media and word of mouth recommendations, helping to boost their operating margins. Advertising is almost always the first cut to be made when savings are needed. However, it is not always the wisest place, as many companies who promote during a downturn increase their market share.

6 **Look at the net contribution** This is the amount of money a brand or product contributes to the overall company, expressed as a percentage. It includes the costs of marketing and making the product

or service but excludes the fixed costs such as people and offices. The higher the net contribution, the higher the inherent profitability. If a net contribution is very high it means that that particular brand or division is subsidising less profitable brands or divisions. Sometimes that is deliberate – for example, companies may use highly profitable home markets to subsidise overseas expansion in the initial years. Similarly, profitable 'cash cow' brands and products are often used to subsidise newer, more innovative growth areas.

7   **Check overheads (sometimes called SG&A – selling, general and administration)** This is the fixed cost of the salaries of all the staff involved, alongside rental costs, and the cost of stationery, travel, etc. It's also one of the most common places to cut costs. These costs are often hard to allocate to specific products, which is why they are separated out from the other indirect costs such as advertising. Well-managed companies keep these at a minimum. I recall John Mars, the famous owner of Mars, explaining to me that he kept his overheads down at company HQ by never adding slots to the timecard holders on the wall where all employees had to clock in and out. Simple? Certainly. But very effective.

8   **Consider the overall financial shape and benchmark it against other companies and brands** Although you will not have access to internal management accounts for competitors, basic data is available from annual reports. Use it to benchmark your P&L. Are you more or less profitable? Is your gross margin lower or higher? What about advertising and selling expenses? Overheads? Net margin?

Balance sheets

Balance sheets include the balance of every account in the accounting system, aggregating all P&L accounts. An accurate balance sheet provides a sound understanding of an organisation's financial position at a given time. When compared with previous balance sheets, trends can be discerned. However, a balance sheet is a snapshot of the financial position, so it can quickly become out of date. Balance sheets must be prepared at the end of the company's financial year, but they can be prepared for internal use as and when required.

The fundamental formula of balance sheets is that all of the assets of a company must be equal to its debts + equity. It means that all of the value of the company, its assets, as described as plant and equipment, inventory, cash and accounts receivable, are equal to its debts, both short and long term, plus the amount of shareholder equity.

Assets = liabilities + shareholder equity

One of the most useful measures on a balance sheet for managers is working capital. The management of working capital involves managing inventories, accounts receivable and payable, and cash. Efficient working capital means that you are collecting your debts on time and in full, that you are drawing out the payment period to your creditors (although not by so much that they go bankrupt) and that you are managing inventories efficiently.

Business financial measures you need to know

Here is a brief compendium of commonly-used financial measures.

Evaluating financial returns

There are various different financial measures for financial returns. In my experience, payback, NPV and IRR tend to be used for new launches, whilst ROI might be used for shorter-term investments. The main thing is to have a consistent measure across the organisation so that comparisons are valid.

Here's a brief look at the most popular.

Payback: This looks at the amount of time it takes for an investment to pay back its cost in terms of additional sales it generates. It is straightforward to calculate; however, it does not allow for the fact that different investments, such as a new brand, may generate revenue over a longer period than others. Neither does it account for the time value of money.

Example: If investing in a sampling effort and a new machine costs £100,000 and generates £50,000 of new sales, it will pay back its cost in two years. So it has a two-year payback. Payback is often confused with break-even analysis – the break-even point is a point in time when total revenues equal total costs.

ROI: Similar to payback, but ROI takes into account the incremental profit generated by the investment. It is very helpful for evaluating additional expenses in adding sales people or investing in marketing. However, it still doesn't consider the time or value of money, or the total time frame of the investment.

Return on Investment (ROI) = Gains from Investment – Cost of Investment/ Cost of Investment

Example: You invest £1,000,000 in a marketing campaign you project will generate an extra £5 million in sales. You would be tempted to say it has an ROI of 500 per cent – that is, it returns 5x the initial investment. However, if you only make a 20 per cent margin on the £5 million, then your investment will only generate an extra £1 million in profit, so its ROI could be 1x the initial investment, or 100 per cent.

Net Present Value (NPV): This looks at the cash flows generated by a project as well as the timing of those flows. NPV compares the value of cash invested today to the value of that same cash in the future, taking inflation and returns into account.

Example: You buy a fruit shop to grow your fruit business. You look at the amount of cash it would take to buy the business (your outflows plus the amount invested in merging and supporting the business) versus the amount of cash you would take in (additional sales plus the amount of cash you could save by combining operations). You would then discount these cash flows over the time horizon of the investment – to account for the interest you would make on the cash if you invested it elsewhere. It might be five or ten years, as you would expect the shop to last that long. If the NPV of all the cash outflows and inflows is £600,000 and the fruit business costs £500,000, it would be a good deal. If it costs £750,000, you may balk and walk away.

Internal Rate of Return: IRR also measures cash inflows versus outflows over the time horizon of an investment, and discounts these according to the time value of money and inflation. But rather than look at the value of the cash invested today, it looks at the rate of return the project generates over time. (In effect, the IRR is what will bring the Net Present Value to zero.) If that rate of return is higher than the company could get from the average cost of its capital (i.e. borrowing from a bank or other means of raising it), then it is a good project. If it is lower than the company's cost of capital (sometimes called internal hurdle rate), then it's not. Cost of capital varies, but is typically around 7 to 8 per cent.

Investor benchmarks

Investors use balance sheets to calculate financial ratios to benchmark a company's performance. Here are some of the most popular:

ROS: Return on Sales. The amount of profit a company makes on its total sales.

ROE: Return on Equity. The amount of net income returned to shareholders divided by the total shareholders' equity.

ROE = Net income after tax/Shareholders' equity.

ROA: Return on Assets. This looks at the capital intensity of a business and how efficiently it uses its total assets to generate income. In manufacturing and heavy industries this figure will be low, because it requires huge capital investment. In software industries it will typically be higher.

ROA = Net Income after tax/Total assets (or Average Total assets)

ROCE: Return on Capital Employed. Measures efficiency and profitability of use of capital. It should always be higher than the rate at which the company borrows, otherwise shareholders' earnings will be diluted.

ROCE = Earnings before Tax/total assets – total liabilities.

P/E ratio: Price–earnings ratio. This determines whether to invest in a given stock. It is the ratio of the market price per share over the earnings per share. It is also sometimes referred to as a 'p/e multiple'. The higher the multiple, the more the market is willing to pay for the company's earnings, because they think it will continue to outperform the market.

Note: a helpful glossary can be found at: investopedia.com/terms

Top tips, pitfalls and takeaways

Top tips

- Make the Finance Director your friend.

- Use key metrics such as Return on Investment and Net Present Value, but use them appropriately and be aware of the aspects that they don't measure.

Top pitfall

- Subjecting budgeting and forecasts to too much revision, neglecting the actual business.

Top takeaway

- All managers should be financially literate, as this is the ultimate measure for commercial success and viability, and a business case must incorporate financial analysis and projection of returns.
- Know the ins and outs of building a budget and reading a P&L. Encourage benchmarking and a good understanding of the financial 'shape' of your business or organisation.

19

Understanding digital and Big Data

What you will learn in this chapter

- How to understand 'Big Data' and why it's important
- How to create Customer and Business Insight that's used not deleted
- How to appreciate your website as a powerful shop window from the user's perspective
- How to understand why IT and Thinking Digitally is for everyone

It used to be that the 'guys from IT' were geeks who sat in darkened rooms by big computer servers. No more. These days, we are all in the business of data and knowledge, and almost all of us use our website as one of our main routes to market and 'shop window'. Moreover, you won't 'get' your customer, or the possibilities of today, unless you 'get' digital. The amount of data created today is truly astronomical. Indeed, experts claim that all the words ever spoken by humans up until 2003 equals 5 exabytes of data, the amount that is now created inside of 24 hours. It's mind-boggling.[1]

In the digital age, everyone knows much more about what everyone else is doing, as the internet is totally traceable. Every website you visit, every link you click on, every transaction you complete, is recorded – with or without the users' knowledge. If you can accurately trace this

---

[1] Yates, Mick, CMI President's Lecture, 7 May 2013.

online activity and combine it with offline knowledge, you get a very compelling picture of how people behave. The implication for managers is clear: get digital or get dinosaured. This chapter explores the basics every manager needs to know.

Big Data, Little Data

Big Data, cited as one of the top ten trends by leaders such as Sir Martin Sorrell, is about taking the various sources of information a company has about its customers and bringing them all together in one place. If you have one source of data, say your credit card info, or your online shopping delivery, that is 'Little Data'. 'Big Data' combines 'structured data' in databases with 'unstructured data', such as what you post on Facebook or websites you visit, and then mines them systematically for customer insights.

Big Data is changing the way we do business. Although customer information has long existed, it has tended to be in isolated pockets that did not connect to each other. People didn't know which customers were buying which products, in which countries, and what motivated them to do so. Nor did they know much about these customers outside of their behaviour in their particular part of the customer's world. Technology enables us to connect these databases and mine them for insight into customer behaviour. By using rapid a/b testing, predictive modelling and algorithms, you can create analytics that help to better understand and anticipate customer behaviour.

Big Data can be a force for good, but only if you harness it well. Few companies do that. And there are privacy concerns. Ultimately, most experts believe the consumer, not the company, is in control of the data, and most consumers are willing to give up their data only when they get something in return.[2]

I can honestly say that every success I've enjoyed over the years as a manager has been down to data. Back in the days of direct marketing

---

[2] Yates, Mick, dunnhumby Head of International, presentation at CMI President's Lecture, 9 May 2013.

on Pampers it might have been 'Little Data', but it was absolutely the same principle. Here are some more contemporary examples.

Troy Carter, manager for pop star Lady Gaga, related the following at the *FT*'s Innovation Conference in 2012. If a rock star is touring globally, there is typically a list of venues chosen for a few days round the world. Today, given the internet, the manager can identify which cities download her songs the most and plan the tour so that it stays longest there. He also works with downloader Spotify to see which songs in which areas are most popular, to help select the playlist for each gig. If he uses fans' drawings on Facebook to design the tour T-shirts, merchandise sales increase 30 per cent. And by connecting the fans on Gaga's social networks, he can get those in France talking with those in Korea using translation software in chat rooms.[3] At a more modest level, a plumber in Manchester wants to put an ad in Yellow Pages. Using data mining, coupled with customer research, the Yellow Pages publisher can estimate the number of leads that plumber should receive, as well as the average job value, to calculate an estimated ROI from the ad. The plumber places the ad and is given a dedicated phone number and web micro site so he can actually track the number of leads received.

Tesco, one of the big data pioneers, began mining data using its Clubcard, and many attribute its meteoric rise to the world's third largest retailer to its ground-breaking use of customer analytics. Big Data enabled Tesco to identify and nurture high-value customers. When store managers wanted to remove organic bread to make more room for baked beans, Tesco knew that those organic bread customers were buying more frequently and spending more per visit than others. Recently, Tesco could marry their Clubcard database and info with your Facebook profile. They could discover you love the colour blue in photos, and make sure they only send you emails in your favourite shade of blue.[4]

BSI wanted to know what benefits customers were gaining from audits beyond the audit certificate. By connecting the auditor's reports and their customer satisfaction study they were able to produce a sophisticated benchmark report for their 70,000 audit customers which became

---

[3] FT Innovation Conference 2012, interview with Troy Carter.
[4] Yates, presentation at CMI President's Lecture, 9 May 2013.

a differentiator – as well as a source of potential leads for other products. Using the same metrics they could predict which customers were likely to lapse.

Experts recommend five steps for creating successful data plans, all of which tally with my own experience:

1 Have a game plan for assembling and integrating data.

2 Make sure you agree to use the best data available – otherwise you'll lose months arguing over whether it's accurate.

3 Make sure you have the right talent that can master database design and analytics.

4 Make use of advanced analytic models to try to predict customer and behaviour trends.

5 Have easy-to-use tools and applications for managers and front-line users to understand.

Equally, we agree on three big planning challenges:

1 Match the data agenda with the needs of the business and strategy – don't go off and spend a fortune.

2 Demonstrate real-life quick wins so colleagues buy into the programme.

3 Ensure you focus on getting front-line users to use the data tools correctly and give them the capabilities to do so. Otherwise you'll end up with garbage in/garbage out.[5]

Who owns the data? and the importance of the 'golden record'

Pick a customer, say it's John Smith of ABC Company. In most organisations, John will exist many times over as a separate data record. In some cases his first name will be present, in others it will be Mr Smith, or J. Smith. In some entries his company will be entered, perhaps as

---

[5] Biesdorf, S., Court, D. and Willmott, P., 'Big data: what's your plan?', *McKinsey Quarterly*, no. 2, 2013.

ABC Company, and in others it will be missing, or entered as A. B. C. Company. Because he is entered differently everywhere, no one will know that the different records refer to the same person, so the organisation misses opportunities to understand John's buying habits and spending potential.

Many databases get choked up with invalid names, or multiple different entries. In one company I worked in, we supposedly had over 1 million 'leads' on the system. The only problem was, all but 150,000 of those leads were bad data. In one division of the same organisation, the sales team had a 90 per cent close rate – because they only entered customers into the system they had already signed.

The 'golden record' is one version of a data entry. One version of a customer's name, title and contact details that is consistently used throughout the company. It is worth paying attention to those on the front line and rewarding them for correct entry.

To promote data quality:

- Establish who has ownership of the data and make them responsible for its quality.

- Establish a data governance policy and a data quality initiative. Any initiative should aim to be more than a piece of paper – people and processes need to be taken into account.[6]

- Use quality improvement methods such as Six Sigma.[7]

- Ensure everyone understands the importance of good-quality data, and the impact of poor-quality data on their ability to perform well.

- Build KPIs on correct data and monitor the performance of it frequently – and ensure successes are shared when data has been used well.

---

[6] O'Brien, T., 'Poor data can cost you money and get you sued', submitted for CMI's Management Articles of the Year competition, 2012.

[7] Stephen, M.K. and Kleiner, B.H., 'Better data means better decisions', *Industrial Management*, Vol. 53, no. 4, July 2011.

Business insight

Business insight is taking data and information and turning it into news you can use – whether it is information about your market, your competitor or your customers. Too often I see business insight generating reams of unwieldy reports and PowerPoint presentations that no one reads.

This is something that you can programme into your business insight team design. Ensure you focus your initial intelligence on real business issues: things the organisation wants and needs to know to achieve its strategic objectives. Make people 'hungry' for your outputs.

Share the design of any reports or tools that emerge from your intelligence. Allow internal customers and stakeholders to ask questions and make comments – ultimately, they must 'act' on your data, so unless they own it, it will be difficult to get any results from it.

Keep analytics simple, sharp and user friendly. They need to be actioned by busy sales people and customer service reps. Remember KISS (Keep It Simple, Stupid) definitely applies here.

There are four things you will always need to do:

1 **Gain commitment from senior management** Creating business intelligence will have costs and resources implications. Also, make sure it has a commercial focus, and not just a technical one.

2 **Plan** Business insight takes time and money. Data warehouses must be built, often enterprise systems upgraded. It's important this is done in a methodical manner with clear objectives. Developing a research plan could be useful here. Start with the key questions you are trying to answer. Make sure they are business-relevant. If you are not sure, ask your key internal customers. If you cannot answer the question 'What will we do with the answers from the research?' then it's not the right research!

3 **Analyse the information** Information is of no use if it is not analysed and summarised effectively. Keep it short. Decide who the audience for the report is, and make sure it's relevant. Include recommendations and suggested actions as well as key findings.

Have a session or three to discuss and refine these with operational business people.

4 **Use the data to make actionable decisions** If you can't do this, then it's useless information.

A guide to creating insight that's used

1. **Start with the internal accounting system, especially sales analysis and customer records.** Analyse your customer transactions over a period of time and reconcile each one back to your financial transactions. This will enable you to see who your biggest customers are and what they buy. Do this for each of your product lines, and major geographies. Then cross-compare. Look at average values and retention rates. Check industry sectors and business size. There is a wealth of information to be gained from this exercise. Because you are tying the data back to the financials it's much more likely to gain acceptance.

2. **Other internal databases.** Maybe you've got customer complaints databases. Or website hits, or downloads. Or content and social media sites. What trends and habits can you find when you correlate their transactions with other databases?

3. **Market intelligence.** Once you've identified your key customers, and some of their behaviours, look to the broader market. What are the habits of your lead sector, who are the leaders there? Who are your main competitors? How are you and your customers positioned in the market?

4. **Market research.** Once you've understood more about your customers, use research to get the rest of the answers. You can use online research to speed things up.

5. **Other information sources.** Most organisations already hold, or have access to, 80 per cent of the information required for assessing their competitors. Do not overlook the importance of front-line staff as sources of information – they are likely to pick up all sorts of information through dealing with customers.

6. **Social media.** Don't forget your customers are people when they leave you. They may interact with lots of other internet and social media sites and organisations. The more you can link these up, the more you can understand about them.

IT is for everyone

It's no longer possible for employees at any level to avoid the use of technology – and nor should they. From the use of multi-million-pound IT systems that make processes more efficient, to free social media tools that help us to promote brands, there are a huge number of technical tools at our disposal. Managers should select those digital tools that will help their organisation operate more effectively. You don't need to know every technical detail but you do need to have enough knowledge to keep pace with the digital age and to encourage the use and development of IT.[8]

Try a reverse mentoring scheme, where younger people who are digital literates team up with tooled folk who are technology Luddites. Consider sending everyone on a 'learn to code in a day' course. The more you can demystify technology, the more you can benefit from it.

Your IT needs will vary hugely depending on the size of your organisation. Some investment in IT will often be required, but most businesses are not software developers. Apart from very large companies, it is advisable to use custom-made software packages rather than employ a team of in-house developers. It is so very easy to get bogged down and waste time and money developing your own solutions when you can use 'off-the-shelf' things that will work just as well. This is another reason to have IT as an integral part of your commercial team – it will militate against the tendency to develop everything 'in-house'. Also, whatever new product or services your commercial folks are developing, chances are very high they will need IT time and support to pull it off. Integrating IT into your core commercial functions will ensure that people spend time thinking about the IT requirements their projects are generating.

In the 1990s, many organisations invested in IT systems in a bid to increase productivity. Nowadays, whilst there still may well be efficiency savings to be made by investing in IT, there are a number of other advantages of concentrating time, effort and money on your IT operation.

Visa gained market leadership in the payments platform by being a relentless adopter of technology to make payments simpler, safer and faster for customers and banks alike. Technology investments made a competitive difference. New technologies help to improve operating models, and, crucially, the selfsame technologies also make it possible to replicate improvements across the board. Indeed, manufacturing in the USA is being revitalised using high-tech solutions which, coupled

[8] De Kare-Silver, M., *e-shock 2020: How the Digital Technology Revolution is Changing Business and All our Lives*, Palgrave Macmillan, 2011.

with lower energy costs, are making it cheaper for firms to manufacture in-house than to outsource to countries like China and India.[9]

Who owns your web? It's your first point of contact

Never underestimate the importance of your company's website. It is estimated that 35–45 per cent of multichannel companies' business comes through the web. Your website is an information tool, but increasingly it's also your best source of leads and enables potential customers and stakeholders to engage with you wherever they are in the world. It is also a major source of revenue and cost savings, as you can engage with many people very efficiently online. The web drives disintermediation, which means it eliminates the middle man.

Many websites are not fit for purpose. They are overcrowded, complex and clunky. People throughout the company ask that their content is posted with no regard for how useful it will be for users. The site may be structured along internal company lines rather than the way the external users need to use it. It can be almost impossible to discern what a company does based on the site.

In one company I worked in, there were over 1,500 pages of content. And yet 90 per cent of the traffic went to just 7 per cent of the pages. In searching for the nearest store, the customer had to go through fifteen clicks – over 80 per cent of them dropped out. There were over 190 ways in which customers were urged to contact the company – with the result that less than half of those did. Almost half never made it past the home page. The site had been built from the company's point of view, rather than from the users' point of view. User-centric design means you build your site around the different types of users you know you will have and make it easy for them to find what they want. If you are a university, for example, a prospective student will want information on how to apply; a current student to sign up for a course; alumni will want to buy reunion tickets and so on.

[9] *Time Magazine*, 22 Apr. 2013, pp. 23–9.

Digital is everyone's business: Management 2.0

Technology should not just be the preserve of the IT department. There needs to be recognition of the importance of IT throughout the organisation, including an understanding of how the use of technology affects the business.

There's more. Does technology have the potential to reinvent management? A group of leading thinkers and practitioners, known as Management Innovation Exchange, or MIX, thinks the answer to that question is yes, and I would tend to agree. The problem is that much of management is still done in a pre-digital, Management 1.0, way. It's based on slow-moving, inflexible, hierarchical organisations characterised by inertia, instrumentalism and disempowerment. The solution? Transparency, Collaboration, Meritocracy, Community, Speed and Agility – the same principles upon which the web is built. If we can apply these to organisations we can reinvent management for the better – welcome to Management 2.0! The data would tend to support them, in that, generally speaking, agile, community-based, collaborative organisations outperform those that aren't. And are a lot more fun.[10]

Here are some ideas:

■ Hire some digital entrepreneurs to get agile.

■ Remember that flexible working can boost productivity.

■ Embrace technology and the values of the web 2.0 and you will boost your managerial performance.

■ Understand eCommerce metrics below (figure 19.1). How does your company's website stack up? If you aren't doing eCommerce, why not? Are you missing out on a vital route to market for your organisation?

---

[10] MIX (Management Innovation Exchange) http://www.managementexchange.com/but

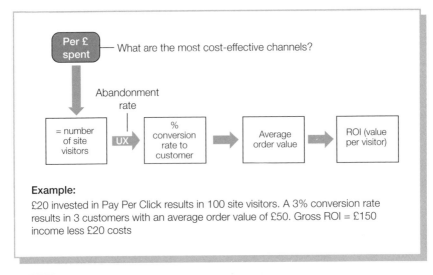

figure 19.1   eCommerce metrics

Top tips, pitfalls and takeaways

Top tips

▪ Always remain commercially focused: data is never an end in itself, and its use should be geared to tangible business goals.

▪ Combine data gathering with real insights, such as buying patterns over time and by geography, and other dynamics.

Top pitfalls

▪ Obsessing over data, rather than the underlying objective.

▪ Confusing data with real insights.

▪ Neglecting the website, and making it user-unfriendly

Top takeaways

▪ Big Data is having a transformational impact on the way in which businesses operate, especially in the areas of marketing and understanding customers.

■ IT is something that everyone in the business has to understand, including a grasp of how it affects the business.

■ Think about the user perspective. When you want more info from your customer, give them something in return – and respect their privacy!

part

7

The last word

20

Views from the front line

For this chapter I have gathered the views of some of the many managers I have met and worked with over the years. I asked them to share their 'Management Cheat Sheet', consisting of three things:

1 **Top tip** Your Practical Pearl of wisdom to help others achieve it.

2 **Top pitfall** The trap that you see yourself and others falling into time after time that just doesn't work.

3 **Top takeaway** Your headline thought on what great management and leadership looks like.

I can think of no better way to end this book. Remember:

'In times of drastic change it is the learners who survive. The learned find themselves fully equipped to live in a world that no longer exists.'

(Author unknown – submitted by Joan Zimmerman)

Steve Axe: General Manager, Belgium, Mars

Top tip

Great leadership is about being able to work on three levels – to develop yourself, to develop your people, and to deliver outstanding business results. Each requires true listening and the ability to ask great questions.

Top pitfall

Believing that as the leader you need to have the answers and be 'right'. You need to have questions, and have the courage to make mistakes, admit them, and move on.

Top takeaway

Leadership means going first, and in doing so creating the environment for your people to be the best they can be.

Peter Ayliffe: President and CEO of Visa Europe, CMI President

Top tip

The most important quality of leadership is integrity – people must believe in you and trust you. The decisions you take as a leader impact the reputation of your business, the reputation of your colleagues and your personal reputation. Nothing is more important than integrity.

Top pitfall

Not listening to the views of others: when leaders have all the answers and don't listen to the views of their subject-matter experts they will invariably fail. As a leader, yes, you have to make decisions, but ensure they are informed decisions.

Top takeaway

Communicate your vision with a passion. Leadership is about creating a compelling vision, developing the long-term goals and plans to deliver that vision and then communicating the vision and plans. However, what determines great leaders is their ability to communicate their vision with passion; they are able to inspire and motivate people to excel.

Lena Benjamin: Founder of Ones Company Ltd

Top tip

Taking personal responsibility by taking action no matter how small you think it is. Join a group either online or offline because the humanity and humility comes from sharing and working towards a collective goal that will sustain civilisation for the next generation.

Top pitfall

Letting fear take over. The reason why most people, particularly women, do not take responsibility and take action is because they fear they are not good enough, not smart enough, not rich enough or not pretty enough.

Top takeaway

It's about truly embracing humanity and humility in order to sustain civilisation – socially, economically and politically.

It is responsible and ethical behaviour that actually enables and inspires customers and employees to collaborate and co-create. The new era of twenty-first century management and leadership is not sustainable without embracing diverse opinions. Management and leadership is no longer a dictatorship, it is a democracy that truly embraces the values and purpose of the organisation.

Louise Bevan: Director of Customer Insight, BSI

Top tip

Don't be scared of talented people, embrace them and put their skills to good use. Should you be lucky enough to have high achievers in your team, even for a short time, then help them achieve their aspirations whilst learning something yourself. It's like 'Pay it Forward'.

Top pitfall

Fruitlessly managing weaknesses instead of focusing on strengths is a costly and destructive pitfall that can negatively impact the individual and the business. Managing strengths will raise the bar that people aspire to reach and can even help someone who is not achieving choose a different path.

Top takeaway

I have always looked to be inspired by exceptional leadership. I find inspiration in leaders who are always prepared to be measured by the success of those they are responsible for, and earn respect through the decisions and actions they take every day.

Dame Carol Black, Chair, Nuffield Trust

Top tip

A high-minded mission statement is empty rhetoric unless reflected in attitudes, behaviours, working relationships and organisational arrangements. Fulfilling its promise depends on employees who are valued and feel valued, and are enabled and supported to do their best.

Top pitfall

Seeing too readily that failings are someone else's problem; or – worse – shutting your eyes and hoping the problem will go away; and – worse still – denying there is a problem.

Top takeaway

Excellence in leadership and management shines out in every encounter. It is declared in the bearing, demeanour and conduct of employees at all levels. There is a tangible sense of organisational well-being, with employee commitment to values and goals that are honestly shared; there is engagement.

Britta Bomhard: General Manager, Europe, Church & Dwight

Top tip

Seeing is believing! There is nothing that beats seeing yourself in action as a leader or manager for receiving honest feedback. So, if you have the chance to video yourself – be it giving a presentation to the full team or conducting smaller meetings, go for it! You will see how you come across and what reactions you produce in other people. And no one else will ever give you such honest feedback. Of course, you can also use this technique for leadership development of your team or managers.

Top pitfall

Being soft on people! As much as you can understand the personal circumstances of a manager, if they don't live up to the task of leading others, you need to address this immediately.

Top takeaway

Great leadership is one that adapts itself to the circumstances and people involved. There is not one leadership style that always fits the bill. Great leaders, therefore, need to have first of all the ability to judge any situation quickly in order to know the best management style right now. The second important ingredient is self-awareness and knowing what is authentic behaviour for you. And after that it is practise, practise and practise. Great management behaviour can be learnt.

Stefan Bomhard: Regional President, Europe, Bacardi

Top tip

Your strategy and key action on a page: lay out your strategy on one page in a simple and easy-to-understand way so that everybody throughout the organisation can understand it. This allows you and your team to know every day what is important and what 'moves the needle' in the business. Personally follow up if things fall behind, as it also sends the signal that you care.

Top pitfall

Communication: You always think that once you have communicated things that are important to you the organisation has understood it. You learn over and over again that you need to use every opportunity to communicate the things that are important to you using all kinds of different methods as often as possible.

Top takeaway

Define the future and then motivate and lead the team to achieve it. Help everybody understand what their role is and how they can make a difference.

Helen Brand: CEO, ACCA

Top tip

Always communicate in an open and transparent way in order to build trust and confidence.

Top pitfall

Conducting important conversations by email or in writing.

Leading and managing through rules rather than values and principles.

Top takeaway

People with integrity and authentic passion for their business, who inspire others to deliver.

Sir David Brown: Chairman, BSI

Top tip

It is impossible to innovate alone. So don't try to. Engage your team and anyone else who can contribute.

Top pitfall

Don't ever believe that you know best. Nobody has a monopoly on wisdom, yourself included.

Top takeaway

Great management is the feeling of confidence a team gets from knowing that it is controlling what it can control, understanding what it cannot control and mitigating the risks to the very best of its ability, and still having enough bandwidth to innovate freely. Great leadership is exploiting that bandwidth to the full, each and every day, habitually.

Alex Cheatle: CEO and Founder, TEN

Top tip

Keep talking a lot to enough of the people who do *the* critical roles in your business. In my business, I try to keep a personal connection with the lifestyle managers. If I ran a newspaper I hope I'd be in touch daily with the journalists. This connection allows you to short-cut middle management and have your own pulse to sense check the data and reports that you get as you scale.

Top pitfall

Don't rush the big messages. Many of your team won't get what you mean the first time you say it. You may need to say what you mean in many different ways and repeatedly before everyone 'gets it'. I certainly used to think that something communicated once, well, should do the trick. It doesn't.

Top takeaway

Think about focusing on communicating and leading through values and vision far more than profit and cash. The meaning you create in the lives of your customers, employees and even shareholders is rarely best explained in financial metrics.

Peter Cheese: CEO, CIPD

Top tip

Begins with self-awareness, understanding your own strengths and weaknesses and leadership style, courage to build the right team around you, ability to listen and openness to take on other ideas, taking time to understand the strategic context of your role and your teams, setting clear and broad objectives and empowering your team to deliver.

Top pitfall

Thinking you are empowering, but actually not delegating and trusting others to do their job. Not providing continual and clear feedback and guidance, including the tough messages which then need to be acted on – courage to move people on when necessary. Listening as well as talking – when you hear your team express your ideas as theirs and take them forwards, you know you have progressed.

Top takeaway

In today's world with so much change we need great management and leadership to be inspiring, able to understand the bigger picture and set context, to be empowering and facilitative with an emphasis on stewardship and growing others, authentic and open, which are critical to building trust and integrity.

Lori Collins: Strategic Advisor, Emerging Ventures

Top tip

To keep that constant perspective on what's most important, one of my favourite maxims is Dr Stephen Covey's theory of 'big rocks' – know what's most important in your life, and let all the 'little rocks' fill in around the boulders. How easily we can get distracted by other people's priorities!

Top pitfall

Ah, get that monkey off my back! Originally discussed in the *Harvard Business Review* in 1974, the politics of responsibility and delegation are still a trap, as I see myself and others take on responsibilities that 'are not my/our job' and get on the slippery slope of being stuck with the ugly monkey.

Top takeaway

Clear vision is just another term for *focus* – the key to both long- and short-term success. For leaders in organisations both large and small, focus can be a constant challenge. Entrepreneurs who chase today's shiniest star, or corporations who creep into far-afield business lines, rarely have a winning strategy, just a constant temptation. Jim Collins, author of *Good to Great* and *Built to Last*, addresses focus in his 'hedgehog' concept and quantifies the impact on business results.

Neil Constable: CEO Shakespeare's Globe

Top tip

Within the arts sector, it is always important to remember that an artistic decision is also a business decision and vice versa. Without both being in the mind's eye, it is impossible for the business to enable and serve the art and in turn support risk-taking and innovation.

And remember sometimes 'good enough' is good enough – don't waste energy worrying about the past!

Top pitfall

Not owning an issue or a problem and then wondering why no one else has. If you don't want to deal with it, who will? And occasionally stay long enough in an organisation to see if the management changes you plan and implement actually work in the longer term.

Top takeaway

Great management and leadership in any organisation is demonstrated by a strong and dynamic synergy between the board, executive and staff, with a proper shared understanding of vision and goals, an open preparedness to question and challenge and a leadership style that does not take either its staff or customers/users for granted. It is a many-headed animal and in my world the satisfaction that all is good is taken once the curtain has gone up!

John Curtiss: President (ret.) of North America, Mars Pet Food

Top tip

Spend the time up front on your strategy and be ruthless about mission and objectives.

Top pitfall

Being unclear about strategic mission and objectives or changing them along the way or not even having a written and agreed-to strategy. The more time you spend up front the less confusion downstream. I believe this is critical. All the best product innovation and advertising campaigns I have ever been involved with began with simple and singularly focused strategies.

Top takeaway

Great management is inspiring and focused. Great accomplishments begin with clarity of mission and aligned resources. Everyone on the same page.

Patrick Dunne: Chairman, LEAP and CMI Board of Companions

Top tip

Try and listen to what people think as well as what they say and treat everyone with integrity, respect and decency, especially those who make you cringe. Decent 'thought-bubble' thinkers have a natural advantage over manipulators, who usually get found out and become mistrusted.

Top pitfall

A humility bypass can prove fatal for even the most gifted of leaders. Arrogance undermines judgement, ****** people off and puts a great big muffler on your antennae.

Top takeaway

To lead you need:

- **A galvanising purpose** there's only any point if you want to achieve something,

- **Great judgement** one of the most under-used words in business,

- **Superb interpersonal skills** to bring those judgements to bear,

- **Positive energy and empathy** to inspire people and overcome the inevitable challenges, and finally

- **Finely tuned antennae** to ensure that your judgements are well informed.

Francesca Ecsery: Non-Executive Director

Top tip

No matter how qualified and good at your job you are, office politics can have a perverse impact on your success and on how much you enjoy your time at work. But it does not necessarily have to be so. Start by identifying the key influencers within your firm and their different agendas and priorities.

You will then have the awareness to understand which ones you can do something about in your role and help influence your professional destiny. Think of it as part of your job description, albeit unwritten.

Top pitfall

It would be a mistake to think that corporate politics are only created by others. We all have our own weaknesses, habits and behaviours which can generate issues for others as well. Being aware of this will help to manage difficult situations.

Top takeaway

Recognise 'office politics' as unavoidable and make them work for you.

Richard Ellis: Director of CSR, Alliance Boots

Top tip

You don't know what you don't know.

Top pitfall

Doing the same things time and time again and expecting a different result.

Top takeaway

Management is about following the rules and procedures properly;

leadership is how you behave when you are faced with a situation not covered by these. You follow the company's values and do what you know is the right thing.

Susan Farr: Director of Chime PLC

Top tip

Surround yourself with brilliant people and success will surely follow.

Top pitfall

If something needs sorting, sort it quickly, decisively and fairly. Don't give problems the time to take root.

Top takeaway

A great leader has a clear vision, well expressed and easily understood. He or she sets the course and empowers a well-motivated and collegiate team to achieve their goals.

Ian Filby: CEO DFS

Top tip

Listen to EVERYONE inside and outside of the organisation for a long time. Then co-create an exciting future vision with your top team.

Top pitfall

Dropping down into the detail, i.e. moving from leader to the successful manager/operator you once were!

Top takeaway

Think like Sir Alex Ferguson! Put together a great team of complementing skills and characters. Treat them all individually according to their nature. Set clear high goals. Then walk the talk.

Paul Geddes: CEO Direct Line Group

Top tip

Focus on the important; leave enough time and energy to think.

Top pitfall

Don't confuse good luck with talent or ability – for yourself or your team. In other words – don't believe your own hype!

Top takeaway

Great leadership is seeing the future and pulling your organisation towards it fast. Great management is building an ecosystem that grows talent and lets that talent deliver results.

Werner Geissler: Vice Chairman, P&G

Top tip

Keep things simple. If you want to align an entire organisation and especially a big one, you have to be understood by everyone. If you are too theoretical or too abstract nobody will understand you, nobody will follow you, and the organisation will move in too many different directions, i.e. nowhere.

Top pitfall

That we begin to believe in our own propaganda and don't renew ourselves, our teams, and game plans before it is too late.

Top takeaway

First, there is no difference between great management and leadership. Leadership without managerial skills to penetrate issues and organisations is a 'walk in the park'. Management without leadership sounds like a short-lived one-man (or one-woman) show. Both are needed to be able to deliver winning results consistently over time and across business units.

Mike Harrison: Global Brand Director, Timberland

Top tip

Be authentically and transparently YOU. *Know* what you stand for and will fight for (values and principles), *know* what drives your inherent biases and preferences (personality type, past successes and failures) and make sure your team knows this too. Build your leadership style on *who you are*, rather than trying to adopt someone else's leadership model. But make sure you compensate for your blind spots – for example, by hiring people who complement your strengths and weaknesses.

Top pitfall

Staying too long with 'what worked in the past', or, worse still, staying with a vastly over-simplified, over-sanitized view of 'what worked in the past'. Leaders need to be conscious of the evolving external environment and challenging their teams to explore new approaches or ideas.

Top takeaway

Great leadership starts when an individual has a powerful long-term ambition, and the ability to assemble and inspire a strong team to share that ambition. Then the 'nuts and bolts' of leadership kick in – being articulate and consistent about strategy, priorities, accountabilities and so on, and having the right culture and systems to objectively review progress and make necessary adjustments.

Tamara Ingram: President and CEO of Team P&G, WPP

Top tip

Listen to all your stakeholders – your people, your clients, your customers and your influencers.

Top pitfall

When you have decided what to do, make the changes fast.

Top takeaway

Leadership is about understanding the power of VISION. The ability to define a vision, shape it, share it and keep a relentless focus on it – and most importantly take your people with you towards that vision. A vision on its own is not enough. You need attention to the detail because only through the execution does the vision come to life. And finally, great leaders have great people around them.

Debbie Klein: Chief Executive of Engine and Chairman of WCRS

Top tip

Whatever you do, and wherever your career path takes you, always be true to yourself. In my career I have seen people who haven't been really clear on what their values are, what they stand for and where they will and won't draw a line in the sand. As opposed to those who have always been clear on their beliefs and values and lived by them no matter what. The latter are the people I have been most inspired by, and learnt the most from. As someone famous once said, be the best you that you can be, because you'll be a lousy somebody else.

Top pitfall

Not trusting your instinct. If your gut instinct is that something doesn't feel right, it probably isn't right. We all have a little voice in our heads that tells us which path to follow in many situations – listen to it and learn to trust it. It will not let you down.

Top takeaway

The best leaders embody three qualities – cool head, firm hand, warm heart.

Austin Lally: President, Braun, P&G

Top tip

The answers we need are usually within reach: with customers, distributors, consumers, in-store consultants. The important behaviour is to travel, to make sure this direct insight from the marketplace reaches you candidly and unfiltered.

Top pitfall

Don't keep pursuing an ineffective approach with more urgency and determination. It is wheel spinning. Change the approach.

Top takeaway

Figure out what is really needed to win. Distinguish carefully between what is needed and what people say is possible. As a leader, refuse to settle for today's possible – you have a responsibility to mobilise everyone to create what's needed.

Derek Mapp: Chairman, Informa

Top tip

Never speak first at the meeting: 'Confucius says "He who speaks last is the most clever".'

Saying thank you is the cheapest but the most effective and under-used management tool in British industry today.

Top pitfall

Believing your own bulls**t and detaching yourself from your customers. Customers do make pay days possible – cherish them and ensure everyone else does.

Top takeaway

You can tell if a company is well managed and reflecting the importance of its people. Are there director car parking places? (I am more important than you – yuk!) Are people proud of how their business looks externally? Are people happy? Leadership is not necessarily a pyramid of command; it should be allowed to shape itself as ability is more important than status.

Steve Marshall: Chairman, Balfour Beatty

Top tip

Be authentic and be yourself. You are trying to mobilise emotional, selfish but largely well-meaning human beings. If the person you are trying to be at work is different from the one you are at home, you will not be at ease and you will be found out anyway!

Top pitfall

Failing to filter out the clutter. All executive teams massively underrate the serious damage that diluting their personal and collective focus causes. This is partly because they tend to massively overrate their ability to intervene in areas where in practice they add no value. A great Chairman is a great de-clutterer.

Top takeaway

Great management is knowing how to get things done through people and through organisations. It is a vital skill, but is a lesser skill than leadership. Great leadership is determining what you collectively need to achieve as a group, and having the conviction and capacity to express it, then convince and mobilise your colleagues to want to achieve it as much as you do.

Deanna Oppenheimer: Founder and CEO, Camelotworks

Top tip

PAPS! *Passion* – Inspiration transfers energy from the leader to the led so they are enthused by passion to achieve the impossible. *Appreciation* – A handwritten thank-you note from the boss will be saved for a lifetime. *Presence* – Develop social skills in a social media world. *Service* – Model authenticity by showing true vulnerability.

Top pitfall

Becoming myopic in any one direction within a large company. I finally learned this when I listened twice as much as I spoke, reflecting my mother's saying: 'You've got two ears and one mouth for a reason!'

Top takeaway

Top leaders speak humbly: everyone already knows they are the boss; decide consistently and break down silos by bringing diagonal groups of teams together. By leading with teams created from cross divisions and a variety of employee grades, the leader can forge his/her culture, break the paradigms of the past and innovate.

Dimitri Panayopotopoulos, Vice Chairman, P&G

Top tip

Focus on results and the rest will come. Too often, we get drawn into non-value-added work. Every time this happens it's a distraction from a leader's core deliverable: results.

Top pitfall

The biggest pitfall I have seen is a leader's ability to say 'no'. We have to be the ones to make priority calls and be masters of stopping work to enable our organisations to focus on the most significant choices that will truly drive the business.

Top takeaway

Strong leadership is in touch with the external environment and deeply connected with what is happening internally. Great leaders know their operations inside and out and the people who are getting the work done. They spend more time outside of their offices connecting with the business, employees and key stakeholders, and making critical connections to simplify, drive action, and produce strong, sustained results.

Gavin Patterson, CEO, BT

Top tip

Use all parts of your brain when making decisions. Develop your intuition and learn to complement the rational side of your decision making with the intuitive side. Learn how you interpret people because you often have to make a decision based on whether you can rely on the individual. And if someone seems uncertain, always probe deeper to help you to manage any risk.

Top pitfall

Be modest and don't believe your own PR. There will be moments when you think you can walk on water, but as soon as you begin to believe your own publicity you'll find it's the beginning of the end. So don't be complacent, get carried away with your own success or be capricious. Always acknowledge your weaknesses and build a team that complements your skills and experience.

Top takeaway

Great leadership is about anticipating the need to change, making change happen and about tailoring your style to the situation. In moments of crisis you need more authoritative leadership and when the business is thriving, a more consultative and supporting style encourages people to achieve more and to change the way they think or act. It's also about using influence not power.

John E. Pepper Jr., former CEO & Chairman of P&G and Chairman of Walt Disney Company

Top tip

Make everyone know they count: by listening to them; getting the benefit of their ideas without ever losing the compass of your own values, judgement and experience. Remember: trust is the greatest gift we give to another. *Expecting the best in others empowers others.*

Top pitfall

Failing to address misalignment in an organisation and in relationships with others in a timely and decisive manner.

Let me add one other: failure to listen carefully to my spouse when it comes to judging other people.

Top takeaway

Establishing an empowering vision, sound strategies, maniacal commitment to outstanding execution; enrolling a great team, growing people (they relish having worked for/with you) and never stopping learning on how to do better.

Empowered by a special combination of competence, character, caring and commitment.

Tony Pidgely: Chairman, The Berkeley Group Holdings

Top tip

Whenever I get more than 200 people in one division I tend to create a separate unit so that they can work better together as a team.

If you involve people in projects and give them ownership you always get better results. We employ the single mothers on our estates to look after the gardens. You'd better not mess with their gardens.

When I was first a director I used to stand up in front of the Board and deliver the bad news. I'd always start with the bad news. I got fired for it, and that's how Berkeley got started. But I still operate that way today.

Top pitfall

That's easy. One word. Greed.

Top takeaway

Good management is all about common sense, decency, collaboration and treating others with respect. You also need to give people autonomy. And have a vision for the long term.

Richard Pinder, Founder and CEO, The House

Top tip

As the military leader of Gulf War I, General Norman Schwarzkopf said: 'When put in charge, take charge.' Too many people on being appointed to a leadership role they have so badly wanted, then fail to actually lead. And his second top tip which I also live by: 'When in doubt, do what's right.' These are the best two top tips I have ever heard and I use them daily.

Top pitfall

Forgetting that real leadership is not to do the fishing yourself but to inspire others to do the fishing themselves. Ego, distrust, time ... all conspire to stop us from remembering this simple but crucially important pitfall and time and again we will step right back into it.

Top takeaway

I believe inspirational leadership is the best way to describe and enact the role of manager or leader in any organisation. The act of inspiring others to achieve what they thought impossible while at the same time encouraging them to co-create the goals and approaches themselves.

Then using your own skills and judgement to sort the good ideas from the bad and not being afraid of explaining clearly to the team why you did what you did. That's inspiring and it's clearly leadership.

Paul Plant: Mentor, Wayra

Top tip

Never be afraid to recruit people who are better and more talented than yourself.

Top pitfall

In today's ultra-competitive, disruptive, digitally influenced commercial environment, success is dependent much less on having the right strategy, but far more on how well you execute the strategy you decide to run with. Great companies, and therefore great leaders, are all about impeccable strategic execution – think Amazon, think Apple, think GE, think Google, think Virgin.

Too many leaders fall into the trap of spending disproportionate time developing their strategy, and then do not apply anywhere near enough rigour or focus on ensuring that their strategy is properly executed.

Top takeaway

Great leaders align the objectives of their people and their teams with those of the broader business – and almost always, customer excellence is right there in the mix.

Paul Polman: CEO, Unilever

Top tip

Ask yourself what you can do to become part of the solution. An African proverb says, 'If you want to go fast, go alone. But if you want to go far, go together.'

How can you make sustainable and equitable growth part of your business model? How can you make it a force for good? Less bad is simply not enough any more. More than ever, we need leadership and the courage that comes with it where the interest of the common good is put ahead of someone's own interest.

Top pitfall

Avoid being on a journey without passengers. Spend a lot of time on forming the needed coalitions and bring others along. And don't get sidetracked by the cynics who unfortunately still get too high a share of voice. Remember simply that it's the easiest form of abdicating responsibility.

Top takeaway

Capitalism and globalisation has lifted many out of poverty over the past few decades. Yet we have not yet figured out how to grow without over-consumption, enormous levels of public and private debt and frankly leaving too many people behind. A long-term prosperous future now and for generations to come also means a more equitable and sustainable growth model. We have the means and knowledge to eradicate poverty once and for all and make future growth inclusive. The cost of inaction increasingly outweighs the cost of action, be it around food security, nutrition, climate change, youth unemployment or some of the other major challenges. In this journey, business has to be an active participant and can no longer be a bystander in a system that gives it life in the first place.

Shafi Saxena: CMO, Microsoft India

Top tip

Be curious. Be engaged. Be brave.

Top pitfall

Being over-protective of today at the expense of tomorrow. Fear of cannibalising existing business can paralyse companies and is one of the most common leadership failures. If you don't self-cannibalise in a virtuous cycle of continual innovation, others will chomp away at your business for you. Trying to withstand the winds of market change instead of learning quickly to ride with them is never a successful business strategy.

Top takeaway

Great management is different from great leadership. Great leadership is prescient, able to envision the future as clearly as it can see the past, to shape the current to galvanise for continued leaps of growth. Great management is all about the here and now, with a laser-like focus on the current to ensure optimum operational efficiency. Leadership inspires with vision. Management inspires with behaviour.

Martin Schlatter: VP, Global CMO, Wrigley, Mars

Top tip

It is as important to win the hearts of the associates as it is to win their minds. In order to do this, it is key for a leader to provide associates with a higher-order purpose that makes a difference to consumers' lives. This will give them a sense of belonging and significantly drives engagement.

Top pitfall

Micro-managing versus setting an overall aspirational direction and enabling associates to take initiative, be creative and self-actualise.

Top takeaway

Great leaders create an environment for associates to be fully engaged and able to do their best every day.

Cilla Snowball: Group CEO and Group Chairman, AMV BBDO

Top tip

Obsess about customer satisfaction. Delighting customers is key to growth and reputation in every organisation.

Top pitfall

The mark of outstanding leadership is not just how good a leader you are but how many leaders you develop. Overlook succession planning at your peril. The best organisations prioritise it.

Top takeaway

Leadership is about delivering great results by motivating people and growing organisations in all senses – culturally, commercially, operationally and, in our case, creatively.

Andrew Summers, Chairman, Companies House

Top tip

Always be strategic and focus on what's really important – but always be grounded in the reality of what's achievable.

Top pitfall

The pitfall is talking the talk and thinking that is enough to inspire people. It's not – you have to act it out and make things happen.

Top takeaway

Great management and leadership is about inspiring others and inspiring yourself. You always need to lift people's vision above the day-to-day and give confidence that something better can be achieved.

To do this you need always to be inspiring yourself to achieve more than you think you can.

Rebecca Taylor: Dean, Open University Business School

Top tip

Personal reflection and self-awareness – make time for it. It can be a difficult journey to reconcile differences between how we perceive ourselves and how others see us, but really knowing yourself has to be the starting point for leading others effectively.

Top pitfall

Effective communication isn't simply a matter of passing on information. It's about making a personal connection with people. So make sure you've created enough space in your diary to regularly meet with your staff. If you don't you'll miss out on all their great ideas as well as miss opportunities to recognise effort and success – expressing your appreciation is essential in making people feel valued.

Top takeaway

Great leadership is about knowing yourself and what you stand for – understanding your own values and those of your organisation. If you are confident in your role, the chances are that both sets of values will be aligned, which I believe is essential to leading your team successfully. If you are clear about what you and the organisation believe, making complex decisions is much easier.

Jan Von Bon: President, European Petcare, Mars

Top tip

Bring positive ENERGY to your organisation and relentlessly attract and coach top talent.

Top pitfall

Avoid unnecessary change in vision and strategies: repeat, repeat and value consistency!

Top takeaway

Providing direction (vision), developing and implementing clear strategies (steer the HOW) and putting an efficient and effective infrastructure in place to make it happen.

Chris Warmoth, former Executive Vice President, HJ Heinz

Top tip

Building on strengths almost always delivers more return than fixing weaknesses. This is true of brands, businesses and people. Of course, one has to work on weaknesses to neutralise them. But too often we put in more effort against weaknesses than strengths – a big mistake.

Top pitfall

Play the cards you have, and don't spend time regretting the cards you don't have. Most 'hands' have sufficient strengths in them to leverage.

Beware the 'law of unintended consequences'. An action we take has implications we never thought about – often in a place or way we didn't even consider. This is the cause of nearly all major mistakes.

Top takeaway

We should always be as externally focused as possible – looking to consumers, customers and competition. Our customer is not World HQ or regional management or ourselves. Do have a clear strategy, what you want to achieve and then communicate it relentlessly and often. It really does make a difference.

Mick Yates: Head of International, Dunn Humby

Top tip

Building on strengths almost always delivers more return than fixing weaknesses. This is true of brands, businesses and people. Of course, one has to work on weaknesses to neutralise them. But too often we put in more effort against weaknesses than strengths – a big mistake.

Leadership is a process not a position. Anyone can have a vision and bring lots of energy to a task – but the really critical thing is to turn it into a plan that your team can execute. This is the 'enabling' step in all leadership processes and is usually the difference between success and failure.

Top pitfall

Trying to do too much too quickly is, if anything, even more deadly than not doing enough. Getting the balance and speed of change right is the biggest difference between great leaders and the rest of us!

Top takeaway

Great leaders have values congruent with their teams, create a strong vision and action plan to make change happen, ensure everyone has the right training, and then personally energise their organizations by consistently 'walking the talk'.

Joan Zimmerman: Founder and CEO, Southern Shows

Top tip

Building on strengths almost always delivers more return than fixing weaknesses. This is true of brands, businesses and people. Of course, one has to work on weaknesses to neutralise them. But too often we put in more effort against weaknesses than strengths – a big mistake.

Surround yourself with people who understand and appreciate your vision, and then learn to listen – to what is being said, and what is not being said. Learn how to communicate – one to one, one to many, in writing and in person. Never stop reading and learning.

Top pitfall

Cutting corners on salaries, quality and service. Never hire an individual or company because they will work for less – good people and talent pay for themselves many times over.

Top takeaway

Management and leadership are different – but the skills can be combined in one person. Great management, and leadership, appears relaxed, confident, open and current. It is diversified by age, ethnicity and gender. When the manager–visionary is the same person, companies are more likely to be results-oriented, financially savvy, future-focused, brand conscious and customer-centric.

21

Views from the FT's finest

Ryanair volte-face shows feedback is best given face-to-face

By Lucy Kellaway

Earlier this month Ryanair decided that being horrid to customers was not a great business strategy and declared it would be a bit nicer. This was pretty remarkable and has, indeed, been much remarked upon.

Yet even more remarkable was what caused chief executive Michael O'Leary to make this U-turn. It was not market research. It was not social networks. It certainly was not anything to do with management consultants, whom Mr O'Leary once said he would shoot if they ever darkened his doorstep. Nor was it due to pressure from the board.

Instead, the trigger was people who periodically accost him in McDonald's to moan about his airline while he sits trying to enjoy a meal with his kids. As he said to shareholders at last week's annual meeting, he is sick and tired of it.

So never mind big data. When it comes to bringing about change it is criticism delivered in person by random strangers that counts. Mr O'Leary is unusual in many ways, but in this one I suspect he is just like the rest of us.

On the face of it, placing so much emphasis on such meetings is irrational. The people who bearded him were surely no more disaffected than the thousands who for years have been posting their hostilities online. In the brief time since I started writing this article, several dozen angry tweets have been written, including this one, which I rather like: "That £50-100 difference between Ryanair and BA is taken not from your wallet, but from your soul."

Such stuff is both endless and up there for the world to see, and yet turns out to be easier for executives to ignore than half a dozen cross customers they meet in person.

You might have expected that, as the virtual world has grown and data proliferated, the value of the real encounters would have shrunk, but the reverse seems to be happening. The more bewildering the virtual world, the more we fall back on "real" evidence, no matter how subjective, presented by strangers under our own noses.

It is not just Mr O'Leary who puts disproportionate weight on chance meetings while he is eating his supper. Richard Dawkins recently told The Times that he realised atheists such as him had won the battle over God because at the dinner parties he goes to he no longer meets anyone religious. When even scientists trust the anecdotal evidence of the dinner party more than data, you know something pretty fundamental has happened.

Just now I bumped into a fellow columnist. I was about to explain to him my theory about the inflated trust we place in face-to-face encounters but before I could open my mouth he started boasting. He told me he had just got back from the US where he had been stopped twice by perfect strangers, once in a bookshop and once in an airport, both of whom told him they loved his writing. There was no need for me to ask his view of my theory: he was providing me with living proof of it. This man gets a vast amount of adulation on email and Twitter, but by comparison to the real thing, they do not touch him at all.

Yet if praise delivered in person by strangers is powerful, criticism delivered in the same way is even more so. I can remember exactly the dinner party I went to about 15 years ago, when a fellow guest who I had never met before looked me in the eye and said that she thought my columns were fatuous. I can remember the food, what I was wearing – everything.

This sort of thing is memorable partly because it is so unusual. Most people do not relish being nasty in person: we have all been brought up to be polite to strangers, especially if we are breaking bread with them.

By contrast, on the internet our upbringing is non-existent. No one seems to think there is anything wrong with being gratuitously horrible – so long as we cannot be seen. So the dinner party/McDonald's test may not be unscientific after all. The person who approaches an off-duty chief executive to complain is not just another internet troll. They are someone who really means it and really wants an answer.

The executive is then put on the spot, in a way that almost never happens in the course of a normal day in the office. At a dinner party or at McDonald's there is no PR person at hand to draft a sanitised reply. There are no underlings to delegate the tricky question to. There is no time to think it through: a convincing answer needs to be given in public, then and there.

This means that the test set by the angry fellow diner is invaluable. If the chief executive cannot muster a good defence, then it suggests that Mr O'Leary's response is the only honourable one. A U-turn is signalled.

Source: Kellaway, L. (2013) Ryanair volte-face shows feedback is best given face-to-face, *Financial Times*, 29 September 2013

Profits are the route to sustainable business

By Andrew Hill

Ask chief executives to make controversial public statements about their core business and they tend to be shy. I know this because I spent a few years trying to coax them into print as editor of the FT's comment page. But provide them with an opening to tell the world about their sustainability initiatives and they are often impossible to shut up.

The UN Global Compact and consultants Accenture have just given 1,000 of them their triennial opportunity to sound off, in what they say is the largest ever chief executive study on sustainability. But the noise the world's bosses are making is a depressing cacophony of moaning and self-congratulation: two-thirds of them think business is not doing enough to meet environmental, social and governance challenges, but three-quarters are satisfied with the speed and effectiveness of their own companies' sustainability drive.

The study's authors are polite. It would not do to alienate business leaders who are committed, through the global compact, to promote core values in important areas such as human rights and the fight against corruption. They refer to the "frustrated ambition" of chief executives who have now reached a "plateau" on their ascent to a more sustainable future.

This is, however, a plateau where most chief executives will be happy to pause for a while. The proportion who regard sustainability as "very important" to their companies' future has dropped since 2010 and 83 per cent of them are looking for governments to help pull them up to the next level. In short, they are about as "frustrated" as climbers who look up from their warm tents to see their more adventurous rivals clinging desperately to the rock face as a storm closes in on the summit.

Self-interest is, as it always has been in the area of corporate social responsibility, a great motivator. Carlos Brito, chief executive of AB InBev, says in the study: "Embedding sustainability is easier when it makes sense as the right thing to do and makes business sense." But as Gavin Patterson, new chief executive of BT, told me last week, other companies have recently "deprioritised" some of their sustainability ambitions: in western economies, at least, "on the face of it, there have been more pressing things to worry about, [such as] paying the bills".

Many still whine that two of their most important constituencies – customers and investors – are equivocal about the benefits of pushing on. Even pioneers sometimes send a mixed message. Siemens wins praise from the UN report for its clean energy initiatives, which helped make eco-friendly products and services its fastest growing business last year. Yet in July an avalanche of shareholder and board anxiety about profit warnings and narrowing margins swept away Peter Löscher, the German company's chief executive.

But these are easy excuses. The business case to take bolder steps is becoming stronger. Ioannis Ioannou of London Business School has co-authored a study showing that a consistent sustainability strategy leads to better long-term operational and stock market performance. He says the UN report is good news. At a few companies, frustration will lead to innovation – as it did when manufacturers first sought to reduce the size of mainframe computers and widen the market – while those that fail to adapt will be overtaken.

To progress, the fastest climbers must collaborate more closely with suppliers and customers. To promote a "circular economy", they need to design and build kit – from a BT router to a Philips lighting system – for recycling and reuse. To improve trust, they need to show that radical plans – such as Syngenta's counter-intuitive new programme to encourage farmers to do more with less of the pesticide and fertiliser it sells – are more than mere "greenwash" and do yield benefits for the company, the customer and the community.

As with any innovation, chief executives require courage to make this sort of leap. But they need something else as well: a determination to prove publicly that common sense and business sense on sustainability are one and the same.

One chief executive quoted in the UN study puts it well: "Business is absolutely not doing enough: we're being held back by timidity, by a lack of understanding, by a lack of a more holistic approach." By the time the 2016 report comes out, perhaps he or she will have the guts not to remain anonymous.

 Source: Hill, A. (2013) Profits are the route to sustainable business, *Financial Times*, 23 September 2013

Mandela's lessons in how to negotiate

By Michael Skapinker

Assessments of Nelson Mandela's achievements rightly focus on his talent for the conciliatory gesture and South Africa's relative post-apartheid peace and institutional stability. (If you contest the last two, compare the country with Syria, Egypt or even Russia.)

Less often discussed are the long negotiations that produced a political settlement. They are worth recalling as Israelis and Palestinians return to tentative talks.

And, although similarities between politics and business should not be overdone, anyone involved in negotiations, whether between unions and management, or over a corporate merger, or even an office desk reshuffle, should consider the lessons of South Africa's transition.

What are they? • Know your pre-negotiation strengths and weaknesses. In his autobiography, Long Walk to Freedom, Mr Mandela recalled evaluating his position and that of the African National Congress from his prison cell. A military victory over the white government was "a distant if not impossible dream".

So where did his negotiating strength come from? What could he offer that would persuade his adversary to concede?

We get the answer from that adversary's autobiography. In The Last Trek – A New Beginning, FW de Klerk, South Africa's last apartheid president, outlined what persuaded him that a deal with the ANC was necessary. He, too, realised outright military victory was impossible. South Africa's international isolation was holding back growth. Its companies needed access to world markets. The advent of democracy would bring international legitimacy. "The government had the power and the authority and the ANC the numbers," Mr de Klerk wrote. • You don't need to be friends with the people on the other side of the table, but you do need to keep talking. A startling feature of Mr de Klerk's autobiography is his constant complaint about how little of Mr Mandela's famous forgiveness and reconciliation he felt were directed towards him. The two argued frequently over the violence that plagued the country between Mr Mandela's release in 1990 and the first democratic election in 1994.

After one acrimonious exchange, Mr de Klerk slammed the phone down on Mr Mandela. Yet they made sure that contact, between themselves or their teams, continued. "We would both frequently have to rise above our personal antipathy," Mr de Klerk said. • Don't pay too much attention to what the other side says in public. Negotiations, whether in politics or business, are often accompanied by posturing, designed both to reassure supporters and to put pressure on the other side. In a speech in Cape Town immediately after his release, Mr Mandela upset many whites by reaffirming his commitment to armed struggle and to the ANC's alliance with the South African Communist party.

There was a reason for that. Mr Mandela knew many in the ANC were suspicious of his talks with the government while in prison. "I was aware that they had heard rumours that I had strayed from the organisation, that I was compromised, so at every turn I sought to reassure them."

For his part, Mr de Klerk said that Felipe González, who became Spain's prime minister after fighting the Franco dictatorship, had warned him the ANC "would say one thing at the negotiating table one day, and something completely contradictory the next day in public". • Focus on the other side's bottom line. Mr de Klerk knew that democratic elections would almost certainly bring the ANC to power. Mr Mandela understood that Mr de Klerk needed to assure whites that they wouldn't be crushed in the new South Africa. The key to an agreement came when the ANC proposed a power-sharing government for five years and the honouring of the mostly white civil servants' contracts.

Mr de Klerk said he was happy to have ensured that the new South Africa ended up with a liberal constitution and a free-market economy. But he did not achieve his hope of a rotating presidency.

Once elections had happened, Mr Mandela saw the need to ensure that whites and other minorities felt secure. "From the moment the results were in and it was apparent the ANC was to form the government, I saw my mission as one of preaching reconciliation."

This is the final negotiating lesson: • Try to ensure the other side doesn't feel it has lost.

Source: Skapinker, M. (2013) Mandela's lessons in how to negotiate, *Financial Times*, 31 July 2013

Management – overview

By Andrew Hill

Peter Drucker, who did more than most to promote the study of modern management, once pointed out that when Karl Marx's collaborator Friedrich Engels was running a mill in the 19th century, its 300 employees had no managers as such, only "charge hands" who enforced discipline on "proletarians".

As Drucker wrote in The New Realities (1989) management's "fundamental task" is to "make people capable of joint performance through common goals, common values, the right structure, and the training and development they need to perform and to respond to change". Management, he continued, explains why "for the first time in human history, we can employ large numbers of knowledgeable, skilled people in productive work".

In other words, "management" has a fair claim to be the most revolutionary business idea of the past 150 years – if only managers could pin it down and apply it.

Harvard Business Review has dubbed the years between 1911 – when Frederick Winslow Taylor published his book The Principles of Scientific Management – and 2011 "The Management Century". Taylor's breakthrough was to see that production line productivity could be improved by using "scientific" methods of organisation.

The approach has been criticised for imposing a mechanistic regime on workers in the interests of pure efficiency, but it triggered more research into psychological and sociological ways to make manufacturing more productive.

Plenty of management techniques have helped to improve the ability of managers to fulfil their fundamental task. China-based car manufacturers, for example, are using the production line efficiency methods pioneered by Japan's Toyota and others.

But the overarching management ideas that have shaped the way in which people run any large organisation – and plenty of small ones – are mostly broader and less changeable.

The FT judges chose leadership, ethics, strategic management and the spread of business educators and advisers for the list of the 50 big business ideas. But we steered clear of singling out individual management theories.

Even successful management theories, such as those espoused by Tom Peters and Robert Waterman in In Search of Excellence or by Jim Collins and Jerry Porras in Built to Last, tarnish with time, as the companies studied fail to keep up with the latest business trends.

Management writers would love to think that their ideas shape business. Some theories, including those mentioned above, did affect managers' thinking and practice, particularly between 1990 and 2000 as globalisation took hold. But unlike solid inventions that can be installed and put to work until the next upgrade – such as fibre optics, robotics or the microchip – "management" is a concept which users must constantly reshape to meet new organisational challenges.

As Charles Handy, the veteran management thinker, now in his 80s, told the FT in a recent interview: "The most that I can do is to cast [managers'] problems and opportunities in a different light so they see them more clearly. But what they do about it and what the answers are, no, I don't have them. So I'm never going to have three rules for success, or this is the answer to leadership … that's impertinent and bound to be wrong anyway most of the time because … every problem is different."

Source: Hill, A. (2013) 50 IDEAS – Management – Overview, *Financial Times*, 12 June 2013

The multilingual dividend

By Andrew Hill

Speaking two or more languages develops cognitive skills that are ideal for top managers, writes Andrew Hill

Afew years ago, when Antonella Sorace visited the European Central Bank in Frankfurt to talk about her research into bilingualism, she was astonished to find the bank's multinational staff worrying about what should have been one of their families' principal assets. "They had all kinds of doubts about the benefits of multilingualism for their children; they worried that their children weren't learning to read or write properly – in any language," she says. "I found it very instructive."

The Italian-born University of Edinburgh professor of developmental linguistics should set their minds at rest. Prof Sorace's research has shown that speaking another language offers not only utilitarian communication advantages, but also has cognitive benefits. Her message to business is: "Hire more multilingual employees, because these employees can communicate better, have better intercultural sensitivity, are better at co-operating, negotiating, compromising. But they can also think more efficiently."

Big multinational companies recognise the importance of language skills. McKinsey counts more than 130 languages spoken across the management consultancy, and offers a bursary to those who wish to learn another language before joining. Unilever estimates that up to 80 of the consumer products group's 100 most senior leaders speak at least two languages. Standard Chartered seeks out bilinguals for its international graduate training scheme.

These companies understand the functional benefits of having enough Mandarin-speakers to deal with suppliers in Shanghai, or French speakers sufficiently fluent to smooth relations with a customer in Carcassonne.

But at a recent FT roundtable in partnership with Bilingualism Matters, a project led by Prof Sorace, executives and consultants said they also believed that companies benefited from the diverse background and skills of multilingual leaders – and would benefit more in future.

"Multilingualism will be better valued and better leveraged by companies," says Laurence Monnery, co-head of global diversity and inclusion at Egon Zehnder, the executive search company. "Multiculturalism makes better leaders."

"Do multilinguals make better managers?" asks Ann Francke, chief executive of the UK's Chartered Management Institute. "Probably the answer to that question is yes."

Research shows bilinguals have an enhanced awareness of other people's points of view, born from their deeper understanding, from an early age, that some people have a different perspective. They are also better than monolinguals at giving selective attention to specific features of a problem, while ignoring misleading elements, and at switching between different tasks. Prof Sorace points out that bilinguals do not switch off their "other" language, meaning their brains grow to be more adaptable than those of monolinguals – a vital asset in a complex business world.

Most companies still value the practical rather than cognitive advantages of employing linguists. HSBC is one of the world's most multinational employers and emphasises hiring and cultivating multilingual staff. But Jorge Aisa Dreyfus, the Spanish-born co-head of learning, talent, resourcing and organisational development, says the bank is "probably still paying too much attention to [the fact] that you speak German, so you [can] handle all my German business".

In any case, for many companies from English-speaking cultures, pressure to employ a multilingual workforce has eased as English has spread as the language of business.

Academics worry that this will make national policy makers and educators complacent. James Foreman-Peck of Cardiff Business School has assessed the cost to the UK economy of under-investment in language skills as "the equivalent of between a 3 and 7 per cent tax on British exports". A recent study by the British Academy on "the state of the nation" concluded that the UK was entering a "vicious circle of monolingualism".

While the problem is particularly acute in the UK, other countries are also concerned. A 2006 report for the European Commission stated that "a significant amount of business" was sacrificed because of poor language skills across Europe: 11 per cent of small- and medium-sized enterprises had lost a contract as a result.

Prof Sorace says the cognitive benefits of multilingualism can be acquired by adults who become proficient in a second language. But a downward spiral in the quality of language education undermines the potential to develop that proficiency.

Richard Hardie, who chairs UBS's London operation, says the Swiss bank's recruitment website used to specify that it was looking for language skills. But it had to drop the requirement as the quality of linguists it was interviewing fell.

Multinationals have the edge over smaller companies in being able to recruit bilinguals globally, or to give staff with language skills full- immersion assignments.

Will Dawkins, of executive search firm Spencer Stuart, says "most enlightened companies" look for candidates for senior jobs who are not only multilingual but also have "performed a significant leadership task in another language".

Doug Baillie, chief human resources officer of Unilever, agrees: "Our most successful leaders are the ones who speak more than one language and travel to more than one geography."

But big companies can sometimes be complacent. Tracey Roseborough, managing director, international, at the Chartered Institute of Personnel and Development, saw the advantages of multilingualism when working with high-potential managers at Standard Chartered, earlier in her career, but says the quality of language skills at some big American multinationals she has worked for has not matched up. "The quality of the conversations wasn't the same," she says.

Prof Sorace advises companies to help combat prejudice and misconceptions about bilingualism and to exploit the opportunity to integrate expatriates into their local communities, to the advantage of the employees themselves and their families.

But her principal concern remains the failure of education systems – notably in the UK, whose citizens rank last out of EU members in linguistic ability – to promote languages at school. Add the cognitive disadvantage that monolinguals suffer to the more obvious communication deficit and countries' neglect of languages translates into a tale of lost potential.

Get a business brain

* Bilingualism does not mean perfect, balanced fluency in two languages from birth. Bilinguals are people who know, and use regularly, more than one language.

* Early exposure to two languages does not disadvantage children and may bring benefits, such as flexible thinking. The cognitive benefits apply from childhood to old age.

* No languages are "more useful" or "less useful": what matters is having more than one language in the brain.

* Starting early is good for developing cognitive ability, but proficiency and number of languages matter more than age of first exposure to the second language.

* "Late" bilinguals who are proficient in their second language also have cognitive advantages.

Source: Bilingualism Matters

'Our most successful leaders are those who speak more than one language'

Source: Hill, A. (2013) The multilingual dividend, *Financial Times*, 14 March 2013

I've finally found a piece of good corporate guff

By Lucy Kellaway

Why is it, readers often ask, that I never write about good corporate communication, but serve up an unvaried diet of bad.

There are three reasons for this. The first is that the negative is deeply rooted in my psyche. The second is because most of us like reading about guff as it's funnier and makes us feel superior. And the third is an almost complete absence of supply of the good stuff.

For one week only, I'm changing the pattern. Last week I came by chance on some startlingly sharp business writing, made even more freakish as it was in an area where communication is invariably dismal – statements of values and purpose. But before settling down to extol it, I can't resist a small fix of guff, as a reminder of how bad things have become.

Last week Barclays declared that its new purpose was: "Helping people achieve their ambitions – in the right way." On the positive side, the words are nice and short and it's encouraging that after 300 years the bank has decided that the right way is better than the wrong one.

The only snag is that it is hogwash. The purpose of a bank is nothing to do with ambition. It is, as I pointed out a couple of weeks ago, to keep depositors' money safe and to lend it to people who aren't going to run off with it.

The bank went on to state that staff will be rewarded according to "how they live our Values and bring them to life every day. And we'll judge our 'Go-To' success on a balanced scorecard of impact."

Thus Barclays establishes itself as the "Go-To" place for two things: corporate marshmallow and incorrect use of upper case.

Now compare this to Our Credo from Johnson & Johnson, four paragraphs laying out the medical group's priorities. As I read it I got so excited, I resolved to track down the man who wrote this exemplary piece of corporate prose. After a bit of searching, I found him.

His name is Robert Wood Johnson. There is only one thing wrong with him: he's dead. It turns out that the statement was written in 1943, long before corporate guff was invented, but the company has sensibly hung on to it.

It begins: "We believe our first responsibility is to the doctors nurses and patients … who use our products."

This is a strong start. There is none of the modern corporate pretence that the interests of all "stakeholders" point in the same direction. Instead, customers come first. The products, it goes on to say, should be of "high quality". Not excellent, or world-class, or any other overinflated tosh. Just "high".

The company's next priority is to its employees. "We must respect their dignity and recognise their merit," it states. "They must have a sense of security in their jobs", feel able to make suggestions, and their pay must be "fair and adequate". This is exceptional stuff. No dreary waffle about fun or engagement, no passion, no talent. Just the stuff that matters.

But now for the best bit of all: "We must provide competent management, and their actions must be just and ethical." I have never seen this in a statement before. For a company to promise to manage itself competently is, to slip into current language, a very big ask. A big hairy audacious stretch goal.

The third duty is to the community. "We must be good citizens – support good works and charities and pay our fair share of taxes." Starbucks etc, take heed.

Shareholders take their place at the back of the queue. "When we operate according to these principles, the stockholders should realise a fair return." On reading this credo, I find that I believe, too. I enthusiastically sign up to this sort of capitalism.

Alas, since Our Credo was written, there has been some slippage. On Johnson & Johnson's website are examples of "Credo in Action", with dismal, modern mentions of a "Diverse Inclusive Leadership Pipeline" and the "employee experience".

Sadder still is that for all its credo, Johnson & Johnson doesn't noticeably exceed the undemanding standards set by other drug companies. In recent years, jobs haven't always been secure, and customers haven't always been looked after. Only last week there was a story about executives from the company being investigated for allegedly bribing doctors in Greece.

There may be a good reason companies talk flatulently about helping people meet their ambitions and "Go-To" success. Because if they don't live up to such waffly principles, no one will ever know.

If you have to reject me, tell it to me to straight

By Lucy Kellaway

Last December, Elly Nowell was interviewed for a place at Magdalen College, Oxford to study law. When she got home, she sat down and composed a letter to the ancient institution. "I very much regret to inform you that I will be withdrawing my application," she wrote. "I realise you may be disappointed by this decision, but you were in competition with many fantastic universities and following your interview I am afraid you do not quite meet the standard of the universities I will be considering."

This 19-year-old girl has taught me two important things about rejection letters. First is how well they work in the wrong direction: from candidate to interviewer. To have the powerless rejecting the powerful not only does the soul a great deal of good, it may make sense tactically. To dump a complacent boyfriend is a time-honoured ploy; I don't see why the same shouldn't work with jobs and university places.

If there is anyone with any spark in Magdalen's law faculty they will surely be regretting this plucky, funny girl who got away. (Though perhaps wondering if law, that dullest of all dull courses, was right for her.)

Second, by mimicking the standard rejection letter, Ms Nowell reveals what a pathetic form of communication it is. Patronising, disingenuous, all-round beastly. There is only one accepted way of writing these things, used by all organisations everywhere, and it contains three bits that go like this. "Thank you for your interest in," they all begin. "We have had a record number of highly qualified applicants and regret that ..." And then, an upbeat ending: "We wish you all the best for your future."

All three elements are shockers; far from softening the blow they intensify it. First, as a reject, you don't want to be thanked for your "interest", as what you were showing wasn't interest, but desire for a position. Neither is it remotely comforting to know how many other great applicants there were. Worst of all, no one appreciates hollow good wishes from someone who is telling them to shove off.

When putting rejection into words, less is more. When one of my children was rejected from a university it was less upsetting to see the naked word UNSUCCESSFUL against the entry on the online application form than to read the letter that arrived a couple of days later with its bad tidings routinely packaged with insincere good wishes.

One might think there were nicer ways of saying no. Howard Junker, the founder of literary magazine ZYZZYVA, used to return short stories with a covering letter that began: "Gentle writer, Please forgive me for returning your work and not offering comments. I would like to think of something to make up for my ungraciousness, but I don't think a few quick remarks would really help." He signed off with a handwritten, "Onward! J".

How charming, I thought. But then I read a blog from a not-so-gentle writer who had received the very same letter on many occasions and found it anything but charming. The point is that no standardised letter can ever soften any blow. Rejection is rejection and it hurts.

Indeed, sometimes a brutal rejection is better. Actor Sir Antony Sher often describes the letter he got from the Royal Academy of Dramatic Art that said: "Not only have you failed the audition and we do not want you to try again, but we seriously recommend that you think about a different profession."

Similarly, about 30 years ago a senior colleague of mine applied for a job at the Economist and got a rejection letter back from the editor's secretary asking him not to contact the editor again. Such rudeness can only make the recipient think "screw you" and fill them with just the right sort of bloody mindedness to fight on until they make it.

The only worthwhile kind of rejection letter is one that gives reasons. Ms Nowell told Magdalen that she thought it stuck up and off-putting to candidates who didn't come from posh schools, a point the college might do well to ponder.

In offering an explanation she wasn't mimicking the normal style: employers almost never give reasons for fear of being sued, or because they don't want to enter into a dispute, or because their hiring processes are so opaque they don't know the explanation themselves.

The best rejection letter I ever received contained a reason I will never forget. I had written to a Mr Ivan Sallon, City editor of the Sunday Telegraph, asking for a job. He replied saying that there were no vacancies and went on: "May I offer you a word of advice? When applying for a job, do take care to get names right." The letter was signed: Ivan Fallon.

Source: Kellaway, L. (2013) If you have to reject me, tell it to me straight, *Financial Times*, 23 January 2013

The value of mentors who have been there

By Michael Skapinker

The vagaries of Cape Town's trains have made Mpho Mbhele an hour late, but it does not take long for a smile to replace her flustered apologies. She is a vital presence, a picture of health, and looks younger than her 41 years.

She is also HIV-positive, having been infected by her former husband who then threw her out. She has lost one of her three children to Aids.

It is a common story. Three-quarters of the world's HIV-positive pregnant women live in 12 African countries, including South Africa. At Chris Hani Baragwanath Hospital in Soweto, 8,000 HIV-positive women give birth each year. This is more than in the whole of the US. Untreated, 40 per cent of those women will give birth to infected babies.

It does not have to be that way. Ms Mbhele is one of an army of HIV-positive mothers who persuade pregnant women to take an Aids test, advise them to submit to the treatment that will help ensure their babies are born healthy and then support them if they need antiretroviral drugs to stay alive to look after their children.

These "mentor mothers" work for an organisation founded in 2001 by Mitchell Besser, an American obstetrician whom I first met when he was an undergraduate in the 1970s. Mothers2mothers (m2m) operates in seven African countries, employing 1,475 mentors and site co-ordinators who deal with 78,000 women each month.

Dr Besser set up m2m after his frustration, while working at a Cape Town hospital, at how few pregnant women agreed to be tested for HIV and how little time he and his nurses had to counsel those who did take the test and proved positive.

The mentor mothers not only help to compensate for the dire African shortage of doctors and nurses. Pregnant women are also more likely to listen to HIV-positive women who have had children themselves.

That the mentors look so well is one of the keys. When I visited a clinic in the South African province of KwaZulu-Natal in 2010, the chubby-cheeked mentors made a strong contrast with the drawn and coughing patients.

The mentors, who are trained and paid a salary, provide the answer to the many women who say they don't want an HIV test because they don't want to discover that they are going to die. "Do I look like I'm dying?" the mentors ask.

Their other central role is helping defeat the HIV stigma. Speaking in m2m's central Cape Town office, Ms Mbhele waves away my question of whether she minds her name appearing in a newspaper published world-wide. She doesn't believe people should hide being HIV-positive. Women who come to the two clinics she supervises aren't all as brave about their status. "They say 'we can't disclose like you'," she says.

She knows what it is like. It took her time to tell people she had HIV. She knows, too, that antiretroviral tablets, while life-saving, are not easy to take. "Three in the morning, three in the evening. It's very hard to remember," she says. There can be side effects. For three months at the beginning, she suffered numbness in her leg. But she tells the mothers that they have a duty to their children. "I say, 'You must live long, you must take your ARVs.'"

These mentoring lessons apply elsewhere too, including in business. Dr Besser says patients are often readier to listen to their peers than to sup-posed authority figures. He also asks whether, with health costs under pressure in both developed and developing countries, doctors and other medical professionals are always the most effective deliverers of care. As populations age, isn't there a role, for example, for the more robust elderly to support those whose health has declined?

Peer mentoring exists elsewhere; Alcoholics Anonymous is a leading example of people who have changed their lives supporting others who are struggling to do so.

What of companies? A 2007 review of the research literature into corpo-rate mentoring by Barry Bozeman and Mary Feeney of the University of Georgia shows it is overwhelmingly seen as something senior people do for their juniors. "A mentor is generally defined as a higher-ranking, influen-tial individual in your work environment who … is committed to providing upward mobility and support in your career," is a typical example.

There is a role for people like that, although they might better be called sponsors than mentors. As with the mentor mothers, someone who started where you are would surely be more credible and effective.

Source: Skapinker, M. (2012) The value of mentors who have been there, *Financial Times*, 4 January 2012

22

A guide to the gurus

Thirty years ago books on management were largely confined to dusty library shelves and written in dull, dense prose that was begrudgingly digested as part of one's academic study. But then, along came the one-minute manager in search of excellence and before you could blink, a populist bestseller business genre was built to last. According to the *FT*'s Andrew Hill, nearly 20 million business books a year are sold in the US, the world's largest market for such fare, a figure that excludes downloads.[1] And the bestselling business book of all time? Spencer Johnson's colourful *Who Moved My Cheese*, with 23 million copies sold, underscoring the point that the most popular books combine business advice with self help.

So just who are these gurus and what do they have to say on the subject of management? In this chapter, I take a quick romp through the best-sellers and the most admired and attempt to summarise their main points. To make navigating easier, I've organised them as follows:

The Top 5 Hall of Famers
The Top 5 Behaviour Buffs
The Top 5 Strategy Sages
The Top 5 Framework Folks
The Top 5 Practitioners

---

[1] Andrew Hill, *Financial Times*, 15 Oct. 2012.

The Top 5 Hall of Famers

This is my top selection of the bestsellers that you'll find on the shelves at any airport bookstore. They are easy to read and are brimming with action-based, self-help advice and tips. Some have spawned significant business empires and bestseller series off the back of their first book, and all have impacted popular culture well beyond the management genre in which they began. Their legacies are 'built to last' by any measure, and no doubt they will continue to inspire generations of future managers and leaders.

1. Tom Peters, In Search of Excellence (9 million sold)

The original rock star of management gurus, Peters not only writes his advice, he positively performs it, leaving audiences applauding wildly in appreciation. With the publication of *In Search of Excellence* in 1982, Peters and Waterman, two McKinsey consultants, helped to change the audience and outlet for management books from academics to ordinary working people in bookstores and cafés around the world. At a time when most boardrooms were drowning in a sea of strategy, Peters reminded us that customers come first. Peters exhorts us to embrace change and innovation, rather than get stuck in a rut of routine and risk getting left behind. His work was based on interviewing his 'list' of 43 excellent companies and distilling their common characteristics down to eight key principles:[2]

1 **A bias for action, active decision making** 'getting on with it'. Avoid bureaucratic control.

2 **Close to the customer** learning from the people served by the business.

3 **Autonomy and entrepreneurship** fostering innovation and nurturing 'champions'.

4 **Productivity through people** treating rank-and-file employees as a source of quality.

5 **Hands-on, value-driven** management philosophy that guides everyday practice – management showing its commitment.

6 **Stick to the knitting** stay with the business that you know.

[2] http://www.tompeters.com/toms_world/toms_books.php#Excellence

7 Simple form, lean staff some of the best companies have minimal HQ staff.

8 Autonomy in 'shop-floor' activities plus centralised values.

The go-to guru for: a comprehensive checklist of what makes an organisation excel and deliver on its promises; good for checking out what a great culture looks like.

2. Ken Blanchard, The One Minute Manager (13 million sold)

Ken Blanchard is the storyteller supremo. He wrote *The One Minute Manager* (OMM)[3] as a simple, easy to understand manual of allegories and anecdotes, helping 'normal' people to believe they too could be a manager and a good one at that. In the book, our aspiring manager-hero seeks an inspiring manager but finds such beings elusive, as those he encounters are either results-driven and too autocratic or people-driven and too democratic. Blanchard's premise is that good managers focus on both results and people, and that if you can master one-minute goal setting, one-minute praising and one-minute reprimands, you can master good management techniques.

One-minute goals are 250 words or less and are clearly communicated, linked to behaviour, and reviewed daily. Similarly, one-minute praises are specific, immediate, and accompanied by shared feelings and a handshake. One-minute reprimands are also specific, focus on the behaviour, not the person, and also include the impact of the bad behaviour on the manager and the organisation. The OMM spends his time going around looking for people 'doing the right things' so he can praise them, and also looking for people 'doing the wrong things' so he can encourage them to get back on track. Blanchard applies the principles used to train animals to train people, relying on specific, immediate positive reinforcement to encourage right behaviours. Blanchard went on to write over twenty *One Minute* books which collectively have sold over 100 million copies.

[3] http://www.kenblanchard.com/Store/Books_Audios/The_One_Minute_Manager_Essentials/ One_Minute_Manager_The/

The go-to guru for: advice on how to line manage when you are newly promoted. A refresher course on how to line manage when you're stressed, complacent, unclear, or in a new role.

3. Jim Collins and Jerry Porras, Built to Last (5 million sold)

Jim Collins and co-author Jerry Porras advocate taking the long-term view and anchor much of their work in historical research. They argue that great companies are built on lasting principles rather than quick fixes or miracle mantras. By studying eighteen visionary companies, those that are most admired in their field and have been around for ages, Collins and Portas debunked a lot of the 'myths' surrounding success. These include: 'it takes a great idea to start a great company'; visionary companies require a great and charismatic leader; the most successful companies exist first and foremost to maximise profits; and 'highly successful companies make their best moves by brilliant and complex strategic planning'.[4] Collins included loads of practical examples alongside his research from companies such as Procter & Gamble, Boeing, 3M and Wal-Mart. He also coined the expression BHAG (Big Hairy Audacious Goals) to describe the kind of inspirational – but a little scary – organisational mission these exceptional companies embrace.

The go-to guru for: inspiring yourself when you are about to embark on setting out a strategy or taking on a new organisational challenge.

4. Dr Spencer Johnson, Who Moved My Cheese? (23 million sold)

Johnson was Blanchard's partner in *The One Minute Manager*. A medical doctor, he uses principles of medicine and biology to encourage us to deal with change, and has become a fixture on bestseller lists along the way. *Who Moved My Cheese?* tells the tale of two mice, Sniff and Scurry, and two little people, Hem and Haw, who live in a maze but seek cheese for nourishment and happiness. Cheese is a metaphor for what you want in life – be that love, health, money or a job. The 'maze' is the place you go to find what you want – be that family, com-

---

4 http://www.jimcollins.com/article_topics/articles/building-companies.html

munity or workplace. Spencer is helping us to anticipate, prepare and adapt to change in work and in life, and to find fulfilment. He wants us to 'see the handwriting on the wall', i.e. monitor the cheese so you know change is coming. Don't be afraid of the maze, get out of your 'comfort zone' and go out and search for new and better cheese. Keep anticipating that someone will also move that cheese, so be ready to change again. Ironically, companies have been known to give this book out to employees during downsizings, prompting cynics to say they are misusing its message in an attempt to position such organisational moves in a positive light.

The go-to guru for: learning how to adapt to a new or changing environment either at work or in life generally. A boost to help you get out of a rut when you're stuck.

5. Steven Covey, The Seven Habits of Highly Effective People (over 5 million sold)

Covey combined business and personal with this book,[5] which encouraged managers to be people first and behave in the same way as managers. Taking a holistic approach to both work and life, he championed the 'natural laws' he believed governed both human and organisational effectiveness. He built his 'habits' concept on the notion of 'interdependence' – the idea that the optimal outcome comes from everyone giving their best, aligned to a common goal and vision, but using their own individual best judgement as to how to go about achieving that goal.

The seven habits have since found their way into common parlance. They are:

Habit 1: be proactive
Habit 2: begin with the end in mind
Habit 3: put first things first
Habit 4: think win/win
Habit 5: seek first to understand, then to be understood
Habit 6: synergise
Habit 7: sharpen the saw

---

[5] https://www.stephencovey.com/7habits/7habits.php

On a personal note, I recall being given this book as a middle manager at Procter & Gamble in the early nineties, and then sent on a four-day course to practise the 'habits'. Covey's maxims, such as begin with the end in mind, seek first to understand, then to be understood, and think win–win became deeply ingrained in the popular culture of the company.

The go-to guru for: great principles to set out ways of working in a new team or a new job; simple steps to get back on track when you feel a role or a situation is becoming ineffective.

The Top 5 Behaviour Buffs

Given that about 80 per cent of a company's assets are its people, it's little wonder most leaders cite the mantra that 'people are our greatest asset'. As a result, understanding and effectively engaging your people is arguably the most important management skill you can master. Management thinking from the days of Maslow has drawn heavily from psychology by building up an understanding of individual behaviours and key motivators. The latest thinking has focused on crowd psychology, as captured through Malcolm Gladwell's *Blink*.

1. Abraham Maslow, Hierarchy of Needs

Many of us who studied this in psychology class may not associate Maslow with management, but he is one of the first management thinkers to focus on people rather than task. Maslow's significant and widely used contribution was to class human needs in the form of a hierarchy.[6]

When one set of needs is fulfilled it ceases to become a motivator and people move up to the next level. If a manager can understand which level his employees are at, then he or she can better understand how best to motivate them. Maslow also spawned thinking in terms of people focus and task focus. His work continues to inform lots of employee surveys and checklists.

The go-to guru for: figuring out what makes others tick and how best to motivate them; understanding people's different perspectives and approaches to work.

---

[6] http://www.simplypsychology.org/maslow.html

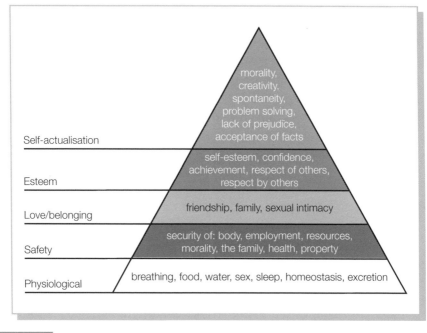

figure 22.1   **Mastow's hierarchy of needs**

Source: From Maslow, A. H., 'A Theory of Human Motivation', *Psychological Review* 50(4), 370–96 (1943).

2. Daniel Goleman: Godfather of EQ

Goleman popularised the notion that emotional intelligence (often referred to as EQ) is more important than IQ when it comes to living life successfully.[7] And Goleman equates business acumen with emotional intelligence (EQ) rather than intellect, arguing that the ability to read people well and respond with highly developed interpersonal skills often makes the difference between success and failure. Goleman characterised 25 EQ competencies, many of which have since been simplified. However, his core idea, that we can use our intelligence to better manage our emotional intuition to guide our thinking, is one that has significantly shaped modern management thinking.

The go-to guru for: helping you to stay in top form as a manager when dealing with different stakeholders and situations; getting to grips with understanding your own and others' behaviour.

---

[7] http://danielgoleman.info/topics/emotional-intelligence/

3. Dale Carnegie, How to Win Friends and Influence People

Carnegie wrote his famous work[8] in 1936, but it foreshadowed much of modern-day thinking with regard to managing interpersonal relationships successfully. It's all about promoting self-esteem. Carnegie believed great leaders refrained from criticising or condemning others and focused on praising them and understanding their point of view. He believed most folks were primarily interested in their own desires, so that by uncovering others' motivations you could persuade them to do your bidding willingly, and thus succeed at almost anything. Carnegie was proof of his pudding – he made a fortune peddling his business philosophy of self-confidence and self-esteem, and his books still sell millions today. The 'How to Win Friends and Influence People' catchphrase has become iconic, widely used in all sorts of cultural references.

The go-to guru for: boosting your confidence when faced with the unfamiliar; networking with a roomful of people you don't know; helping you to persuade others to get what you need to progress.

4. Rosabeth Moss Kanter

Our first female guru is best known for her work on change management and innovation, as well as pioneering work on diversity expressed in her *Men and Women of the Corporation*.[9] Many of her ideas have gained in relevance and become anchored in popular management wisdom. They centre on empowerment, participative management and employee involvement. Moss Kanter has a 'how to' approach that considers the social as well as management aspects of issues such as change. Her view is that a leader's job is to manage change and her tips for doing so are simple, practical and compelling. 'People will often resist change for reasons that make good sense to them, even if those reasons don't correspond to organisational goals. So it's crucial to recognise, reward and celebrate accomplishments.'[10]

---

[8] http://www.dalecarnegie.co.uk/secrets_of_success/?keycode=google06uk.
   GBBranded&gclid=COL9suC4-bQCFfHJtAodVzAAuw
[9] http://www.questia.com/library/3697902/men-and-women-of-the-corporation
[10] http://thinkexist.com/quotes/rosabeth_moss_kanter

The go-to guru for: managing change and insights into dealing with human behaviour and expectations in companies; help in boosting employees' morale in difficult times.

5. Malcolm Gladwell: Blink, Outliers and the Tipping Point

In his entertaining and provocative treatise, *Blink: How to Think Without Thinking*,[11] Gladwell argues that the best decisions are snap decisions, where we trust our instincts rather than rely on the evaluation of information and risk. His book is still the number two management book on Amazon at the time of writing, which demonstrates he has indeed hit a nerve. Like Stephen Covey, Gladwell blurs the distinction between work and life, and calls on us to pay attention to something he calls 'rapid cognition'– the first two seconds in our decision-making, which he says are often the best. He says it's not about intuition, but about using our instincts and our gut reaction to things to get a better result. He also distinguishes between good and bad rapid cognition: good is doctors in Chicago relying on gut to better diagnose heart attacks at a major hospital; bad is most Fortune 500 CEOs being tall because people instinctively believe tall folk make better leaders. In addition to Blink, Gladwell's 'Tipping Point' is often used in management as a predictor of trends, while his 'Outliers' talks about how the idiosyncratic can be successful.

The go-to guru for: inspiring, quirky but brilliant ideas and approaches to things; making sense of the modern world in ways that make you go 'Aha'; tips on decision-making and creating trends.

The Top 5 Strategy Sages

Strategy can be a vastly over-used word, with many managers aspiring to move to the loftier world of strategic decision-making beyond the perceived operational doldrums of delivering daily business success. However, most excellent strategies emerge from knowing the realities of your business and particularly through knowing your customers really well. And all strategies require excellence in execution to succeed. The

---

[11] http://www.gladwell.com/blink/index.html

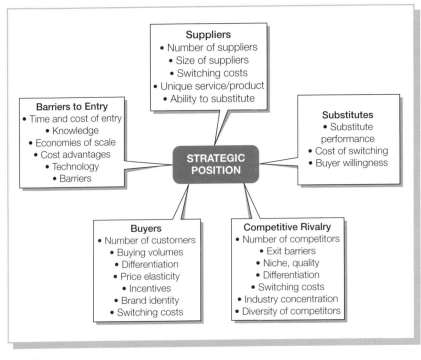

strategic sages I have selected will help you to better understand how to pull all of these aspects together using tools and frameworks that will help you to strategise well and to expand the horizons of your thinking.

1. Michael Porter, The Five Competitive Forces That Shape Strategy (over 1 million sold)

Competitive Strategy is one of the few business bibles to gain widespread academic as well as practitioner acceptance. Porter created a lasting framework for strategic analysis by shifting the focus away from individual companies or markets into the broader arena of industries, and varying the approach according to whether the industry was emerging, declining, fragmented or global. Porter defined three generic strategies: low-cost, differentiation and focus. He coined the phrase 'value chain' and also gave us the now widely used 'Five Forces', pictured in Figure 0.1.[12]

More recently Porter has coined the phrase 'shared value' to describe combining capitalism with social benefit as a new force for good.

The go-to guru for: a primer in undertaking any fundamental strategic analysis; benchmarking your existing or future company in terms of how clear your positioning and strategy is – or isn't.

2. Gary Hamel and C.K. Prahalad, Competing for the Future

This is regarded as one of the most influential books[13] on strategy. Hamel and Prahalad argued against the traditional notions of strategy in terms of market share and value chain and introduced broader, more multifaceted concepts that were emotional as well as analytical. They championed notions such as 'strategic intent' and 'core competence'. To be successful over time, they argued, companies needed to shift focus away from monitoring short-term operational efficiencies in day-to-day operations and start to plan for the future by building new business ideas around their 'core competencies' – the things they were fundamentally good at, which weren't always obvious. A core competency meets the following criteria:

■ Provides benefit to the customer.

■ Is difficult to imitate.

■ Can be leveraged widely to create many products (or operate in many markets).

■ Uniquely identifies the organisation.

■ Is difficult to pin down, because it seems to be a combination of things such as technology, process, and know-how.

The go-to gurus for: a simple and very effective way to understand what your organisation is truly and uniquely good at – and not good at. Sharpening or correcting strategy now or in the future.

---

[12] http://hbr.org/2008/01/the-five-competitive-forces-that-shape-strategy/ar/1?referral=00269
[13] http://hbr.org/product/competing-for-the-future/an/7161-PBK-ENG

3. Clayton Christensen: The Innovator's Dilemma

Christensen[14] introduced the notion of 'disruptive innovation' – the idea that successful companies will get pushed aside by new entrants who introduce cheaper products that still meet customer needs. Over time, the innovations meet these needs better than the existing leaders and top them. The leaders typically miss these newcomers until it's too late because they are operating in less attractive, low-cost markets. Christensen was trying to answer the question, 'Why do good companies fail?' Because they are too busy listening to their customers and focusing on larger, more profitable markets. They are more likely to introduce what he calls sustaining technologies rather than disruptive ones – technologies that improve the performance of their existing products in line with customer needs. Disruptive technologies, however, focus on typically lower-cost, simpler and easy to use innovations that are at first appreciated only by a few. But as the new markets grow, the products improve until they are so good they displace their larger competitors. Christensen advocates setting up smaller separate divisions to allow them to pursue smaller gains, plan and learn from failure, and avoid obsession with 'big breakthrough' mentality.

The go-to guru for: driving more innovation in your organisation's outcomes, products and services; understanding your market and competition better; improving sluggish performance.

4. W. Chan Kim and Renée Mauborgne: Blue Ocean Strategy

Kim and Mauborgne, professors at INSEAD, refer to traditional notions of companies competing as red ocean strategies. To seize new profit and growth opportunities, companies need to go beyond red ocean strategies and create blue ocean strategies.[15] Red ocean strategies focus on competing for a larger share of a fixed market – dividing up the red ocean, which doesn't grow. Blue ocean strategy, on the other hand, is based on the view that market boundaries and industry structures are not given and can be re-imagined in managers' minds and actions. Blue ocean strategy means extra demand is out there, largely untapped

---

[14] http://www.businessweek.com/chapter/christensen.htm
[15] http://www.blueoceanstrategy.com

– one needs only to create it by focusing on value innovation and breaking the cost/value trade-off. By expanding the demand side of the economy, new wealth is created. Such a strategy therefore allows firms to largely play a non-zero-sum game, with high pay-off possibilities. Apple's invention of the iPod, iPhone and iPad are all examples of blue ocean strategies.

The go-to gurus for: kickstarting innovation and a new approach to growth in mature markets; coming up with new ways of looking at current markets and situations to define opportunities.

5. John Kotter

Harvard Business School Professor Kotter's research and writings[16] focus upon change management from the leadership perspective. He believes that 'Most organizations are over-managed and under led.' He identifies eight critical stages that leaders need to follow in order to achieve effective organisational transformation:

1 Establish a sense of urgency.

2 Form a powerful guiding coalition.

3 Create a vision.

4 Communicate that vision.

5 Empower others to act on the vision.

6 Plan for and create short-term wins.

7 Consolidate improvements.

8 Keep the momentum for change moving and institutionalise the new approaches.

The go-to guru for: a step-by-step guide to leading change and creating the platform from which to transform an underperforming organisation.

---

[16] http://www.kotterinternational.com/aboutus/bios/john-kotter

The Top 5 Framework Folks

Many view management as an organising discipline, and as such these gurus provide frameworks to help organise your own thinking on management. They rationalise and try to make sense of management as a discipline, using tools to help your understanding and aid the practical application of management theory. Indeed, Drucker is often credited with creating management as a discipline in itself. The other gurus selected here apply their frameworks to many different aspects of management ranging from quality through to measuring the right things. They also help you to understand the importance of collaboration and continuous learning in the digital age.

1. Peter Drucker: Father of Management?

Peter Drucker (1909–2005) is regarded by both practising managers and writers throughout the world as *the* management guru. He disliked the term guru – likening it to charlatan – and preferred to be known as a writer. Drucker did concede, however, that he discovered management, not merely as a discipline, but rather as a way of life that is central to the wellbeing of society as well as to the economy. With more than thirty-three books published over seven decades (and translated into at least thirty languages) Drucker was, by common consent, the founding father of modern management studies.

Drucker coined the 'management by objectives' term in his 1954 book, *Principles of Management.*[17] Management by objectives involves the employee and his boss sitting down together and defining goals, agreed roles and responsibilities and measures. Drucker believed that by participating in setting objectives, managers would be more motivated to achieve them. Clarity of communication, agreed roles and responsibilities and SMART objectives (Simple, Measurable, Actionable, Relevant and Time-bound) are still very widely used. He also coined the equally popular distinction between efficiency (doing things right) and effectiveness (doing the right things).

---

[17] http://books.google.co.uk/books?hl=en&lr=&id=1GJzVRYOCkgC&oi=fnd&pg=PA5&dq=principles+of+management+drucker&ots=xS8toK1nJm&sig=jxY0lylCD56M-EBfSXHu8HCOXU4#v=onepage&q=principles%20of%20management%20drucker&f=false

The go-to guru for: understanding the principles upon which much of modern management is based; learning about how to set objectives and measure them; gaining clarity around responsibilities.

2. W. Edwards Deming: Total Quality Management

Deming has been universally acclaimed as one of the founding fathers of Total Quality Management, if not *the* founding father. The revolution in Japanese manufacturing management that led to the economic miracle of the 1970s and 1980s has been attributed largely to Deming. His Fourteen Points have now been adopted, assimilated and integrated into management practice in the 1990s as well as continuously debated and taught in business schools around the world. Deming's Fourteen Points[18] add up to a code of management philosophy which spans the two major schools of management thought which have dominated since the early twentieth century: scientific (hard) management on the one hand, and human relations (soft) management on the other. Over half of his Fourteen Points focus on people as opposed to systems. Many management thinkers veer towards one school or the other. Deming, like Drucker, melds them together. Deming believed in employees developing quality as a team and building it into the product or service. He also recognised the importance of pride and a sense of accomplishment in boosting productivity.

The go-to guru for: a framework for improving the quality of output in any organisation; ensuring that you are balancing an approach to tasks with an approach to people.

3. Robert Kaplan and David Norton: The Balanced Scorecard

Robert Kaplan and David Norton are jointly recognised as the popularisers of the balanced scorecard and their approach to it was first introduced in a 1992 *Harvard Business Review* article, 'The balanced scorecard: measures that drive performance'.[19] Kaplan and Norton turned the popular saying 'What gets measured gets done' on its head

---

[18] http://www.mindtools.com/pages/article/newSTR_75.htm
[19] http://hbr.org/product/balanced-scorecard-measures-that-drive-performance/an/ R0507Q-PDF-ENG

and began with 'What you measure is what you get', and championed setting key performance indicators (KPIs). The scorecard is flexible, and can be adapted for use by individual organisations or business units across the private and public sectors. It is practical, straightforward and devoid of obscure theory. Most importantly it moves away from measuring an organisation's success in purely financial terms and looks more broadly across other areas of the business such as customers, employees and communities. The balanced scorecard has become increasingly popular; Bain and Company's 2007 survey of management tools suggests that 66 per cent of companies are using it worldwide, with usage at its highest in Asia and in large companies.[20]

The go-to guru for: adopting a comprehensive and well-respected system for measuring your success at any level of an organisation, whether it is a single store, a division or an entire company.

4. Don Tapscott: Wikinomics

Tapscott's claim to fame is that he saw the impact of the digital age well before most of us, and the impact that technology and the internet would have on businesses, individuals and society. In his best-selling book, *Wikinomics: How Mass Collaboration Changes Everything*, he argues that the web creates new powers of democracy for people everywhere and enables users to participate en masse.[21] By working together, people can create 'open source projects which redefine the way things are produced and replace traditional hierarchical structures with self-organised collaborative communities'. 'Wiki' means quick in Hawaiian.

The go-to guru for: understanding how technology and the internet have changed the way we work; gaining insight and inspiration on how to create a more collaborative culture and ways of working.

5. Peter Senge: The Learning Organisation

Senge coined this phrase in his major work, *The Fifth Discipline*.[22] In it he argued that a learning organisation believes that competitive advan-

---

[20] http://www.bain.com/management_tools/management_tools_and_trends_2007.pdf
[21] LCCN 2006-51390
[22] Senge, Peter M., *The Fifth Discipline*, Doubleday/Currency, 1990.

tage and value stem from continued learning of both individuals and collectives. Senge combined the approach to management with that of biology, the environment and the social sciences, believing that organisations were organisms and that all of these were linked in both approach and outcome. Organisations, to succeed, must continue to adapt, change and transform on a regular basis if they are to become learning organisations. In order to move forward, managers have to give up control and enable learners to make mistakes – easier than in theory, perhaps, than in practice.

The go-to guru for: nudging yourself or others out of complacency and inertia by encouraging ongoing development, change and learning from failures and mistakes as well as successes.

The Top 5 Practitioners

My final selection of gurus are those who have been there and 'got the T-shirt'. They have been instrumental to managing and leading phenomenal success in their respective companies. They are excellent story-tellers and provide fascinating insights into their own management careers, which make for inspiring reads. As individuals they have all had very different journeys to get to the top and are testament to the fact that great leaders are not born, but are made by sheer hard work and determination and often have a lucky break thrown in. They all describe experiencing setbacks on the way, providing lessons in resilience for us all, as well as popular holiday reads. I am now just waiting for the first female poster practitioner …

1. Steven Jobs

Universally celebrated as the creative and irascible genius entrepreneur and impresario behind Apple, Steven Jobs' business contributions are chronicled in a best-selling biography he commissioned shortly before his death from cancer at 56, written by Walter Isaacson. Jobs was famous for being iconoclastic, obsessed with excellence, and for bending the world around him to suit his amazingly strong will. He also referred to Apple as 'the world's largest start up', and abhorred corporate decision-making by committee. At Apple, he championed the right individuals and put them in teams that came together once a week for three hours to share ideas and progress – arguing that the best ideas win, not the best hierarchy. No one will doubt his genius and ability to shape the future. He was brilliant at user-centric design and elegance, combining both with intuitive and user-friendly function. He also led on what is regarded as one of the greatest successful corporate comebacks ever. Ousted at Apple in 1985, he returned in 1996 and led the company back into the black, via the invention of the iPod, iPhone, iPad, apps and the Apple stores. He reinvented our relationship with technology and changed how we consume media, making Apple the most admired company and valuable brand in the process. No wonder Jobs also tops the Forbes list of most valuable CEOs ever.[23]

The go-to guru for: the story of how a brilliant, iconoclastic individual changed the world and reinvented how people interact with technology. A dramatic lesson in the value of user-centric design and 'blue ocean' innovation.

2. Warren Buffett: The Sage of Omaha

Rising from humble beginnings in Omaha, Nebraska, Buffett is one of the world's wealthiest men and enjoys a reputation as the world's most successful investor. His company, Berkshire Hathaway, takes stakes in everything from Coca Cola to Geico to Tesco, and the market impact of Buffett investing in something can be significant. Buffett espouses the value investing approach, which is to buy shares in companies for less than their 'intrinsic' value – in other words, buy the stock of a great company at a sensible price, and sell it when the value is realised. He teaches this approach for free on a website and in many books. Famous for combining folksy humour, modesty and simplicity in his approach, Buffett has also become the populist voice of authority for millions of private investors. Thousands travel each year to Berkshire Hathaway shareholder meetings. A major philanthropist, Buffett has pledged to give away over 99 per cent of his multi-billion-dollar fortune, most of it to the Gates Foundation.

The go-to guru for: a common-sense, real-world approach to investing and value creation in a world obsessed with complexity and leverage. A

---

[23] http://tnerd.com/2010/03/29/steve-jobs-is-the-most-valuable-ceo-in-the-world-says-forbes/

great believer in just getting on with it – read him when you're feeling overwhelmed by the uncertainty of it all.

3. Jack Welch

Jack Welch was perhaps the first CEO whose ways of working spawned a management doctrine. As CEO of GE from 1980 to 2001, he pioneered a number of practices that became incredibly influential and were not without controversy. Among them were GE's ruthless performance management: every year, the bottom 10 per cent of performers were fired, whilst the top 20 per cent were rewarded with stock options and bonuses. Welch was ruthlessly driven to weed out inefficiencies and bureaucracy, and in the process he shed over 100,000 from the GE workforce, and earned the nickname 'neutron Jack'. A big proponent of Six Sigma, Welch also believed that unless a company was number 1 or 2 in its industry it couldn't compete. During his tenure at GE he built the company's market value by over 4000 per cent, and in 1999 *Fortune Magazine* named him 'Manager of the Century'.[24] Since leaving GE he has, among other things, founded his own Management Institute, which claims to be 'the only online executive education program built on the proven principles and practices of one of our country's most celebrated business leaders'.

The go-to guru for: a hard-hitting guide to improving business performance via a tough, no-nonsense approach to people management and stamping out organisational bureaucracy.

4. Richard Branson, Losing My Virginity

This aptly titled biography[25] chronicles the 'life and times of Britain's' most famous entrepreneur. He has built a business with over eight separate billion-dollar companies, spanning everything from airlines to gyms. Branson is regarded as both an iconoclast and a branding genius. He is also a daredevil – frequently taking off on adventures many would

---

[24] 'FORTUNE – GE's Jack Welch Named Manager of the Century – November 01, 1999'. Timewarner.com. 1999-04-26. http://www.timewarner.com/corp/newsroom/pr/0,20812,667526,00.html. Retrieved 2010-07-12.

[25] Branson, Richard, *Losing My Virginity: How I Survived, Had Fun, and Made a Fortune Doing Business My Way*, Three Rivers Press, 1999.

regard as foolish, such as travelling around the world in a balloon or trying to break world speed records. His own advice is simple and with a rebel's edge – he started Virgin when he was 20, as a self-confessed hippie who never went to business school. Not surprisingly, 'Be visible', 'Choose your name wisely' and 'Take risks' are among the Branson bon mots of business advice. He also advocates picking up the phone, and laments that the email age is damaging business relationships.[26]

The go-to guru for: understanding the importance of building a personal as well as a business brand, of not being afraid to challenge conventional wisdom and of staying true to your brand and yourself. Also good for reminding us all to have fun and not take it all too seriously!

5. Bill Gates

The world's second richest man, Bill Gates is currently worth $65 billion. A Harvard drop-out who founded Microsoft in his garage, Gates is now almost as famous for his philanthropic efforts as for the company he built that pioneered web software with Windows. The Bill Gates Foundation champions the eradication of infectious diseases and the provision of education in Africa and throughout the world. He also founded the 'Giving Pledge', where the world's wealthiest pledge to give away half their wealth (Buffett is a member). Ranked the fourth most powerful person in the world by Forbes, and the highest business person on the list, Gates is a soothsayer when it comes to technology – he accurately predicted Amazon, Netflix and Facebook.[27] He was also the most influential proponent of geek chic and is quoted as saying, 'If geek means you're willing to study things, and if you think science and engineering matter, I plead guilty. If your culture doesn't like geeks, you are in real trouble.'[28]

The go-to guru for: understanding that it's not enough to be rich for the sake of it. You've got to use your vast wealth to improve the lives of the people and the planet. Philanthropy is CSR for CEOs.

---

[26] http://business.financialpost.com/2012/09/22/richard-bransons-18-tips-for-success
[27] http://www.forbes.com/profile/bill-gates/
[28] http://www.telegraph.co.uk/technology/bill-gates/8073946/Bill-Gates-If-you-dont-like-geeks-youre-in-trouble..html

Top tips, pitfalls and takeaways

Top tips

1 **Be eclectic** Not one of these thinkers is 100 per cent right – or wrong. Put together your own personal 'menu' of advice based on the circumstances you face. If you are stuck for ideas in a competitive market then maybe 'blue ocean' thinking will help; if you're not getting the people results you need, maybe some One Minute Manager techniques will be helpful.

2 **Use free resources to stay current** There are many really useful summaries of management thinkers which can save you a fortune in time and money. I've listed some of these below:

■ Business Book – http://800ceoread.com

■ Top 50 Thinkers – www.thinkers50.com

■ Mind Tools – www.mindtools.com

■ HBR – www.hbr.org

■ Mix – www.visitmix.com

Top pitfall

Use sparingly and stay grounded No one is going to welcome you spouting forth management theory in your meetings or over-quoting Harvard Business School professors or Dale Carnegie. Try to apply the principles of the gurus to your own situation using your own words.

Top takeaway

Focus on the main message The overwhelming message from all the gurus is it's about people and behaviour, at least as much as about task or process. Most managers get into trouble because they forget that, and forget that too easily. Remember: business is simple, people are complicated! Even if you are using advanced strategic techniques, if you ignore the people element you won't succeed.

Index

Comprehensive. Authoritative. Trusted.
FT Guides will tell you everything you need to know about your chosen subject area

Buy now from your favourite bookshop
or www.pearsoned.co.uk/bookshop